American Literature and Culture
1900–1960

Blackwell Introductions to Literature

This series sets out to provide concise and stimulating introductions to literary subjects. It offers books on major authors (from John Milton to James Joyce), as well as key periods and movements (from Old English literature to the contemporary). Coverage is also afforded to such specific topics as "Arthurian Romance." All are written by outstanding scholars as texts to inspire newcomers and others: non-specialists wishing to revisit a topic, or general readers. The prospective overall aim is to ground and prepare students and readers of whatever kind in their pursuit of wider reading.

Published

American Literature and Culture 1900–1960

Gail McDonald

Blackwell
Publishing

BLACKWELL PUBLISHING
350 Main Street, Malden, MA 02148-5020, USA
9600 Garsington Road, Oxford OX4 2DQ, UK
550 Swanston Street, Carlton, Victoria 3053, Australia

First published 2007 by Blackwell Publishing Ltd

1 2007

Library of Congress Cataloging-in-Publication Data

McDonald, Gail.
American literature and culture, 1900–1960 / Gail McDonald.
p. cm.—(Blackwell introductions to literature;15)
Includes bibliographical references and index.
ISBN-13: 978-1-4051-0126-4 (hardcover : alk. paper)
ISBN-10: 1-4051-0126-1 (hardcover : alk. paper)
ISBN-13: 978-1-4051-0127-1 (pbk. : alk. paper)
ISBN-10: 1-4051-0127-X (pbk. : alk. paper) 1. American literature—
20th century—History and criticism. 2. National characteristics,
American, in literature. 3. Literature and society—United States—
History—20th century. I. Title. II. Series.

PS221. M394 2006
810.9/358—dc22
2005034697

A catalogue record for this title is available from the British Library.

Set in 10/13pt Meridien
by Graphicraft Limited, Hong Kong
Printed and bound in Singapore
by COS Printers Pte Ltd

The publisher's policy is to use permanent paper from mills that operate
a sustainable forestry policy, and which has been manufactured from
pulp processed using acid-free and elementary chlorine-free practices. Furthermore,
the publisher ensures that the text paper and cover board used have met acceptable
environmental accreditation standards.

For further information on
Blackwell Publishing, visit our website:
www.blackwellpublishing.com

Contents

List of Illustrations

Timeline

Historical events	*Cultural events (discussed in the text)*
1900 McKinley elected to second term as President	Dreiser, *Sister Carrie*
	Roosevelt, *The Strenuous Age*
Hurricane kills 6,000–7,000 in Galveston, Texas	American Arts and Crafts movement continues from 1890s
	Frank Lloyd Wright establishes architecture studio in Oak Park, Illinois
1901 President McKinley assassinated; Theodore Roosevelt becomes president	Washington, *Up From Slavery*
J. P. Morgan founds US Steel Corporation	
First wireless communication between US and England	
Socialist Party of America formed	
1902 United Mine Workers' strike	James, *The Wings of the Dove*
1903 Henry Ford founds Ford Motor Company	*Camera Work* begins publication (Stieglitz)
Wright brothers fly motorized plane at Kitty Hawk, North Carolina	Du Bois, *The Souls of Black Folk*
	James, *The Ambassadors*

Historical events	Cultural events (discussed in the text)
New York City opens subway	11-minute narrative film, *The Great Train Robbery*, shown in theaters
US Departments of Commerce and Labor created	
1904 Work begins on Panama Canal (completed 1914)	James, *The Golden Bowl*
	Tarbell, *The History of the Standard Oil Company* (published 1902 in *McClure's* magazine)
	Weber, *The Protestant Ethic and the Spirit of Capitalism*
1905 Industrial Workers of the World organized in Chicago, Illinois	Hall, *Adolescence*
	Wharton, *The House of Mirth*
Stieglitz opens 291 Gallery, New York City	
1906 Catastrophic earthquake and fire in San Francisco, California	Gilman, *Women and Economics*
	Sinclair, *The Jungle*
Pure Food and Drug Act passed	
Roosevelt first uses term "muckraker" to describe work of investigative journalists	
1907 Oklahoma admitted to Union	Adams, *The Education of Henry Adams* (privately printed)
J. P. Morgan averts financial panic with his own $100 million in gold	James, *The American Scene*
	New York Edition of Henry James (1907–9)
	First staging of the Ziegfeld Follies in New York City
1908 Taft succeeds Roosevelt	Zangwill, *The Melting Pot*
	Ash Can school of painters exhibit
	Singer Building in New York City first US "skyscraper"

Historical events	*Cultural events (discussed in the text)*
1909 Founding of the National Association for the Advancement of Colored People (NAACP)	W.C. Handy writes down the "Memphis Blues"
	Wright's "Robie" house
First White House Conference on Children	
1910 Boy Scouts of America founded	Addams, *Twenty Years at Hull-House*
Mann Act prohibits transportation of women across state lines "for immoral purposes"	
First Ford Model T produced	
1911 Triangle Shirtwaist Factory fire	*The Masses* begins publication (until 1917)
	Taylor, *The Principles of Scientific Management* (efficiency in the workplace)
1912 *Titanic* sinks	*Poetry* magazine founded in Chicago, Illinois
Progressive Party established	
New Mexico and Arizona admitted to Union	Antin, *The Promised Land*
	Pound, *Patria Mia*
Wilson elected President	
Department of Labor and Federal Reserve Bank established	
1913 Thomas Edison demonstrates the Kinetophone (for talking motion pictures)	Bourne, *Youth and Life*
	Pound, "A Few Don'ts by An Imagiste"
Ford begins assembly-line manufacturing	New York Armory Show introduces American public to modern art
16th (income tax) and 17th (popular election of US Senators) Constitutional Amendments	

Historical events	Cultural events (discussed in the text)
1914 First transcontinental telephone conversation (New York to San Francisco) World War I begins in Europe	*Vanity Fair*, *The Little Review*, and *The New Republic* begin publication Brooks, *America's Coming-of-Age* Frost, *A Boy's Will* Sandburg, *Chicago* Painting: Hartley, *Portrait of a German Officer*
1915 Taxi-cab business begins Iron and steel workers strike	Eliot, "The Love Song of J. Alfred Prufrock" Frost, *North of Boston* Masters, *Spoon River Anthology* Provincetown Players founded
1916 Wilson re-elected Beginning of Great Migration of African Americans from South to North National Park Service established Margaret Sanger opens birth-control clinic in Brooklyn, New York Eight-hour workday for railroad employees	*The Seven Arts* and *The Dial* begin publication Brooks, "On Creating a Usable Past" and "Young America" Frost, "Out, Out –" H.D., *Sea Garden* Painting: Weber, *Chinese Restaurant*
1917 US enters World War I Immigration act excludes Asian workers (except Japanese) Pulitzer Prize established	*Cambridge History of American Literature* (4 vols., 1917–21) Millay, *Renascence*
1918 Global influenza epidemic, kills between 20 and 40 million Armistice signed, ending World War I	Cather, *My Ántonia* Williams, *Kora in Hell*

Historical events	Cultural events (discussed in the text)
1919 Major race riots in Chicago and Washington, DC	Anderson, *Winesburg, Ohio*
	Frank, *Our America*
18th Constitutional Amendment makes sale of alcohol illegal (Prohibition)	
Treaty of Versailles; formation of League of Nations (rejected by American lawmakers)	
Chicago "White Sox" baseball team accused of gambling in the World Series	
Steel and mine workers strike; Boston police strike	
1920 Urban population exceeds rural population	*Contact* magazine begins publication
	Eliot, *Poems* and *The Sacred Wood*
Transcontinental airmail available	Fitzgerald, *Flappers and Philosophers*
Prohibition in effect	Lewis, *Main Street*
19th Constitutional Amendment grants women the right to vote	Millay, *A Few Figs from Thistles*
	Pound, *Hugh Selwyn Mauberley*
"Red Scare" and Palmer raids	Santayana, *Character and Opinion in the United States*
American Civil Liberties Union (ACLU) founded	Turner, *The Frontier in American History*
Arrest of Nicola Sacco and Bartolomeo Vanzetti	Wharton, *The Age of Innocence*
	Yezierska, *Hungry Hearts*
Harding elected President	Painting: Sheeler, *Church St. El*
1921 First regular radio broadcasts in US	Dos Passos *Three Soldiers*
	Joyce's *Ulysses* imported to US; all 500 copies burned by US Post Office
Emergency Quota Act strictly limits immigration	

Historical events	*Cultural events (discussed in the text)*
American Birth Control League organized	Moore, *Poems*
	Robinson, *Collected Poems*
	Music: Louis Armstrong with the Creole Jazz Band in Chicago; Blake and Sissle, *Shuffle Along* (first all-black musical)
1922	*The Fugitive* and *The Soil* begin publication
	cummings, *The Enormous Room*
	Eliot, *The Waste Land*
	Fitzgerald, *Tales of the Jazz Age*
	Hughes, "Mother to Son"
	Johnson, *The Book of American Negro Poetry*
	Lewis, *Babbitt*
	Stearns, *Civilization in the United States*
1923 US Steel institutes eight-hour workday	*Time* magazine begins publication
	Frost, *New Hampshire*
"Teapot Dome" scandal in President Harding's administration. Leasing of Wyoming Naval oil reserves to private companies	Lawrence, *Studies in Classic American Literature*
	Stevens, *Harmonium*
	Toomer, *Cane*
Harding dies; Coolidge becomes President	Williams, *Spring and All*, "The Red Wheelbarrow"
Members of Osage tribe in Oklahoma targets of violence	Music: Bessie Smith's "Downhearted Blues" sells 780,000 copies
1924 Daily airmail service between East and West coasts of US	*The American Mercury* founded (Mencken and Nathan)
	Ferber, *So Big*
Second strict curb on immigration	Hemingway, *in our time* (published in Paris)

Historical events	Cultural events (discussed in the text)
	Moore, *Observations*
First women governors elected in Wyoming and Texas	Ransom, "Bells for John Whiteside's Daughter"
Coolidge elected President	Seldes, *The Seven Lively Arts*
	Music: Gershwin, "Rhapsody in Blue"
	"Little Orphan Annie" comic strip debuts
1925 "Scopes" trial. Tennessee teacher found "guilty" of teaching theory of evolution	*The New Yorker* magazine founded
	Anderson, *Dark Laughter*
Ku Klux Klan's march on Washington	Cather, *The Professor's House*
	Cullen, "Incident"
	Dos Passos, *Manhattan Transfer*
Land boom in Florida	Dreiser, *An American Tragedy*
Standard Oil adopts eight-hour workday	Eliot, *Poems 1909–1925*
	Fitzgerald, *The Great Gatsby*
	Glasgow, *Barren Ground*
	H.D., *Collected Poems*
	Hemingway, *In Our Time* (revised and enlarged)
	Locke, *The New Negro*
	Pound, *A Draft of XVI Cantos*
	Stein, *The Making of Americans*
	Williams, *In the American Grain*
	Yezierska, *The Bread Givers*
	Music: Copland, *Music for Theater*; Charleston dance craze
1926 Ford introduces eight-hour, five-day working week	Book-of-the-Month Club initiated
	New Masses magazine begins publication
Transatlantic wireless telephone	Faulkner, *Soldier's Pay*

Historical events	Cultural events (discussed in the text)
	Ferber, *Show Boat*
	Hemingway, *The Sun Also Rises*
	Hughes, *The Weary Blues*
	Ransom, "Janet Waking"
	Music: Copland, *Piano Concerto*; Josephine Baker stars in *Le Revue Nègre*
1927 Sacco and Vanzetti executed in Massachusetts	*transition* magazine begins publication
Charles Lindbergh completes first non-stop, transatlantic flight	Charles and Mary Beard, *The Rise of American Civilization* (4 vols., 1927–42)
First television transmission, New York to Washington	Cather, *Death Comes for the Archbishop*
	Cullen, *Caroling Dusk* and *Copper Sun*
Amelia Earhart first woman to complete non-stop transatlantic flight	Mourning Dove, *Cogewea, the Half-Blood*
	Hemingway, "Hills Like White Elephants"
	Hughes, "Mulatto"
	Lewis, *Elmer Gantry*
	Parrington, *Main Currents in American Thought*
	Williams, "The Dead Baby"
	Film: Al Jolson sings in *The Jazz Singer*, the first successful "talkie"; Academy of Motion Picture Arts and Sciences founded (first Academy Awards, 1929)
	Music: Antheil, *Ballet mécanique*; musical *Showboat*
	Painting: Hopper *Automat* and *Light at Two Lights*; Sheeler photographs of the Ford Motor Company plant

Historical events	Cultural events (discussed in the text)
1928 Hoover elected President	Frost, *West-Running Brook*, "Acquainted with the Night"
Kellogg–Briand treaty outlaws war (US approves, 1929)	Larsen, *Quicksand*
St. Francis Dam breaks in California, killing over 500	Film: Mickey Mouse debuts in *Steamboat Willie*
1929 Gangster activity given national visibility by Chicago "St. Valentine's Day Massacre"	Cullen, *Black Christ and Other Poems*
	Dewey, *Individualism Old and New*
	Faulkner, *The Sound and the Fury*
Stock market crashes; Great Depression begins	Hemingway, *A Farewell to Arms*
	Larsen, *Passing*
	Helen and Robert Lynd, *Middletown – A Study in Contemporary American Culture*
	Founding of the Museum of Modern Art (MOMA)
1930	*Fortune* magazine begins publication
	Crane, *The Bridge*
	Dos Passos, *The 42nd Parallel* (first of *USA* trilogy, completed 1936)
	Faulkner, *As I Lay Dying*
	Hammett, *The Maltese Falcon*
	Twelve Southerners, *I'll Take My Stand*
	US Customs seizes copies of Joyce's *Ulysses*
	Sinclair Lewis becomes first American to receive Nobel Prize for literature
	"Golden Age" of radio begins
	Painting: Sheeler, *American Landscape*

Historical events	Cultural events (discussed in the text)
1931 First Scottsboro trial (nine young African Americans accused of raping two white women)	Buck, *The Good Earth*
	Rourke, *American Humor*
Empire State Building completed in New York City	Whitney Museum of American Art opens
1932 "Bonus Army" (war veterans) march on Washington	Farrell, *Studs Lonigan* (trilogy completed 1935)
	Hughes, "Mother to Son"
1933 Franklin Delano Roosevelt (FDR) elected President	*Partisan Review* begins publication
	Cowley, *Exile's Return*
New Deal begins promotion of economic recovery	Fitzgerald, *Tender Is the Night*
21st Constitutional Amendment repeals Prohibition	West, *The Day of the Locust*
	Film: *42nd Street; Gold Diggers of 1933*
	"L'il Abner" comic strip debuts
1934 "Dust Bowl"	Painting: Douglas, *Aspects of Negro Life* mural; "Machine Art" exhibit at MOMA
Creation of National Labor Relations Board	
Major strike by millworkers in the South	
1935 Second phase of New Deal; WPA established	Lewis, *It Can't Happen Here*
	Odets, *Waiting for Lefty*
	Rukeyser, "The Trial"
	Cavalcade of America radio program
1936 FDR re-elected	*Life* magazine begins publication
Jesse Owens wins four gold medals in Berlin Olympics	Faulkner, *Absalom! Absalom!*
	Frost, *A Further Range,* "Desert Places," "Design"
Spanish Civil War begins	
	Hughes, "Let America Be America Again"
	Mitchell, *Gone With the Wind*

Historical events	Cultural events (discussed in the text)
	Taggard, "Mill Town"
	Wright completes "Fallingwater"
1937 Golden Gate bridge opened	Barnes, *Nightwood*
Hindenberg explodes	Solomon R. Guggenheim Museum opens
1938	Brooks and Warren, *Understanding Poetry*
	Luce, "The American Century"
	Millay, "Say That We Saw Spain Die"
	Wilder, *Our Town*
	Music: Copland, *Billy the Kid*
	Radio: Broadcast of *War of the Worlds* causes national panic; series, *Americans All*
1939 New York World's Fair	Steinbeck, *The Grapes of Wrath*
World War II begins	Film: *Mr. Smith Goes to Washington*
1940 FDR re-elected	Hemingway, *For Whom the Bell Tolls*
	MacLeish, "The Irresponsibles"
	O'Neill, *Long Day's Journey Into Night*
	Wright, *Native Son*
	Film: *The Grapes of Wrath*; *His Girl Friday*
	Painting: Lawrence, *The Migration of the Negro* series (completed 1941); Hopper, *Gas* and *Office at Night*; MOMA adds photography department
1941 FDR's "Four Freedoms" speech	Evans and Agee, *Let Us Now Praise Famous Men*
Bombing of Pearl Harbor; US enters World War II	Fitzgerald, *The Last Tycoon*
	Kazin, *On Native Grounds*
	Matthiessen, *American Renaissance*

Historical events	Cultural events (discussed in the text)
	Thurber, "The Secret Life of Walter Mitty"
	Film: *Citizen Kane*
1942	Faulkner, *Go Down, Moses*
	Rourke, *The Roots of American Culture*
	Film: *Sullivan's Travels*; *Casablanca*
	Music: Copland, *Rodeo*
	Painting: Hopper, *Nighthawks*
1944 FDR re-elected	Moore, "In Distrust of Merits"
D-Day	Music: Copland, *Appalachian Spring*
G.I. Bill of Rights passed	
1945 Germany surrenders	Brooks, "kitchenette building"
Atomic bombing of Hiroshima and Nagasaki	Williams, *The Glass Menagerie*
	Film: *Mildred Pierce*
Japan surrenders	
World War II ends	
FDR dies; Truman becomes President	
1946 1946–64 sees "baby boom"	*Literary History of the United States* completed
	Lowell, *Lord Weary's Castle*
	McCuller, *The Member of the Wedding*
	Petry, *The Street*
	Spock, *Common Sense Book of Baby and Child Care*
	Williams, *Paterson* (completed 1958)
	Film: *The Best Years of Our Lives*; *The Big Sleep*; *It's A Wonderful Life*
1947 Freedom Train begins travels across US	Hughes, "Genius Child"
	Williams, *A Streetcar Named Desire*

Historical events	Cultural events (discussed in the text)
1948	Mailer, *The Naked and the Dead*
	Pound, *The Pisan Cantos*
1949	Miller, *Death of a Salesman*
1950 Korean war (ends 1953)	Riesman, *The Lonely Crowd*
"McCarthyism" begins	Gwendolyn Brooks first African American woman to receive Pulitzer Prize
	Abstract Expressionism dominates art scene throughout decade
1951	Jones, *From Here to Eternity*
	Lowell, *The Mills of the Kavanaughs*
	Salinger, *The Catcher in the Rye*
1952 Eisenhower elected President	Ellison, *Invisible Man*
1953 Department of Health, Education, and Welfare established	Miller, *The Crucible*
	Film: *Shane; The Wild One*
Subcommittee on Juvenile Delinquency formed	
1954 First restaurant in the McDonald's chain	Cheever, "The Country Husband"
	Williams, *Cat on a Hot Tin Roof*
Supreme Court rules racial segregation in public schools unconstitutional	Film: *On the Waterfront*
	Television: *Father Knows Best*
McCarthy censored by Congress	
1955 Salk polio vaccine	Auden, "The Shield of Achilles"
	Ginsberg, "A Supermarket in California" and "Howl"
	Film: *Blackboard Jungle; Rebel Without a Cause*

Historical events	Cultural events (discussed in the text)
1956 Bus boycott in Montgomery, Alabama	Whyte, *The Organization Man*
	Film: *Invasion of the Body Snatchers*; *The Man in the Gray Flannel Suit*
Khrushchev's remark: "We will bury you!"	Television: Elvis Presley performs on the Ed Sullivan show
"In God We Trust" adopted as official motto of US	
1957 Launching of Sputnik: space race between US and USSR	Chase, *The American Novel and its Tradition*
President Eisenhower authorizes federal troops to impose order during school integration in Little Rock, Arkansas	Kerouac, *On the Road*
	Musicals: Bernstein, *West Side Story*; Willson, *The Music Man*
Establishment of the Civil Rights Commission	
1958 Alaska admitted to Union	Barth, *The End of the Road*
	Television: *77 Sunset Strip*
1959 "Kitchen Debate" between Nixon and Khrushchev	Lowell, *Life Studies*
	O'Hara, "The Day Lady Died"
Hawaii admitted to Union	Television: *Dobie Gillis*
1960 Kennedy elected President	Brooks, "We Real Cool"
	Fiedler, *Love and Death in the American Novel*
	Lee, *To Kill a Mockingbird*
1961 First manned US space flight	Heller, *Catch-22*
1962	Salinger, *Franny and Zooey*
	Harrington, *The Other America*
	Kesey, *One Flew Over the Cuckoo's Nest*
	Film: *The Manchurian Candidate*
1963 Assassination of Kennedy	Friedan, *The Feminine Mystique*
	Martin Luther King, Jr., "Letter from Birmingham Jail"

Acknowledgments

The University of North Carolina at Greensboro, until recently my academic home, generously supported this project. I am especially grateful to Rosemary Wander, Denise Baker, and my colleagues in the English department for the gifts of time and money. At the University's Jackson Library, the British Library, and the Rothermere American Institute, the librarians and desk assistants made doing research a pleasure. Tony Aarts and Blythe Winslow performed even the dullest research assignments promptly and cheerfully. I am indebted to Ron Bush, Andrew Delbanco, Kevin Dettmar, Barbara Packer, and Patricia Tatspaugh for friendship and intellectual challenges. Although I cannot thank them individually, the members of the Modernist Studies Association have profoundly influenced my understanding of the twentieth century. I can thank Russ McDonald individually but never adequately for his generous criticism and advice.

Every member of the Blackwell Publishing enterprise has been enormously helpful: Emma Bennett, Kitty Bocking, Janet Moth, Leanda Shrimpton, Karen Wilson, and Astrid Wind were models of patience, efficiency, and good humor. Andrew McNeillie, whose energy is irresistible, set the project in motion and became a friend in the process, enriching my life.

Countee Cullen, "Incident," from *On These I Stand*. New York: Harper & Row, 1947. Copyright © 1947 by Countee Cullen. Copyrights held by Amistad Research Center Tulane University administered by Thompson and Thompson, Brooklyn, NY.

Frank O'Hara, "The Day Lady Died," from *Lunch Poems*. San Francisco: City Lights Books, 1964. Copyright © 1964 by Frank O'Hara. Reprinted by permission of City Lights Publishers.

Robert Frost, "Design," from Edward Connery Latham (ed.), *The Poetry of Robert Frost*. New York: Henry Holt & Co., 1979. Copyright © 1923, 1969 by Henry Holt and Company; copyright © 1942, 1951 by Robert Frost; copyright © 1970 by Lesley Frost Ballantine. Reprinted by permission of Henry Holt and Company, LLC, and The Random House Group Ltd.

Robert Frost, "Desert Places," from Edward Connery Latham (ed.), *The Poetry of Robert Frost*. New York: Henry Holt & Co., 1979. Copyright © 1923, 1969 by Henry Holt and Company; copyright © 1942, 1951 by Robert Frost; copyright © 1970 by Lesley Frost Ballantine. Reprinted by permission of Henry Holt and Company, LLC and The Random House Group Ltd.

Allen Ginsberg, "A Supermarket in California," from *Collected Poems: 1947–1980*. New York: HarperCollins, 1984. Copyright © Allen Ginsberg, 1955, 1984, 1995. Reprinted by permission of HarperCollins Publishers and The Wylie Agency (UK) Ltd.

William Carlos Williams, "The Red Wheelbarrow," from *Collected Poems: 1909–1939, Volume I*. New York: New Directions, 1963. Copyright © 1938 by New Directions Publishing Corp. Reprinted by permission of New Directions Publishing Corp and Carcanet Press Limited.

Every effort has been made to trace copyright holders and to obtain their permission for the use of copyright material. The publisher apologizes for any errors or omissions in the above list and would be grateful if notified of any corrections that should be incorporated in future reprints or editions of this book.

Introduction

Almost without exception companions and introductions to literature begin with questions of nomenclature. In the present instance, the difficulty of defining terms is inherent to the subject. What is "America"? What is "literature"? And what in the world do we mean by "culture"? Given the contested meaning of every term it undertakes to introduce, the title of this volume must seem an exercise in effrontery. Aware as I am that every example and every sentence in the book say as much about its author's tastes and predilections as about its titular subject, I make no pretense of comprehensive "coverage." Rather, the materials discussed and examples employed are ones that have proven useful to my students in understanding what are generally agreed to be some important aspects of twentieth-century American writing and its contexts. Because my objective is to be both clear and suggestive, I focus on a few big ideas about America and, by the marshaling of examples and counter-examples, show that these ideas are, and should be, subject to interpretation, revision, supplementation, and debate.

On the cover of this volume is a painting by Jasper Johns entitled *Target with Four Faces*. So large a "target" as the USA's literature and culture in the first six decades of the twentieth century cannot be fully explored via four of its "faces" but, then, four hundred faces would not exhaust the topic either. One must begin somewhere. The chapters are based on four significant perceptions of America: that it is big, rich, new, and free. Clearly, all these terms are relative and require further definition, and that is the main business of the book. It is intended for students and general readers who, knowing something about America, its literature, and its culture, are inclined to learn more.

"America," as it is used in these pages, refers to the United States of America and, as will quickly become clear, also to a set of ideas. I've chosen "America" because of its rich connotations and because crucial ideas in circulation in the first decades of the twentieth century employ that term: for example, the American Way, the American Dream, and the American Century. Whether for its brevity or for its euphony, "America" seems to have been the preferred term among the historians, critics, and cultural commentators writing between 1900 and 1960. I have followed their lead.

"Literature," also a vexed and loaded term, is here used to refer to poetry, drama, novels, short fiction, and, occasionally, autobiography. Given the voluminous written materials from which to select examples, I have chosen to be literal about "literature" – that is, as defined by "the letter" – referring to written and published materials. Therefore, I do not consider oral traditions. The emphasis is primarily on the category of writing designated as imaginative or creative, what once was called *belles lettres*. Because this book is intended as an introduction to American literature, examples are largely confined to those that may be easily located in standard classroom anthologies and on college and university reading lists. Some readers and teachers will want more – a broader representation of ethnicities, for example. Because of the expansion of the canon over the last sixty years, a persuasive case can be made for this point of view. Limits of space have, in part, determined my concentration on frequently studied texts, but there is another reason, too. The explosion in writing that led to canon expansion is largely a phenomenon of the period just beyond the decades covered here. An introduction to post-1960 American writing would thus have a very different configuration from one focused on the earlier decades of the twentieth century.

Raymond Williams, in his seminal book *Keywords*, declares that "'Culture' is one of the two or three most complicated words in the English language." In fact, Williams is one of the thinkers responsible for complicating the definition still further, influential as he was in defining culture as something "ordinary," as "a whole way of life." In its earliest uses, "culture" was a noun primarily associated with what is sometimes called "high," as opposed to "popular," culture – things like poetry, art museums, opera. One became "cultured" or "cultivated" by exposure to these categories of art, as a plant might be cultivated by exposure to light. Certainly, this book does not ignore so-called "high" culture, but neither does it limit examples to that category. To do so would be a serious distortion of American culture as a whole. In fact, many of its most influential modes of expression – movies and rock-and-roll, for example – are popular arts. In a sense, being in the shadow of the much longer artistic traditions of Europe has meant that "culture" has always been a problematic word for Americans. As with high versus low culture, the separation between *literature* and *culture* in the title of this book should not be taken too seriously. The two are not separate, finally, for literature is a part of a whole way of life. Instead, the title signals that, unlike a purely literary history, this study is *also* interested in aspects of American life such as child-rearing and Broadway musicals. Further, it is interested in the relationships among these various manifestations of American life.

With the rise of social sciences in the late nineteenth and early twentieth centuries; with the introduction of an anthropological perspective examining culture as, for example, kinship structures and foodways; and, much more recently, with the perspectives generated by the theories of "cultural studies," the meaning of "culture" has become far more inclusive. Stephen Greenblatt, a Renaissance scholar who is a central figure of New Historicism, a branch of cultural studies, concedes that "like 'ideology' . . . 'culture' is a term that is repeatedly used without meaning much of anything at all."[1] In short, the inclusiveness may empty the word of any content.

One way of thinking about culture is to consider the ways in which one performs certain actions habitually and without much analysis. Why do I put milk on my breakfast cereal? or Why is that notion disgusting to me? Why do I wear matching shoes? Why do I cover my head? How do I know what behavior is expected of me at a funeral or wedding? Why do I say "hello" or "goodbye" with the intonations I do? Culture is embedded in behavior, and its significance must be brought to the surface by such questions. Thinking about culture requires many of the same skills employed in analyzing a text: paying close attention, noticing patterns, discriminating among nuances of tone and action. Greenblatt makes this connection:

> The world is full of texts, most of which are virtually incomprehensible when they are removed from their immediate surroundings. To recover the meaning of such texts, to make any sense of them at all, we need to reconstruct the situation in which they were produced. Works of art by contrast contain directly or by implication much of this situation within themselves, and it is this sustained absorption that enables many literary works to survive the collapse of the conditions that led to their production.

Some understanding of those conditions is, however, retrievable: "if exploration of a particular culture will lead to a heightened understanding of a work of literature produced within that culture, so too a careful reading of a work of literature will lead to a heightened understanding of the culture in which it was produced."[1]

To promote thinking about relationships among behaviors, beliefs, works of art, places, and other dimensions of "a whole way of life," the chapters that follow are organized less by strict chronology than by exemplary books, ideas, and memorable historical events. Thus, all four chapters range over the entire period. A strictly linear model of presentation, with each chapter dedicated to one decade, would not capture the recurrence of such subjects as racial strife, the persistent division between rich and poor, or the patterns of isolation and involvement that characterize the country's interactions with the world at large. Similarly, a strictly linear presentation almost inevitably suggests progress, that is, a line of development that implies an improvement over the past. Interrogation of what constitutes "progress," suspicion of a positivist view of the nation's growth, marks much of the fiction and cultural commentary of this period; to adopt a teleological, onward-and-upward sort of model undermines the claims of the vocal minority unconvinced that progress was always progress.

To prevent confusion, however, a timeline of the chief events, political, social, and artistic appears on pages viii–xxi. In addition, the chapter subheadings (listed in the table of contents) serve as guide-posts. Chapter 1 contains material, for example, pertinent to the first decade of the twentieth century, such as immigration and assimila-tion. Chapter 2, because of its emphasis on wealth, also contains an overview of labor reform and the build-up to and consequences of the Great Depression. Chapter 3 will be of special interest to students of expatriation (the "Lost Generation") and the artistic experiments of modernism. For readers interested in the Cold War, chapter 4 will be of most use.

Each of the chapters is introduced by a series of quotations. These epigraphs are not meant to be decorative but to display a range of attitudes, expressed over time, toward the chapter's topic. A discussion of their implications begins each chapter. Readers will notice that some of the passages are taken from periods well before the twentieth century, and this retrospection is purposeful. Principal ideas about America and Americans, both of citizens and of those who observe from a distance, are inextricable from the emergence of the very concept of America, comprising its New World aura during a time of discovery and exploration, its Puritan beginnings, its colonial status, and so forth. Despite the rhetoric of newness that pervades writing about the United States, the nation is not *sui generis* or freshly minted. It did not invent democracy or slavery. Its achievements in film and music, to name only two, are impressive, but it is important to remember how many of the achievers in those fields came from elsewhere. The evocation of earlier periods is one way of remembering that the USA, for all its powerful presence in the twentieth century, became so powerful not despite the Old World's human history but because of it.

Every book of this kind must navigate the turbulent waters between the Scylla and Charybdis of breadth and depth. Normally, an introductory text opts for a broad range of examples as best fitting a survey of several decades, and this book does, too. The survey or panorama, however, runs the risk of missing the exceptions that disturb the wide view. Insofar as permissions costs and space allow, I have included specific attention to individual poems, novels, and plays as a reminder of the value of the close-up. So large and various a country as the United States seems to demand sweeping, epic energies, audible and visible in Walt Whitman's "Song of Myself." But Whitman's contemporary Emily Dickinson took the equally persuasive position that the turn inward, the lyric impulse, expresses a particularity that stubbornly refuses to be swept up. Close reading yields the particulars that make a work distinctive, not only a demonstration of a "school" or "type" within a survey.

An effective way to use this book is to think of it as a flexible template. The writing discussed, the music mentioned, the films singled out for discussion – all the examples should be regarded as suggesting still other possibilities. To invoke a third figure from the nineteenth century, Emerson, in "The American Scholar," demands that his listeners practice "creative reading": "One must be an inventor to read well." By pursuing the four lines of investigation outlined in this text, a creative reader will see forty others and thus generate prospects for further study. As Adrienne Rich writes in "Diving into the Wreck," "The words are purposes. / The words are maps." Mapping the USA is an inexhaustible task.

CHAPTER 1

Big

FIGURE 1   Ansel Adams, *Clearing Winter Snow, Yosemite National Park*, 1937
Photograph © Ansel Adams Publishing Rights Trust/CORBIS
Adams was dedicated not only to the beauty of the national park but to
its conservation.

"for wee must Consider that wee shall be as a Citty upon a Hill, the eies of all people are uppon us; soe that if wee shall deale falsely with our god in this worke wee have undertaken and soe cause him to withdrawe his present help from us, wee shall be made a story and a byword through the world."
John Winthrop, "A Model of Christian Charity," ca. 1630

And as the moon rose higher the inessential houses began to melt away until gradually I became aware of the old island here that flowered once for Dutch sailors' eyes – a fresh, green breast of the new world. Its vanished trees, the trees that had made way for Gatsby's house, had once pandered in whispers to the last and greatest of all human dreams; for a transitory enchanted moment man must have held his breath in the presence of this continent, compelled into an aesthetic contemplation he neither understood nor desired, face to face for the last time in history with something commensurate to his capacity for wonder.
F. Scott Fitzgerald, The Great Gatsby, 1925

Between that earth and that sky I felt erased, blotted out. I did not say my prayers that night: here, I felt, what would be would be.
Willa Cather, My Ántonia, 1918

Let America be America again.
Let it be the dream it used to be.
Let it be the pioneer on the plain
Seeking a home, where he himself is free.
Langston Hughes, "Let America
Be America Again," 1936

Yet America is a poem in our eyes; its ample geography dazzles the imagination . . .
Ralph Waldo Emerson, "The Poet," 1844

America's size matters. John Winthrop's image of the New World settlements as a city on a hill did not reflect a tangible reality: the shore may not even have been in his sight as he delivered his sermon. What mattered more was the size of the idea. Still, the vast continent lent itself to grand plans; the life to be undertaken would be exemplary, and to fail would make the pilgrims an infamous "story and a byword through the world." The purpose of this chapter is to consider how the size of the land mass that would become the continental United States contributes to an understanding of American literature and culture. For the imagined Dutch sailors of F. Scott Fitzgerald's famous closing to *The Great Gatsby*, the expanse of land – empty, unspoiled, still fresh and green and virginal – suggests limitless possibility, awe, the thrill of the blank page awaiting the first word. This fantasy of the yet-to-be-named informs not only early exploration literature but the institutionalization of American literature as a discipline. The American male as namer (and thus claimer) generated, for example, the influential concept of "the American Adam," defined by R. W. B. Lewis as "an individual emancipated from history, happily bereft of ancestry . . . standing alone, self-reliant and self-propelling, ready to confront whatever awaited him with the aid of his own unique and inherent resources."[1] Willa Cather's character Jim, however, exemplifies a more somber view. As a child newly orphaned and sent to relatives in the barely settled Midwest, he sees "nothing but land," its emptiness signifying a loss of family and identity. His parents, he is certain, do not look benevolently down from "the complete dome of heaven, all there was of it." The speaker of Langston Hughes's poem turns the mythology of "the endless plain" into an indictment. Emphasizing the disparity between dream and reality, the speaker declares that, for some, America is "the land that never has been yet." In their different ways, then, Winthrop, Fitzgerald, Cather, and Hughes affirm the American landscape as a space to be reckoned with – claimed, admired, feared, shaped.

The land of course was not empty, as the wretched history of Native Americans makes clear. Neither was the Big Sky Country of the West all sagebrush, purple mountains, and laconic cowboys as figured in the popular westerns of Zane Grey or Louis L'Amour. As the country grew skywards as well as westwards, the great urban centers were "alive and coarse and strong and cunning" as in Carl Sandburg's poem "Chicago" (1916). The "City of the Big Shoulders," was, on the one hand, famous for its skyscrapers and, on the other, notorious for its organized crime. The size and rapid growth of the United States support several foundational myths allied with the idea of America: the city on a hill, the virgin land, the American Adam, the wide, wild West. Given the energetic dismantling of these myths over the last century, one is tempted to dismiss the big sky and the big dreams as big lies. But to do so mistakenly denies the power these imaginative constructions of America exercised, for both good and ill, in the twentieth century. The bigness of America, and all that is implied by its size, remains an issue of global magnitude.

What are the implications of immensity? The sometimes contradictory attitudes of Ralph Waldo Emerson toward the perception of landscape can be helpful in addressing this question. In "Nature," Emerson crosses a common at twilight and enjoys a perfect exhilaration. Almost I fear to think how glad I am. . . . Standing on the bare common – my head bathed by the blithe air, and uplifted into infinite space – all mean egotism vanishes. I become a transparent eye-ball. I am nothing. I see all. The currents of the Universal Being circulate through me. . . . In the tranquil landscape, and especially in the distant line of the horizon, man beholds somewhat as beautiful as his own nature. (chapter 1)

The exuberant tone of this passage suggests that to transcend boundaries is to experience a rare ecstasy. But Emerson's mood could be quite otherwise. Elsewhere, in his later essay "Experience," for example, he intimates the potential threat in these circulating currents.

We have learned that we do not see directly, but mediately, and that we have no means of correcting these colored and distorting lenses which we are, or of computing the amount of their errors. Perhaps these subject-lenses have a creative power; perhaps there are no objects. . . . Nature and literature are subjective phenomena; every evil and every good thing is a shadow that we cast. (paragraph 18)

If I am both nothing and everything, where do I begin? If all I see is subjective, then how may I trust my sight?

In Emerson's time and in our own, these questions apply not just to a task to be undertaken or a place to start, but quite literally to the body itself. The curves of the transparent eyeball are permeable – thus open and vulnerable. Mystical elation may be seen as the obverse of a terrifying drop into nothingness. The sheer size of America and the abundance of its natural resources have been, from the writings of the colonists onward, exceptionally tantalizing not only as metaphors but as motives of action. Vastness conjures adventure and the freedom to exploit nature – a sense that there is plenty to do and plenty to go around. Vastness conjures emptiness and isolation, too, as we may observe in the snowy New England landscapes of Robert Frost's poetry. The West to which the newspaper editor Horace Greeley urged young men to go at the beginning of the century and to which, some fifty years later, Jack Kerouac and his companions sped in *On the Road* has served as the Grail of both material and psychic quests; it has also served, in the Los Angeles of Raymond Chandler and the Hollywood of Nathanael West, as the site of profound alienation and apocalypse.

Humankind's relationship to landscape takes many forms. In an essay entitled "The Beholding Eye: Ten Versions of the Same Scene," the landscape historian D. W. Meinig lists ten ways in which an observer might "see" a landscape: nature, habitat, system, artifact, problem, wealth, ideology, history, place, and esthetic.[2] A person's relationship to landscape may also be seen as that of reader to text. As nature, the scene invites speculation about the relative insignificance of the observer; as habitat or system, it presents itself as usable terrain or as a delicately balanced ecology. Other constructions, like those of artifact, problem, or history, emphasize the dynamic relationship between what the landscape is or does and what humans have done or will do to change it. These potential meanings are inherent in every landscape, of course, not just that between the East and West coasts of the United States. But as Emerson noted in 1844, America's "ample geography dazzles the imagination" ("The Poet"). Its size and variety of terrain have had much to do with what many imagine America to be and have generated some of the most stimulating and influential work in the study of American literature and culture: the role of Puritan typology in imbuing landscape with symbolic meaning, as, for example, the equation of wilderness with sin and savagery; the effects of the gendered language of exploration, the land as dis-covered female, with its implications for the ethics of land use and the status of women; the ways in which borders and frontiers are also contact zones, with complex effects on indigenous and settler cultures; and, most recently, the growing field of ecocriticism.

Until the continental United States had stretched, as the anthem "America the Beautiful" has it, "from sea to shining sea," mainstream discourse about settling the land was optimistic and energetic. Two influential concepts that illustrate this phenomenon are Manifest Destiny and the Frontier Thesis. In 1845, writing in *The Democratic Review* on the question of territorial expansion, journalist John L. O'Sullivan declared:

> The far-reaching, the boundless future will be the era of American greatness. In its magnificent domain of space and time, the nation of many nations is destined to manifest to mankind the excellence of divine principles; to establish on earth the noblest temple ever dedicated to the worship of the Most High – the Sacred and the True. Its floor shall be a hemisphere – its roof the firmament of the star-studded heavens, and its congregation an Union of many Republics, comprising hundreds of happy millions, calling, owning no man master, but governed by God's natural and moral law of equality, the law of brotherhood – of "peace and good will amongst men."

This is the rhetoric of American exceptionalism – visionary people, answerable to none but God, granted boundless space and time to achieve a moral zenith. It was deployed strategically and effectively over the next fifty years, despite the resistance of some who, for a variety of reasons, opposed such growth. The historical effects of the idea were substantial and measurable. Under the aegis of Manifest Destiny, cross-country railroads were built; a war with Mexico was fought; Native American tribes were destroyed or displaced, the "slave" and "free" territories became political pawns in the schism that would eventuate in the Civil War.

In 1890 the US Census Bureau declared that, because of the rapid settlement of the West, it was no longer possible to discern a line that could be called the "frontier." Destiny was now manifest. Three years later, in a speech before historians at the World's Columbian Exposition of 1893, the historian Frederick Jackson Turner declared, "American history has been in a large degree the history of the colonization of the Great West. The existence of an area of free land, its continuous recession, and the advance of American settlement westward, explain American development." Turner assumes that if there is land, it cries out to be settled and, further, that if there is no visible frontier at home, then frontiers must be found elsewhere so that the advancement of civilization can continue. The so-called "Turner thesis" or "frontier thesis," has, unsurprisingly, been debated and derided. Contemporary scholars of the "new West," such as Patricia Limerick, dispute the paradigm of values associated with earlier definitions of the frontier. Her now famous example of the heaps of tin cans at the doors of ranch dwellings undermines the image of the self-reliant pioneer; revisions of the history of the West's settlement have significantly altered the conception of the West as home to virtuous pioneers, lonesome cowboys, and wide-open spaces. But, as Limerick herself argues, Turner's thesis has had enormous staying power in American minds.[3] From the space program to cyberspace, from medical diagnostics to the travels of the Starship Enterprise on television's *Star Trek*, the phrase "new frontier" is alive in public discourse.

Sullivan's Manifest Destiny and Jackson's Frontier map an imaginary geography. In the country of this vision, rugged men dominate the landscape, physical energies are directed toward profitable progress, morale is high. Absent from this fantasy are not only women, slaves, scorned ethnicities, and immigrant groups, but also the depressed, the frightened, the hesitant, and the impoverished. The period 1900–1960 offers ample illustration of the darker side of spatial progress, these moves from East to West and, in the cities, from earth to sky. Even as it has celebrated the entrepreneurial spirit, American culture has worried over the poignant, disturbing, and ludicrous characteristics of the go-getter. Consider Arthur Miller's Willy Loman, the salesman who has reached the end of his career but who maintains a habit of baseless optimism almost until the moment of his suicide (*Death of A Salesman*, 1949); he exits with plans to plant a garden, "to get something into the ground." William Faulkner's ruthless Southern empire-builder, Thomas Sutpen in *Absalom! Absalom!* (1936), Sinclair Lewis's eponymous Babbitt (1922) or his preacher Elmer Gantry (1927), James Thurber's sad and comical Walter Mitty (1941), whose daydreams give him the stature that commercial life cannot – all these characters subvert the myth of the self-made man. Today, listeners to National Public Radio relish the irony of radio humorist Garrison Keillor as he broadcasts weekly from fictional Lake Wobegon, where "The women are strong, the men are handsome, and all the kids are above average." If the breadth of the nation has served to expand its powers and wealth and motivate its citizenry, it has also served to bloat and satiate and disgust. Fitzgerald's passage about the Dutch sailors is in fact elegiac: in this novel of the 1920s, futility has already replaced wonder as "we beat on, boats against the current." Indeed, Turner's earlier assertion of the frontier's significance to American history was in part monitory: without a frontier to settle, what would become of the "go-ahead" American character? What vision would now be equal to the capacity for wonder?

This division between elation and despair puts the case too bluntly. Between thrill and terror, fresh starts and exhausted endings, lies a spectrum of attitudes; indeed, given the complexities of art forms, a given work likely comprises a range of contrary attitudes. The remainder of this chapter will examine five forms of response to the size and complex meanings of the American landscape: some psychological effects of expansionism; the delights and horrors of the urban landscape; the photographic and poetic treatment of nature in a post-Romantic landscape; the apocalyptic West; and the reinvention of rootedness in one regional literature.

Expansion and its Discontents

When Henry David Thoreau quipped in *Walden* (1854) that "we do not ride on the railroad; it rides upon us," he was counting the human costs of technological progress. By the opening years of the twentieth century, many of his compatriots believed the costs to have mounted to punishing levels. Analysts of the modernization of the United States often date significant changes in American thought to the traumatic events of the Civil War. The case that Philip Fisher, Louis Menand, and others make for the significance of that struggle to the psychic health or illness of the nation and to the development of influential American thinkers is persuasive and deserving of attention.[4] But since that analysis takes us rather far from the beginning of the twentieth century, this book will consider more immediate anxieties.

We can begin with bodily discomfort. As the century turned and the country grew in both size and population, more and more people complained of nervous disorders. In the final chapter of *The Education of Henry Adams* (private printing, 1907; public, 1918), Adams recalls what America must have looked like to his father in 1868 – "a long caravan stretching out towards the plain." Disembarking at New York in 1905 after a trip abroad, Adams sees instead a "frantic" city, its air full of hysteria, anger, alarm:

> Prosperity never before imagined, power never yet wielded by man, speed never reached by anything but a meteor had made the world irritable, nervous, querulous, unreasonable and afraid. All New York was demanding new men, and all the new forces, condensed into corporations, were demanding a new type of man – a man with ten times the endurance, energy, will and mind of the old type.

Even if we allow for Adams's customarily dark irony, the prospect he describes is daunting. Nor was he alone in believing himself unequal to the demands. Unease about noise, rush, crowding, and rampant materialism was in part a function of the comfort these developments disrupted; that is to say, the strongest objections and descriptions of mental suffering emanated largely from the rich, those not consumed by the daily effort to earn a living wage. In part, of course, we can attribute this impression to the written record. The "recoil from an 'over-civilized' modern existence" that historian Jackson Lears has, in *No Place of Grace*, labeled "anti-modernist" was articulated by people with the leisure to analyze their emotional responses, the education to write about them, and access to venues in which to publish them.[5] It is rare to read of a "factory girl" suffering from neurasthenia.

Neurasthenia was an umbrella diagnosis; the disease was commonly understood to be a reaction to the stimuli of modern life. The physician George M. Beard declared unequivocally in 1881 that neurasthenia was "a product of American civilization." Its symptoms were as numerous as they were vague, ranging from dyspepsia and insomnia to rashes and premature baldness. The number of distinguished Americans diagnosed with the condition is striking: Jane Addams, Henry Adams, Theodore Roosevelt, Theodore Dreiser, Charlotte Perkins Gilman, Owen Wister, Frank Norris – to name a very few.[6] There appears to have been a certain cachet associated with the disease. In Henry James's *Daisy Miller*, Mrs. Miller proudly declares her illness exceptional: Dr. Davis of Schenectady has said "he never saw anything like my dyspepsia, but he was bound to cure it. . . . At Schenectady he stands at the very top; and there's a great deal of sickness there, too." Translation: Americans of my class are martyrs to our highly developed and sensitive natures.

The *locus classicus* of neurasthenia and the "rest-cure" made famous by the physician S. Weir Mitchell is Charlotte Perkins Gilman's "The Yellow Wallpaper" (1892). In her story, a new mother who suffers from an unnamed nervous illness is forced to do nothing but eat and sleep, expressly forbidden by her husband (he is also her physician)

FIGURE 2 Sanitarium photograph, Battle Creek, Michigan
Photograph Willard Library for American Literature and Culture, Battle Creek, Michigan.
Wealthy Americans turned to sanitarium rest-cures to counter the pressures of modern life.

to write or engage in any sort of intellectually stimulating activity. In a period when the New Woman was in an embryonic stage in America, Gilman dramatizes the conflict between stasis and progress; as her character loses her former sense of herself, she increasingly identifies with the woman she perceives "trapped" inside the wallpaper. The story ends ambiguously: the wife has rebelled in a destructive way, ripping down the wallpaper, but she is also on her hands and knees, apparently reduced to madness. Kate Chopin's Edna Pontellier in *The Awakening* (1898) is also stymied and an object of concern to her husband and her physician. Having realized that she is not a "mother-woman" and having attempted to devise other roles for herself – householder, painter, lover – she, too, feels trapped and discontented. The novel's ending, in which Edna strips naked, walks into the sea, and drowns, has been much debated because it is ambiguous. Does Edna actively choose to die or does she, in her dejection, only allow death to come? Finally, in Edith Wharton's *The House of Mirth* (1905), Lily Bart's downward spiral is mirrored in her spatial confinement. A public beauty, Lily has been formed for the marriage market but resists her own commodification and yet can support herself in no other way. Unable to forfeit either her desire for wealth or her desire for an independent "republic of the spirit," she resides in increasingly smaller spaces, insomniac, unable to eat, until, from an overdose of chloral (perhaps accidental, perhaps not), she dies alone in a boarding house.

Gilman, Chopin, and Wharton vividly imagine what their characters reject, but cannot or will not imagine a future for them. All these texts can fruitfully be read as manifestations of the status of women in this period. They can also, however, be studied as narratives that stage the struggle with modernity in spatial terms. Gilman's young mother is pictured in a room at the top of a house, a room in which the windows are barred and there are "rings and things" in the walls. The woman she tries to release from the wallpaper also appears to be behind bars. Attempts to escape her confinement in the yellow-wallpapered room and enter the larger world visible through her windows constitute the main action of her story. Similarly, *The Awakening* begins with the image of a parrot in a cage and ends with a broken-winged seagull flying over an endless ocean. The movement in both stories is from entrapment toward an ambivalently presented freedom; as we move from small space to large, liberation is difficult to distinguish from dissolution. *The House of Mirth* moves in the opposite direction: having established the corruption of her fictional houses of wealth, Wharton's placement of Lily in a narrow bed in a bare room signals a moral victory – Lily's debts are paid. Again, however, it would be wrong to call the ending triumphant. Clearly these stories respond to the contemporary condition of women and may be read as protests against the confines of woman's traditional sphere of influence: home, family, and a highly controlled social circle. We may also, however, consider the movement toward madness and death in each narrative as symptomatic of the fear of transition from one state to another, a distress not confined to women in this period.

We come now to an apparent paradox: how can the conditions of crowding, noise, and hectic activity that seem to have debilitated both male and female neurasthenics, conditions that would appear to make personal space suffocatingly small, be cured by the preferred treatment for female sufferers, still greater confinement? Gilman's young mother is expected to stay not only in her room but in her bed, which in turn is bolted to the floor. The rest cure was designed to calm the nerves by, in effect, radical simplification of the patient's environment. And why, if simplification involved small spaces for women, did the treatment for men require the opposite? Those ministering to male sufferers routinely prescribed physical activity in the great outdoors as the antidote to the distresses of modernity. Teddy Roosevelt not only heeded this advice when he himself was ill but became, as it were, the poster-boy for "the strenuous life." In speeches and essays in the 1890s ("The Strenuous Life," "The American Boy," for example) Roosevelt codified a kind of clean-living manliness as the prescription for the health of both the country and its male citizens. The components of the regime were not original, having been in circulation as the principles of well-established organizations like the YMCA and the dicta of health monitors like John Harvey Kellogg, founder of the well-known sanatorium at Battle Creek, Michigan. Roosevelt's memorable contribution to the discourse was, instead, to link the healthy body–healthy mind paradigm to American expansionism and American superiority. In his speech before the Hamilton Club of Chicago in 1899 Roosevelt admonished his audience to meet the new century strenuously:

> The twentieth century looms before us big with the fate of many nations. If we stand idly by, if we seek merely swollen, slothful ease and ignoble peace, if we shrink from the hard contests where men must win at hazard of their lives and at the risk of all they hold dear, then the bolder and stronger peoples will pass us by, and will win for themselves the domination of the world. Let us therefore boldly face the life of strife, resolute to do our duty well and manfully; resolute to

uphold righteousness by deed and by word; resolute to be both honest and brave, to serve high ideals, yet to use practical methods. Above all, let us shrink from no strife, moral or physical, within or without the nation . . . for it is only through strife, through hard and dangerous endeavor, that we shall ultimately win the goal of true national greatness.[7]

Expansion and domination are here packaged as energizing strategies. Physical exertion and resolute endeavor offer new purpose to citizens Roosevelt fears will become complacent, now that the frontier had closed, without a focus for their energies. Complacency, in the terms he has outlined, would be tantamount to effeminacy.

The obvious explanation for the opposing treatments of female and male neurasthenics lies in the definition of gender roles – the well-documented idea of "separate spheres." While this notion has significant explanatory power, it may cause us to mis-recognize the complementarity of the treatments. However different superficially, at bottom the treatments are the same: remove the patient from the modern world and thereby remove the modern world from the patient. For women, that meant shrinking the world by eliminating the confusion of possible choices beyond traditional roles; for men, it meant expanding the world by simplifying the nature of work. Both strategies sought to restore the neurasthenic to the condition of the "natural" woman or man: for women, mother–housekeeper and indoor domesticity; for men, provider and outdoor activity.

The sources of nervous anxiety, seen from this viewpoint, were related to and indeed a function of the closing of the frontier, when "frontier" is understood as more than a literal geographic line. It is a metaphor describing the space between *what once was* and *what is still to come*. Thus, Edna Pontellier and Lily Bart know what they do *not* want but cannot commit themselves to future plans because the alternatives are still only dimly outlined. Or, to consider a mythical male example, what is a lumberjack like Paul Bunyan to do when there are no more trees? In effect Roosevelt's imperialistic energy redefined the frontier, thus reinforcing a conception of virility that required new fields to conquer. The condition of neurasthenia may be seen as a manifestation of the difficulties of transition, a shift from one set of social customs and assigned roles to other roles still evolving and, in a related if not causal way, from one view of the nation to another. As long as America was defined as a country in the making, with urgent work to be done in establishing a new civilization, the sense of purpose was implicit. Without so clearly defined a purpose, hesitation, apathy, paralysis, complacency set in. And this was the repeated complaint of the neurasthenic, both male and female. Henry Adams ends his *Education* imagining a future America: "he was beyond measure curious to see whether the conflict of forces would produce the new man, since no other energies seemed left on earth to breed. The new man could be only a child born of contact between the new and the old energies." At the beginning of the twentieth century, the old energies were yielding to the new, in Adams's terms, the material power of the dynamo replacing the spiritual power of the Virgin Mary. To live in the world of new energy, he predicted, would require "a new social mind."

Returning from Europe to the United States in 1904, Henry James believed he glimpsed that new social mind in the realm of hotels and Pullman trains. In "The Refrain of the Hotel" in *The American Scene* (1907), the "restless analyst," as James styles himself, sees Americans as "perpetually provisional. . . . [T]he hotels and the Pullmans – the Pullmans that are like rushing hotels and the hotels that are like stationary Pullmans – represent the states and forms of your evolution and are not a bit, in themselves, more final than you are." For him, the "hotel spirit" is cause for dismay, for while the degree of comfort and luxury is notable, he finds that the world of the Waldorf-Astoria is a synecdoche for "the all-gregarious and generalized life [that] suffices to every need." Or is expected to suffice. For James it does not; he fears the "jealous cultivation of the common mean . . . the reduction of everything to an average of decent suitability" that cannot accommodate eccentricity. "Great creations of taste and faith," he reminds himself, "never express themselves *primarily* in terms of mere convenience and zeal." Is James being overly romantic about the sources of art and beauty? Or is he, in the face of a prosperous and complacent populace, taking the snob's view that such conditions are the enemy of art? Assumptions of that sort do appear to affect his view. But the final pages of *The American Scene* movingly project the costs of success, returning us to a version of the question Thoreau asked about the railroads. Were Americans creating the Waldorf-Astorias and Pullman cars – or were these objects creating them? "Where was the charm of boundless immensity as overlooked from a car window?" The "general pretension" of the Pullman car seems to him to say repeatedly, " 'See what I am making of all this – see what I'm making, what I'm making!' " " 'I see,' he replies, "what you are *not* making." Having "caused the face of the land to bleed," having "converted large and noble sanities to . . . crudities, to invalidities," "you so leave them to add to the number of myriad aspects you simply spoil."

For James, despite all that had been done in settling America, there is "a long list of the arrears of your undone."

The City

If log cabins and Conestoga wagons connote expansion from the Atlantic to the Pacific, skyscrapers and traffic jams image another dimension of growth, one characterized by density and height. It is impossible to discuss modern America without reference to the cities – Boston, New York, Chicago, San Francisco, Los Angeles – that became centers and symbols of the country's prodigious development. The city is by definition a complex phenomenon; hence, the bibliography of worthwhile books for study of the American city is dauntingly large and the approaches for study numerous and diverse. One way to define a city is by reference to its autonomy: normally, the city must have a population large enough to warrant a mayor or other managerial structure separate from and supplementary to those of state or federal governments. Thus, a city may be thought of as a set of management challenges. Implicit in that definition is that the city comprises problems requiring solutions. The idea of the city as a cesspool of crime, poverty, and filth is certainly not limited to American culture: numerous Victorian novelists depict London as rife with sickly, exploited child laborers, good-hearted prostitutes and thieves, vicious beadles, and black-hearted businessmen. The Paris of French naturalists like Émile Zola is similarly populated. Because the city is a phenomenon of modernity, and modernity a phenomenon of geographic scope, artistic depictions of the cityscape in many media often cut across national lines. What students of American literature and culture might want to examine, then, is not the exceptional nature of the American city, but the particularities of its depiction, the representations of urban spaces and their populace. In addition, it is useful to keep in view some of the organizing mythologies of America because the realities of city life often severely test those myths. This section describes certain major, if necessarily limited, characteristics of the big city in the first half of the twentieth century: the heterogeneity and distribution of populations; the city as a set of problems; the city as a set of opportunities; the city as a place to run to and a place to run from.

Between 1840 and 1920, 37 million people immigrated to the United States. The effects on cities were profound: Chicago in 1837 had a population of 4,000; by 1890, the number was 1 million. The Statue of Liberty referred to in Emma Lazarus's well-known poem "The New Colossus" (1883) signifies one highly idealized aspect of this immigration history:

> "Keep ancient lands your storied pomp!" cries she
> With silent lips. "Give me your tired, your poor,
> Your huddled masses yearning to breathe free . . ."

For many people fleeing poverty and persecution elsewhere, the approach to New York's harbor seemed a gateway to freedom. "Exodus" is a frequent trope of autobiographical immigrant writing. Mary Antin entitled her autobiography describing her journey from Russia to the United States *The Promised Land* (1912). As a Jewish girl in the Russian Pale, she had felt herself an outcast because of her religion and her gender; Antin presents her assimilation to American culture in the Boston public schools as promising her a nearly unlimited sense of possibility. The image of the immigrant family breathless with expectation at the first sight of American shores may strike contemporary readers as over-simple and sentimental, but it is important not to minimize this moment of expectation, even as we recognize that hope was quickly chastened by the realities of resettlement. These, too, appear in Antin's book, but they do not cancel the general tone of praise and gratitude that, in the first half of the twentieth century, made excerpts from *The Promised Land* a popular selection for classroom anthologies.

Other episodes in immigration history are less inspiring. Legislation designed to halt immigration entirely, such as the Chinese Exclusion Act of 1882, was periodically enacted; quotas or exclusions were set in 1917, 1918, 1921, 1924, and later; various societies, such as the "Know-Nothings," arose from time to time in an effort to smear Roman Catholics or other "undesirables"; in the Palmer raids of 1920, the Federal Bureau of Investigation was authorized to summarily deport "subversives." These measures attest to the mixture of racism, xenophobia, politics, suspicion, and plain ignorance that sometimes prompts policy decisions. They are often also a measure of economic constraints, such as competition for jobs and housing or pressure on the nation's infrastructures and services.

Public policy for the first half of the twentieth century was largely directed at the goal of assimilation. Hence the popularity for many years of another foundational myth about America: the melting-pot. The phrase gained currency in 1908 thanks to *The Melting Pot*, a play by a Jewish immigrant named Israel Zangwill. Well before Leonard

Bernstein's *West Side Story*, the play depicted a contemporary Romeo and Juliet, but this time with a happy ending made possible by the melting away of differences:

> America is God's crucible, the great melting pot where all the races of Europe are melting and reforming. . . . Here you stand in your fifty groups, with your fifty languages, and your fifty blood hatreds. . . . A fig for your feuds and vendettas! Germans and Frenchmen, Irishmen and Englishmen, Jews and Russians – into the crucible with you all! God is making the American.

Here the emphasis is not on what must be forfeited but on what will be gained; in terms of the metaphor – one derived from alchemy – the mixing of lesser metals yields gold.

Arthur Miller would introduce a quite different perspective on this metaphor in his play *The Crucible*, which captures the darker implications of alchemy, the ease with which melting becomes meltdown. For Miller, the demand for assimilation and conformity sickens the body politic. His drama about the Salem witch trials, produced on Broadway in 1953, was written as a rejoinder to the interrogations conducted by the House Un-American Activities Committee. In 1947 and again in 1951, HUAC especially focused on members of the film industry. To be perceived by the Committee as in any way "deviant" in those hearings – whether in terms of one's political philosophy, artistic leanings, or selection of friends – was to risk being labeled a communist or fellow-traveler and thus "blacklisted." At one point over 300 people who worked in the film industry were named on this list. Some of those people were or had been members of the Communist Party; some no doubt wished for the demise of capitalism. But the inquisitorial climate of the hearings permitted no fine distinctions between intellectual sympathy with a utopian ideal and conscious plans for treason. Careers were destroyed, and the force of this self-perpetuating system of accusation is mirrored in the hysteria that overtakes the citizens of Miller's Salem. The fierce interrogations of Senator Joseph McCarthy of Wisconsin, the chief figure in the HUAC hearings, insisting that the witnesses "name names," were so destructive that his name has become a part of the American vocabulary: "McCarthyism" now denotes forms of persecution masquerading as investigation. Periodically, American history has been marked by clampdowns of this kind. Normally they arise in response to a perceived threat from an "outsider" or "other." America's status as a country composed of immigrants – a country in which a claim to native status rarely makes sense – would seem to make distinctions between who's in and who's out pointless, but it has not.

The heterogeneity and size of the population in a city like New York can also be studied from the perspective of how residents use urban spaces and resources. How are the big spaces to be apportioned? If we imagine human interaction on a green or the commons of a small New England village, what will probably come to mind is a central green space surrounded by shops, homes, a school, and a steepled church. As inhabitants go about their tasks, they can make certain assumptions: they will know the other pedestrians they encounter, will conduct leisurely conversation in a language comprehensible to all parties, will likely share with their acquaintances values such as religious faith. Not wholly fantastical, this portrait of village life is the standard against which city growth, and indeed national growth, was measured by the nostalgic. By comparison, a photograph of central Manhattan – whether taken in 1915 or 1955 – teems with bodies and conveyances. And yet these close quarters do not necessarily translate to intimacy or even recognition. Individuals in the crowd may share neither language nor assumptions. Money – earning it, spending it, dreaming about it – may be the only lingua franca.

How to organize this crowd of people, or how will they organize themselves? Where will they live? How will they enter the economy as producers and consumers? What means of transport do they require? Are green spaces like parks too frivolous an expenditure of space? These are the sorts of questions that the new city managers had to answer – and on a large scale. The scale indeed engenders a vocabulary: during the Progressive era, the word "public" was increasingly employed to name not just a political entity, but a mass of bodies to be accommodated in the delivery of spaces and services. This language inevitably served to amalgamate people into an aggregate entity, the behavior of which was often described in spatial terms. Like water, as crowds streamed into the city, their flow was channeled in certain directions, made to pool at certain landmarks, diverted to run-off. Often, too, the imagery of water implies pollution; hygienic measures are called for to eliminate the "dregs" of society.

Attention to the influx of bodies may be malign or benign, of course. Jane Addams, founder of Chicago's Hull House, one of a number of "settlement house" projects in the early twentieth century, had to think in general terms about practical matters of education, nutrition, and childcare in designing services for immigrant families in Chicago. To think of the common problems of life was for her not only a matter of efficiently serving the community in which she had settled; rather, her decision to emphasize what was common was an ethical tenet: "the things that make men alike," she writes in chapter 5 of *Twenty Years at Hull House* (1910), "are finer and better than the things that keep them apart, and . . . these basic likenesses, if they are properly accentuated, easily transcend the less essential differences of race, language, creed, and tradition."

Even when a philanthropist has unassailably good intentions, a project designed to encourage assimilation to a new culture will erode distinctive characteristics of the population it wishes to serve. Nutritionists in the decade from 1911 to 1921 devised healthful American eating plans, emphasizing vitamins (only recently discovered as a component of food) and borrowing largely from British cooking practices. Abundant spicing and garlic were frowned upon as interfering with healthful digestion. The smells of garlic on Mott Street in New York, the pungent sauerkrauts of Chicago, the chicken feet on display in Chinatown windows should be seen as mild forms of rebellion against the standardization and homogenization of foodways by experts. Similarly, projects to teach English and modify Old World practices in every decade have been vulnerable to accusations of cultural bullying. We may observe a similar tension in the development of public education in the US, a powerful tool for "Americanizing" the populace. The language used for instruction, the curriculum, and the standards for testing continue to be sites of contestation, where the values of the various communities that make up the nation are negotiated with the idea of the nation as a single entity.

Mary Antin felt that national entity, by taking her in, enlarged both herself and her chances; it takes little effort to envisage an opposite effect, a sense of being engulfed by the uncontrollable complexities of a modern city. Such culture shock was not limited to immigrants from other countries. The swelling of urban populations may also be attributed to migration. A significant movement of people already resident in the US, for example, was the Great Migration of black Americans from the South to Chicago and New York in the period following World War I. Between 1916 and 1919, 500,000 Southern blacks moved to the North; that figure doubled in the following decade. Some who relocated met with success and improved working conditions. Others, however, found their lives little improved by having fled to the city. In the first chapter of *Native Son* (1940), Richard Wright describes the confined, even suffocating space in which Bigger Thomas resides with his family in Chicago. So small is the apartment that Bigger and his brother must physically turn away from their sister and mother in order to afford the women privacy to dress. Having killed a rat and menaced his sister with it, Bigger begins his day, getting ready for an interview to be the driver for the wealthy Daltons – a job that leads to the series of events concluding in Bigger's jail cell on Death Row. By the novel's end, he has traded one form of imprisonment for another. From the start of the novel, Bigger is enraged by his stasis: "It maddened him to think that he did not have a wider choice of action." The "bigness" of the nation, the city, the range of opportunities, and the range of obstacles can work not to expand but to shrink the sense of self.

To counter the forces of homogenization, some people formed physical or virtual neighborhoods. This strategy has been employed by rich and poor; by races and ethnicities; within ethnicities; around country of origin; around US state of origin; around religious practices. Thus American cities, far from being homogeneous in the way that the "melting pot" implies, typically comprise Chinatowns, Little Italys, Gold Coasts, Strivers Rows, Bohemias, and so forth. At times, these neighborhoods can be demarcated with street names: here is the Polish quarter; here is where the nouveau riche have gathered to gentrify the old neighborhood; here are the cheaper digs where aspiring artists live; here are the buildings with doormen. The neighborhood can also be a matter not of geography but of affiliation. In Edith Wharton's day, the New York 400, those families constituting "high" society, asserted their territoriality not only through the magnificent piles they built to live in but also through a highly codified set of social practices, from card-leaving to at-home days to elaborate dinner parties to summers at Newport, Rhode Island. The same may be said of Harlem: a physical place in Manhattan, bordered by Lenox and Seventh Avenues, it fostered music and art and writing and provided a center for a critical mass of black artists and writers referred to as the Harlem Renaissance (roughly 1915–29). But it was something more. According to the noted scholar Henry Louis Gates, Jr., "Harlem was not so much a *place* as a state of mind, the cultural metaphor for black America itself."[8]

Whether real or imaginary, the boundaries of city neighborhoods are not inflexible. Crossing over those lines has been a rich source for American storytelling, one fundamental both to the upward curve of rags-to-riches narratives and the downward spiral of American naturalist writing. Crossing from one class to another is an idea implicit in the familiar American notion of social mobility; in the "American Dream," the direction of passage is always up, but in the arts that trajectory has been more frequently questioned than accepted. Horatio Alger's popular stories (from the late 1860s through the turn of the twentieth century) are a notable exception. In works such as *Ragged Dick*, a boy's earnest labors and good character are rewarded with material success. Alger's boys are icons of the self-made man. Mark Twain's parody "The Story of the Bad Little Boy" (1875) capitalizes on the moralistic and unrealistic aspects of Alger's stories:

> And he grew up and married, and raised a large family, and brained them all with an axe one night, and got wealthy by all manner of cheating and rascality; and now he is the infernalest wickedest scoundrel in his native village, and is universally respected, and belongs to the Legislature.

The discourse of the success story persists throughout the twentieth century in the business world, in campaigns for public office, and in advertisements for many kinds of products and services – from bodybuilding methods to military recruiting to college prospectuses. In the arts, however, whether music, movies, or fiction, the rising-star protagonist is likely to fall. Despite all the talk of pulling oneself up by one's bootstraps or giving a better life to one's children, change is not consistently portrayed as progress.

"Passing" is a term normally used and probably best reserved for the practice of racial passing – usually a black person passing as white. It has been another mode of threshold-crossing in American literature and culture, quite often marked by the movement to a more prosperous neighborhood, though not without serious consequences to the psyche. Nella Larsen's 1929 novel *Passing* depicts the psychological and social confusion and damage that occur when one moves out of one's "assigned" place. Irene Redfield, who considers herself black, has at the outset of the narrative reluctantly renewed her acquaintance with Clare Kendry, a woman who has "passed" so successfully as to marry a wealthy white man. Previously satisfied with her life and rigidly set in her values, Irene finds that the presence of Clare disrupts every aspect of her life, from her sense of herself as a woman, to her marriage, to her circle of acquaintances. Throughout the text, Larsen emphasizes the "queer" feelings of Irene, a kind of vertigo that makes her irritated, restless, anxious, and finally desperate. The narrative of passing can be seen as a racially charged instance of a common narrative form: an individual forfeits some central aspect of identity – sexual orientation or family ties or cherished rituals of an ethnic culture – in order to move into a "better neighborhood." Recent studies of "hybridity" in sociology and literature make the persuasive point that such narratives assume a binary where none need exist, that the categories of black/ white or self/other don't begin to be adequate to the actual composition of a person or a society.[9] Selves and their categories multiply; this too is a much-discussed aspect of modernity and one that the anonymity of city life can be said to foster.

The meaning of the cityscape changes depending, sometimes quite literally, on the perspective of the viewer. The owner of the five-and-dime store that became an empire, F. W. Woolworth, built his company using the successful formula of observing pedestrians' movements and choosing sites for his stores accordingly. From such a perspective, the size and complexity of life in the city can be measured, codified, and to some extent controlled. Without that specialized information, however, the functioning of a large city can command awe comparable to that felt by Henry Adams as he gazed at the dynamos at the 1893 Exposition in Chicago: how does this enormous machine function and what is my relationship to it? This is the sort of question that can evoke a range of emotions – from despair to exhilaration, from pleasure at a city's beauty to revulsion at its refuse. Some see beauty even in the refuse.

The Ash Can school, a loosely affiliated group of New York City painters active in the early twentieth century, depicted shoppers, outdoor markets, tenements, saloons, boxing matches, and the like, focusing on realistic details of urban life. Observers responded to these paintings with about the same enthusiasm that greeted French naturalism: the paintings were *too* realistic, not elevating; why paint pictures of such sordid subjects? Representative painters of this urban realist style include Robert Henri, John Sloan, George Bellows, George Luks, and William Glackens. Interestingly, some of the painters associated with this group were chief organizers of the 1913 Armory Show, which introduced "modern" art to the American public. It could in fact be argued that these painters, like the realist and naturalist fiction writers, prepared the ground for modernist experimentation; by making ordinary life a fit subject for art, they helped extend the choice of subject matter and alter conventional notions of beauty and value.

The energy and exuberance in the brushstrokes of these painters seem appropriate to their subjects, as does the usually dark palette that records unapologetically the dirtier aspects of urban life. Representations of the city may also evoke busy-ness, variety, and vibrancy, as do the sinuous lines and deep colors of Archibald Motley's Harlem

FIGURE 3   George Luks, *Allen Street*, 1905
Hunter Museum of American Art, Chattanooga, Tennessee, Gift of
Miss Inez Hyder
Like other painters of the Ash Can school, Luks depicted American
urban life without concern for loveliness.

scenes or the abstract, geometric, hot colors of Stuart Davis's Manhattan; or, by contrast, they can exhibit the cool and precise geometries
of Charles Sheeler's paintings of buildings and machines; or they might
suggest narratives of loneliness and disappointment, as do many of
the canvases of Edward Hopper. An imaginary museum of paintings
of the American city would no doubt exhibit a very wide range of styles
and perspectives. What is notable is that, in the twentieth century,
cities have proved a significant subject for painting, the cityscape as
important as the bucolic landscape in other centuries.

Another crucial aspect of city living is the experience of human
proximity. For the Brooklynite Walt Whitman, it was an almost
unbearable pleasure:

> I have instant conductors all over me whether I pass or stop,
> They seize every object and lead it harmlessly through me.
> I merely stir, press, feel with my fingers, and am happy,

> To touch my person to some one else's is about as
> much as I can stand.
>
> ("Song of Myself," 1855)

But proximity also measures the lack of private space, as we have seen in the example from *Native Son*. Consider Gwendolyn Brooks's "kitchenette building" (1945): Its tenants are "grayed in, and gray," so intent upon feeding their families and raising the rent that they have no leisure for dreams. And in any case, the speaker wonders whether

> a dream sent up through onion fumes
> Its white and violet, fight with fried potatoes
> And yesterday's garbage ripening in the hall,
> Flutter or sing an aria down these rooms
>
> Even if we were willing to let it in.

Pervasive smells and sounds make walls irrelevant, and the most one can hope for is get by; the poem concludes with the modest satisfaction of a lukewarm bath. The creation of art – an aria, the poem itself – is an exhausting and perhaps finally a trivial enterprise: "'Dream' makes a giddy sound." The dream ought to be handled as tenderly as one would an infant, should be kept clean and warm, but the cramped spaces and inadequate time prohibit such nurturing. In this environment, the Romantic notion of the solitary artist alone with his rich imagination is a cruel joke.

And yet it was precisely the proximity made possible by urban spaces that, according to modernists like the poet Ezra Pound, enabled the exchanges and confluences of modernism in the arts. In his essays about the possibility of an American equivalent of the Renaissance, a favorite early fantasy, he considers the urban center as crucial to the plan. The attractions of city life were surely one of the causes of the expatriation of American artists to cosmopolitan capitals like London and Paris. A metropolitan center with libraries, museums, galleries, and cafés provides the gathering place for the exchanges that fuel creativity. Students of modernism are used to associating Sylvia Beach's bookstore Shakespeare and Co. with James Joyce, the Paris bistro Closerie des Lilas with Joyce, Ernest Hemingway, and Pablo Picasso. As Hemingway writes in *A Moveable Feast* (1965), his memoir of his early career in Paris, "The people that I liked and had not met went to the big cafes because they were lost in them and no one noticed them and they could be alone in them and be together." There is an

automatic association between the American expatriate and the city
of Paris, but similar and equally important instances of artists being
alone together have occurred in American urban spaces: bookstores
like the Gotham in New York City and City Lights in San Francisco
were unofficial headquarters for writers; Alfred Stieglitz's gallery at
291 Fifth Avenue in New York provided a meeting place for painters
and photographers; humorists like Robert Benchley and Dorothy Parker
exercised their wits at the Algonquin hotel bar; the Cedar Tavern was
the favorite drinking spot of the American Expressionist painters;
jazz is unthinkable without clubs like Roseland in New York's Times
Square and Lincoln Gardens on East 31st Street in Chicago. In these
instances, the spaces of a big city become intimate again, and the
proximity of others stimulates productive *exchange*.

City venues make such good things possible. But scores of American texts expose the less salubrious effects of shared spaces in the
city: dark pool halls, gaudy brothels, greasy diners, squalid flophouses.
These are gathering places for the city's dispossessed, and social realist
writing dwells on these settings. We see for example in James T.
Farrell's *Studs Lonigan* trilogy (1932–5) how an aimless boy's hanging
about in such places leads to violence, nihilism, and an early grave.
The voluminous novels relentlessly present Chicago as destructive of
ideals, ambitions, and hope. The pool hall is also the scene of
Gwendolyn Brooks's devastating "We Real Cool" (1960):

> The Pool Players.
> Seven at the Golden Shovel.
>
> We real cool. We
> Left school. We
>
> Lurk late. We
> Strike straight. We
>
> Sing sin. We
> Thin gin. We
>
> Jazz June. We
> Die soon.

The monosyllabic hopelessness of the poem's speakers makes the pool
hall a synecdoche for the lives of city youths with no place else to go
and no higher ambition than to "strike straight." By 1957, the pool
hall as den of iniquity was so established, even clichéd, that the con-
man in Meredith Willson's Broadway musical *The Music Man* is able,

in the number titled "Trouble," to convince the townspeople of the need for a marching band as a wholesome activity for youth who will otherwise be lost to cues and billiard balls. Interestingly, this hugely successful musical, which ran for 1,357 performances, was popular in part because it was self-consciously nostalgic. The setting of River City, Iowa, a half-century before the show's creation, is innocent. Thus the mostly white residents of River City can afford to worry about pool, juvenile cigarette-smoking, and vocabulary like "Swell" and "So's your old man." By contrast, Brooks's 1960 poem is dead serious, the stakes of the pool game ruinous.

Along with the temptations of city dives are the dangers of the street itself. Losing a boy to "the street" is a recurrent theme. Loitering youths near lampposts, teenagers cruising the streets in souped-up cars, Mafiosi gunned down as they exit their sedans, drugs surreptitiously peddled near a condemned building – these are standard scenes of American film, television, and fiction. In Ann Petry's 1946 novel *The Street*, Lutie is a mother raising her son alone, her energies consumed by the effort to keep him off the street. Having seen a girl bleeding on a stretcher in a hospital, she considers the predictable steps by which her son Bub could be lost to her. "Yes, she thought, she and Bub had to get out of 116th Street. It was a bad street. And then she thought about the other streets. It wasn't just this street that she was afraid of or that was bad. It was any street where people were packed together like sardines in a can" (chapter 8). Proximity resulting from the crowding of urban spaces, then, has context-specific effects. The same may be said of anonymity, another response to crowding, but with the paradoxical effect of isolation. A sampling of walkers in the city will indicate some of the emotions anonymity provokes. The poet Wallace Stevens found himself disgusted by the people he saw on city sidewalks, describing them in a letter to his father: "Everybody . . . looking at everybody else – a foolish crowd walking on mirrors."[10] No *flâneur* or man about town here, sauntering and taking in the view. Like the speaker of T. S. Eliot's "Love Song of J. Alfred Prufrock," for whom the streets are like "a tedious argument of insidious intent," the primary response is one of revulsion. For the cultural theorist Walter Benjamin (and for Charles Baudelaire before him), the *flâneur* is a central character of modernity. Representations of men walking the city streets depict commerce of many kinds, sexual, economic, and social. Frank O'Hara's 1959 "The Day Lady Died" shows how the act of shopping can be stopped cold by another dimension of the city, the artistry of the great jazz singer Billie Holiday:

It is 12:20 in New York a Friday
three days after Bastille day, yes
it is 1959 and I go get a shoeshine
because I will get off the 4:19 in Easthampton
at 7:15 and then go straight to dinner
and I don't know the people who will feed me

I walk up the muggy street beginning to sun
and have a hamburger and a malted and buy
an ugly NEW WORLD WRITING to see what the poets
in Ghana are doing these days
                        I go on to the bank
and Miss Stillwagon (first name Linda I once heard)
doesn't even look up my balance for once in her life
and in the GOLDEN GRIFFIN I get a little Verlaine
for Patsy with drawings by Bonnard although I do
think of Hesiod, trans. Richmond Lattimore or
Brendan Behan's new play or *Le Balcon* or *Les Negres*
of Genet, but I don't, I stick with Verlaine
after practically going to sleep with quandariness

and for Mike I just stroll into the PARK LANE
Liquor Store and ask for a bottle of Strega and
then I go back where I came from to 6th Avenue
and the tobacconist in the Ziegfeld Theatre and
casually ask for a carton of Gauloises and a carton
of Picayunes, and a NEW YORK POST with her face on it

and I am sweating a lot by now and thinking
of leaning on the john door in the 5 SPOT
while she whispered a song along the keyboard
to Mal Waldron and everyone and I stopped breathing

O'Hara's speaker registers the city as a dizzying mixture of the quotidian
and the exotic. Errands – a shoeshine, a trip to the bank, a bookstore,
a tobacconist – are ordinary features of city life. But in the course of
his usual rounds, this person has commerce with the wider world's
productions: art and literature and cigarettes, from places nowhere
near his actual location. We see in the poem a productive chaos of
global commerce, abundance, the labels of places and advertising.
Most of all, we experience the kinetic quality of city life. The only
"still" thing is in the bank-teller's last name and even this suggestion
of respite is coupled with a vehicle of transportation. The sense of
motion is made more pointed, of course, by the elegiac final stanza, in
which breathing stops, and the audience experiences another form of

transport. The "quandariness" of the earlier stanzas is replaced by silence and stasis; time appears to halt, thus placing the performance of Billie Holiday in a transcendent realm. But it would be wrong to see the kinesis and stasis as at odds here: the city is the source of both activities – shopping and art.

The imposed contact of city life suits the gregarious and can, as we heard in the quotation from Hemingway, even offer solitude in company. Crowds may also, of course, induce intense feelings of loneliness. As Holden Caulfield, the adolescent protagonist of J. D. Salinger's *The Catcher in the Rye* (1951) puts it, "New York's terrible when somebody laughs on the street very late at night" (chapter 12). The knowledge that everywhere there are groups of which one is not a part makes singleness seem an oddity. Robert Frost's speakers are often alone, but in most instances they are on farms or in the woods, not in an urban setting. In "Acquainted with the Night" (1928), however, he evokes the solitude of a walker in the city:

> I have been one acquainted with the night.
> I have walked out in rain – and back in rain.
> I have outwalked the furthest city light.

Although the poem is set at night, we sense that this is a speaker whose loneliness does not dissipate at sunrise. The details of the poem – rain, the eyes evading contact, the unnamed things that the speaker is unwilling to explain, the attribution of sadness to city lanes, the faintly menacing sound of footsteps nearby and a cry far away, the circularity of the poem's form – all these suggest an inescapable sorrow. Moreover, Frost's use of *terza rima*, the stanzaic form of Dante's *Inferno*, intensifies the image of the city as private hell.

Theodore Dreiser's *Sister Carrie* (1900) uses the antithetical effects of the city to chart the rise of his heroine against the fall of her older lover, Hurstwood. For Carrie, Chicago acts as a "magnet," focusing her desire to become someone she can admire: that is, visibly successful, beautifully dressed, a feast for the eyes, someone who counts in the great economic machine of the city. Through a combination of talent and accident, Carrie achieves her aim as an actress; with success after success, Dreiser's "little soldier" conquers all before her. As she rises, her lodgings become more spacious and opulent, until the end when she resides in splendor in a New York hotel, her presence providing the management with a form of animate publicity. She embodies Henry James's "hotel spirit." Hurstwood, by contrast, has taken money from his employer's safe and is, again through a combination of forethought and accident, a disgraced man. Unable to find work when he and Carrie move to New York, he tramps the street looking for a job; becomes disconsolate, stops looking, and kills time reading the newspapers; tries to drive a streetcar when the regular workers are on strike; and dies in a room that rents for fifteen cents. Dreiser's novel is intentionally schematic; his aim is to illustrate both what the city can do for you and what the city can do to you. Carrie is made bigger, Hurstwood smaller.

Carrie is one of legions of young women and men who come to the city with the hope of "making it big," the spatial metaphor reinforcing the equation of size with success. The American musical theater, on stage and film, dramatizes story after story about the small-town boy or girl who makes good. An iconic example is Ruby Keeler's portrayal of Peggy Sawyer in Busby Berkeley's 1933 film *42nd Street*. She's the chorus girl who has to go on unexpectedly when the star is injured. The success of the production and the jobs of scores of people depend on her, and thus the director makes her mission clear: "Sawyer, you're going out a youngster, but you've got to come back a star." The film celebrates not only the rise of a sweet kid's talent but the city that made it possible, with Berkeley's stunning black and white geometries of images and bodies capturing the glamour and energy of "naughty, bawdy, gaudy, sporty Forty-Second St." This triumph of the talented innocent is of course balanced by the equally common narrative of the good girl who goes bad in the city – one who falls prey to a seducer or pimp, or who is forced by poverty to prostitute herself. The "fallen woman," a favorite character of the Victorian era in England, has also furnished material for twentieth-century American fiction and film: Stephen Crane's novella *Maggie: A Girl of the Streets* (1893) metamorphoses in Hollywood films of the 1920s and 1930s into *Madame X* and *Sadie Thompson*.[11] In Crane's era, rising panic over the "white slave trade," that is, luring young women into prostitution, led to passage of the Mann Act in 1910, which forbade the transport of persons across state lines for immoral purposes. While the fear of prostitution was not without foundation, most historians now agree that the problems were sensationalized and that the fear was, as much as anything else, a fear of cities themselves. Here as elsewhere in American art and writing, corruption of the female body signals corruption of the nation.

Given such perils, the American small town would seem an appealing alternative. The world's perception of the United States in terms primarily of its cosmopolitan centers misses the historical importance of the small town and the suburb to many Americans' sense of themselves. Sherwood Anderson's group of tales *Winesburg, Ohio* (1919), Thornton Wilder's drama *Our Town* (1938), and Harper Lee's novel *To Kill a Mockingbird* (1960) all depict small towns as simpler than big cities but as nonetheless psychologically complex places. On the one hand the intimate size is a comfort. One knows and is known by one's neighbors; the rituals are familiar; the landscape changes less frequently and residents become attached to particular trees or storefronts or faces. The pace is slower, the manners gentler, and the ethos neighborly. The immense popularity of television shows depicting small towns and rural communities, *Little House on the Prairie*, *The Waltons*, *Mayberry, R.F.D.*, measures the degree to which these smaller living spaces function as a version of American pastoral. Just as the courtiers of Shakespeare's era were entranced by the *idea* of grazing sheep and kindly shepherds, so many Americans are attached to the idea that the small town is the real America, the source of some of its best values: kindness, helpfulness, friendliness.

Unlike the idealized television towns, however, the places created by Anderson, Wilder, and Lee are deceptive in their simplicity. While they offer moving, inspiring, and poignant portraits of small town life, they also present the ways that the smallness can turn in upon itself, making its residents grotesque, sexually perverse, miserable, and cruel. The paradox of the small town as a place in which, despite familiarity, one can feel especially lonely shapes Anderson's connected stories of Winesburg's inhabitants. And, while the stage narrator of Wilder's *Our Town* speaks with tenderness and humor of the lives of the townspeople, particularly the developing romance of George and Emily, the characters speak from their graves in a cemetery. What once was, is no longer; the mood is elegiac. In Atticus Finch, Lee imagines a widower who teaches his children to ignore class and race, a lawyer who heroically fights the town's racism, and a virile man who can shoot a rabid dog with deadly accuracy. He embodies Thomas Jefferson's agrarian aristocrat. But of course Finch is a hero precisely because he is unlike his neighbors, his virtues foiled by the small-mindedness of Maycomb, Alabama.

Another alternative to the big city is the area just outside the city, the place Kenneth Jackson has dubbed "the Crabgrass Frontier."[12] The so called "baby boom" of 76 million infants born between 1946 and 1964 fueled a significant move to the planned communities outside major cities – areas referred to loosely as the suburbs. Suburbs of course existed well before this period, some haphazardly growing up around the edges of cities and some carefully planned and luxurious. They offered an alternative to the less salubrious aspects of city life, but permitted easy access to the commerce of the big city. Places like Levittown, New Jersey, perhaps the most famous of American suburbs, were built specifically with the returning soldiers of World War II in mind. Modest houses, based on a limited number of styles, such as the Cape Cod or ranch, and built of components manufactured on the assembly line, offered an affordable choice to young families who did not want to rear children in the city. In addition, the curvilinear street plans and the careful placement of "village" centers created a nearly instant sense of community. For many Americans, the suburb embodies the comfort and security of middle-class American life.

The fictions of the suburbs, however, are often bleak. The suburbanites of John Cheever's stories live in leafy preserves away from the noise and dirt of the city. The men who commute by train to the city for work return to comfortable homes, attractive wives, country-club golf courses, and dry martinis. Inevitably, the stories reveal that the polished veneer conceals misery. The characters are racked by infidelity, alcoholism, and a sense that their lives are meaningless. Having survived a plane crash in the opening pages, Francis Weed, the protagonist of "The Country Husband" (1954), finds himself suddenly discontented with the rituals of suburban life. "He wanted to sport in the green woods, scratch where he itched, and drink from the same cup." The routines of his family and neighbors deaden him. He wishes to be more like Jupiter, the Labrador retriever who wanders at will over the suburban lawns of Shady Hill: "he broke up garden parties and tennis matches, and got mixed up in the processional at Christ Church on Sunday, barking at the men in red dresses." Francis channels his own anarchic impulses into kissing the babysitter. Cheever writes as a white male observer whose own life resembled that of his characters. Ann Petry's observations of the same sort of neighborhood from the point of view of a black female servant yield similar conclusions. In *The Street*, the contrast between Lutie's family and that of her employers, the Chandlers, is telling: their children are neglected, the mother shallow, and the mostly absent father takes comfort in drink. In a horrific scene, the father's brother shoots himself in front of the whole family, including the children, on Christmas morning. Lutie, who has lived with violence all her life, is not thereby convinced that money isn't everything; on the contrary, "she was interested in the way in which money transformed a suicide . . . into 'an accident with a gun'" (chapter 2). The smaller, more manageable town or suburb is, outside of TV-land, rarely depicted as utopian, despite the careful designs of the planners. Though the poverty and crime may be reduced, or at least less visible, the existential difficulties remain.

Representing Nature

Although the twentieth century can be characterized as an era of cities, the national imaginary continues to include the vast natural spaces of the country as well: the redwood forests of California, the Everglades of Florida, the Great Plains of the Midwest, the Grand Canyon and the Painted Desert of the West. Even in the more densely settled states, painters, photographers, film-makers, and writers find ample material for the representation of nature; here too, some of the most memorable images are those that suggest the wide sweep of the continental United States. The earliest significant movement of American landscape painting – the Hudson River school – depicts natural spaces that appear almost entirely uninhabited. In the work of Thomas Cole (1801–48) and Asher B. Durand (1796–1886) and, later (mid- to late nineteenth century), Frederic Church, Alfred Bierstadt, George Innes, and others, the forces of nature literally dwarf the human figure who, if present at all, is merely a small shape in a corner of the foreground and whose main function appears to be contrast in scale. Nature, majestic and luminous, inspires awe; the spaciousness invites expanse of spirit, in keeping with the Romantic vision of Nature seen earlier in Emerson.

Vigorous conservation efforts have occurred sporadically in the United States, with the result that the system of national parks covers 84 million acres of territory. On the whole, however, the period 1900–45 was not an era of environmental awareness, but rather was marked by the harvesting and exploitation of resources. Forests, mountains, rivers, and oceans remained places of solace and recreation, but widespread concern about the effects of human uses of nature would wait until the 1950s and 1960s. The career of Ansel Adams (1902–84), one of the foremost photographers of the American landscape, suggests some of the ways in which nature was meaningful to Americans during the first half of the twentieth century. A serious student of the piano, Adams expected to make a career in music. His family lived in San Francisco, and as a teenager Adams began hiking in Yosemite; he took his first photograph in 1916. Influenced by the intensity of his experiences in the mountains and by the writings of conservationists like John Muir, Adams had by 1920 begun his lifelong association with the Sierra Club, the oldest and largest of US conservation groups. By 1927 he had published his first portfolio of photographs, *Parmelian Prints of the High Sierras*. His rise was rapid. Respected and admired by his peers, who included most of the important photographers of the period – Alfred Stieglitz, Dorothea Lange, Paul Strand, Edward Weston, Imogen Cunningham – Adams was also a teacher and writer who assisted in the founding of the Department of Photography at the Museum of Modern Art in 1940. His career was marked by multiple passions: technical perfection through knowledge and control of the processes of photography, environmental conservation, and the spiritual nourishment found in his favored subject, the Western landscape. These interests were not always in harmony. Work he did as a commercial photographer during the Great Depression, for example, conflicted with his desire to keep Yosemite free of the more destructive aspects of the tourist trade. His employer, the Curry Company, the result of a merger of the Yosemite National Park Company and the Curry Camping Company, built hotels, skating rinks, ski lifts, and golf courses. "So it goes, nibble by nibble," said Frederick Law Olmstead, Jr., a landscape architect who had followed the profession of his father, the designer of Central Park in New York City. The preservation of the wilderness Adams loved was at odds with the commercial possibilities of the camera. The 1920s were a boom period for advertising and for recreation, and Adams's photographs were used to tout amusements quite unlike the hikes of his adolescence. In the 1950s and 1960s Adams would reverse the promotional potential of the photographic image to further the mission of the Sierra Club. His career required a near-constant negotiation between purist aesthetics and the marketplace, between public and private uses of the landscape.

Commercial interests can make capital even out of the idea of the pristine wilderness, the beauty of which decorates many a travel brochure. To calculate the monetary possibilities inherent in a beautiful landscape seems somehow more grasping than to consider the landscape as a possible source of ore or wheat. That is, the spiritual refreshment of nature would seem to exist, if anything can, outside the realm of getting and spending. Willa Cather's *The Professor's House* (1925) is a meditation on the marketability of nature, intellectual property, and America's history, all of which are intertwined in the structure of her novel. The book is in three sections: The Family, Tom Outland's Story, and The Professor. The protagonist is Professor Godfrey St. Peters, a historian who has built his reputation writing about Spanish explorers. The central conflict of the novel, and the subject of its first section, arises from the decision of his family to leave their long-time home for another deemed superior by St. Peters's wife. St. Peters will not move. Indeed his main action in the novel is refusal: he does not want to move from the study where he has done his writing; he does not wish to travel with his wife, daughter, and son-in-law; he does not want, essentially, to embrace the future.

The focus of the second section is Tom Outland who, killed in World War I, is dead when the story begins. Symbolizing aspects of the past that St. Peters cannot easily surrender, Outland appears throughout the novel as a subject of discussion. He had invented a vacuum and given the plans for it to his fiancée Rosamond St. Peters. After Outland's death, Rosamond marries another man, and she and her husband have grown wealthy from the manufacture of the invention. Tom's abilities as a student had so captivated St. Peters that the professor has neglected his wife and family; his youthful idealism is a standard against which St. Peters measures his own life. For Professor St. Peters, Tom's worth cannot be valued in monetary terms: "my friendship with Tom is the one thing I will not have translated into the vulgar tongue." The central section of the novel is based on Tom's diaries about his life in New Mexico and his archaeological find in the Blue Mesa: evidence of a lost tribe that left behind a sophisticated city carved into the rock. Tom attempts to interest the federal government in the preservation of the city, grows disillusioned in Washington, DC, and finally recognizes that serenity derives not from the physical remains of the tribe but from his imaginative possession of the mesa:

> That was the first night I was ever really on the mesa at all. This was the first time I ever saw it as a whole. . . . It all came together in my understanding, as a series of experiments do when you begin to see where they are leading. Something had happened in me that made it possible for me to coordinate and simplify, and that process, going on in my mind, brought with it great happiness. It was possession. The excitement of my first discovery was a very pale feeling compared to this one. For me the mesa was no longer an adventure, but a religious emotion. I had read of filial piety in the Latin poet, and I knew that was what I felt for this place. It had formerly been mixed up with other motives, but now that they were gone, I had my happiness unalloyed.

Tom's death preserves him, in St. Peters's mind, from the success that results from his invention. In this regard, Tom is St. Peters's Blue Mesa, representative of unalloyed motives, disinterested intellectual curiosity, idealism, and filial piety. He keeps Tom's otherworldly innocence alive in memory. By the novel's end, St. Peters has been rescued by his housekeeper from accidental death by asphyxiation, and has decided that he can live without the "something very precious that he could not consciously have relinquished." Despite St. Peters's accident, the novel's close is muted and undramatic – just as the professor's remaining life will be.

This brief synopsis of the story should indicate that history – private and national – is Cather's central theme. The age difference between St. Peters and Tom not only suggests a father–son and teacher–student relationship but also allows Cather to present a generational shift. Tom's active existence, first as an explorer and then as a scientist, contrasts with the essentially sedentary scholarly work of St. Peters. But both men prize the imaginative possession of the past and the ideal of intellectual exploration as an end in itself. Tom, St. Peters thinks, "had made something new in the world – and the rewards, the meaningless conventional gestures, he had left to others." This praise of unremunerative creativity occurs in the context of St. Peters's university experience, where political and economic interests commercialize intellectual life, where the mandate to "show results" endangers pure scholarship. Without fully endorsing St. Peters's judgment that the world of the future will be one in which he will have to live "without joy, without passionate griefs," Cather's novel movingly registers personal and cultural loss. Developers, politicians, "little black-coated men pouring out of white buildings," as Tom describes them, will clearly dominate the future. The natural landscape of the Blue Mesa is not in fact wholly natural, a key point. It has been the home of a previous civilization. Its existence suggests that there are multiple ways in which humans can live in their landscape. Some ways are superior to others: the Blue Mesa and Tom's life in it suggest that the relationship between humanity and nature can be other than adversarial, other than exploitative.

If any twentieth-century American poet can be said to "own" nature poetry, at least in the popular mind, it is Robert Frost. The association with New England farms and cracker-barrel wisdom is one Frost cultivated. As a result, certain poems of his, such as "The Road Not Taken" and "Stopping by Woods on a Snowy Evening," are read (and misread) at graduation ceremonies, funerals, and other occasions when something poetic seems called for. He is perceived as a nature-poet because of the birds, woodpiles, birches, snow, and wooded paths that make up his usual landscape. Unlike the canvases of the Hudson River painters or Ansel Adams's photographs of Yosemite, however,

Frost's natural settings show evidence of man's engagement with them, as a woodsman or farmer or even only as a walker, rather like the Frost of "Acquainted with the Night." While the outside views in these poems are often tranquil, the speaker rarely is. Indeed the challenges to serenity discerned by Frost's best readers – among them the poet Randall Jarrell – are an effect created by the disparity between what Frost called "inner and outer weather."

In "To the Laodiceans" in the essay collection *Poetry and the Age*, Jarrell describes Frost's poem "Design" (1936) in photographic terms: "it is the terrible negative from which the . . . Kodak picture (with its *Having a wonderful time. Wish you were here* on the margin) had to be printed." The poem reverses the logic of the Argument from Design, the proof of God's power that made colonial writers like Jonathan Edwards exult over sunlight and fear thunder. In Edwards's work, as in most Puritan writing on the subject, it is possible to know the Designer by close inspection of the Design. Frost's observation of mutations in a flower, a spider, and a butterfly lead him to a chilling conclusion:

Design

I found a dimpled spider, fat and white,
On a white heal-all, holding up a moth
Like a white piece of rigid satin cloth –
Assorted characters of death and blight
Mixed ready to begin the morning right,
Like the ingredients of a witches' broth –
A snow-drop spider, a flower like a froth,
And dead wings carried like a paper kite.

What had that flower to do with being white,
The wayside blue and innocent heal-all?
What brought the kindred spider to that height,
Then steered the white moth thither in the night?
What but design of darkness to appall? –
If design govern in a thing so small.

This "albino catastrophe," as Jarrell precisely describes it, seems too patterned to be accidental. The Designer must have a wicked sense of humor, as does the poet. The catechretic combinations of words ("dimpled" and "spider"; "death and blight" and "morning right"; "dead wings" and "paper kite"; "darkness" and "appall") disrupt predictable syntax; the tone oscillates between knowingness and innocence; the "moral" is poised on an "if." It is a disquieting view of the natural world and its supposed Maker.

The Frostian landscape is by and large snowbound and vaguely terrifying, proving that Nature does not necessarily exalt the spirit in the ways that the sunnier poems of Romanticism claim. Frost's take on mankind's relationship to the natural landscape is modern, skeptical, wry. Consider "Desert Places", from *A Further Range* (1936):

> Snow falling and night falling fast, oh, fast
> In a field I looked into going past,
> And the ground almost covered smooth in snow,
> But a few weeds and stubble showing last.
>
> The woods around it have it – it is theirs.
> All animals are smothered in their lairs.
> I am too absent-spirited to count;
> The loneliness includes me unawares.
>
> And lonely as it is that loneliness
> Will be more lonely ere it will be less –
> A blanker whiteness of benighted snow
> With no expression, nothing to express.
>
> They cannot scare me with their empty spaces
> Between stars – on stars where no human race is.
> I have it in me so much nearer home
> To scare myself with my own desert places.

The spaces of nature are both wide and deep. The sleep of the animals is profound and the field blank. The poem does not ask us to fling ourselves across the continent in the panoramic manner of Whitman or his modern inheritor Hart Crane; rather, it is a poem that tunnels into the depths of the speaker's mind. In this poem too, Frost offers a retort to design, this time the literary pattern known as the pathetic fallacy: while employing the usual devices typical of the poem of sympathetic nature – the blankness of snow, the smothered animals, the vacancies between the stars – he explodes the expectations of this pattern. The concept of Nature as sympathetic requires that the poet maintain the fiction that it is Nature that weeps, Nature that sighs, Nature that suffers with the poet. But the lonely speaker of Frost's poem treats Nature not as a comforter but as a rival: he cannot be scared, or soothed, by the vacancy he sees outside, however bleak; it cannot compete with the emptiness inside.

The turn inward is typical of much modernist writing. After all, much of it spoke to a culture in which Freudian vocabulary and psychoanalysis were becoming commonplace. Well before that, of course, William Wordsworth recognized that the scene he observed at Tintern Abbey was a symbiosis of physical and mental landscape: "of all the mighty world / Of eye, and ear, – both what they half create / And what perceive." Frost and other modern American poets increasingly emphasized the "half-created," that is, the subjective nature of perception. A high degree of self-consciousness is characteristic of modern poetry, which, whatever else the topic, seems always to explore the slippery relationship between reality and language. The relevance of these explorations to Nature we have observed already in the disparity between the Emerson of "Nature" and the Emerson of "Experience." Once having recognized the degree to which the subject / observer may alter the object/observed, it becomes impossible not to be self-conscious, and this self-consciousness constantly threatens to overwhelm all other aspects of the scene. William Carlos Williams, who saw his poetry as an antidote to this malady, worried about the status of the thing-ness of things and offered a counter-strategy: "no ideas but in things." This assertion that things count in themselves and not only in what they reflect about the perceiver is one way of making sense of his cryptic poem "The Red Wheelbarrow" (1923):

> so much depends
> upon
>
> a red wheel
> barrow
>
> glazed with rain
> water
>
> beside the white
> chickens

Our attention is directed to the things – the chickens, the wheelbarrow, the rain – because the "so much" that depends on them is undefined, intangible. The poem allows us to recognize perception as a human and thus subjective act, but does not make the things observed merely servants of that act. Marianne Moore's use of animals and natural scenes in her poetry operates according to similar principles. Her poems are a menagerie of pangolins, pelicans, monkeys, plumet basilisks, dock rats, and fish; these are often made to serve a moral turn, as in the fables of La Fontaine. However, Moore's goals of "Humility, Concentration, and Gusto," as she titled one of her critical essays, could not be met by treating creatures only as emblems. As the critic Bonnie Costello expresses it:

> The poems enact and figure a play . . . between the world observed and the observing of it. . . . While other modernists made the major claim of achieving the genuine in form, closing the gap between human constructions and the order of nature, Moore admits the elusiveness of truth, connecting the genuine with the acknowledgement of limits. The poem does not reveal the thing in all its realness, but puts us on the scent with lively images of pursuit.[13]

Thus, in "Poetry," Moore calls for the impossible: "imaginary gardens with real toads in them." Surely this is one of the mental feats that her contemporary Wallace Stevens is exploring in such poems as "Thirteen Ways of Looking at a Blackbird," "Anecdote of the Jar," and "The Snowman."

Nature's manifold meanings register its immense significance. In the United States, as we have seen throughout this chapter, Nature has been construed as a sign of God's beneficent or malevolent design; as a refuge, a place of Edenic simplicity and youthful innocence; as an occasion for introspection, as a source of wealth, as a metaphor for human emotion. So loaded with connotation is any American scene of Nature, indeed so unlikely is the scene to be natural in the sense of being untouched, that no one ever comes to it without dragging most of Western civilization along.

Apocalypse

The Frontier Thesis and Manifest Destiny, terms discussed at the beginning of this chapter, imply endings. Ideas of the ever-receding frontier and the special mission of Americans to settle the continent were designed to spur development and keep the American Dream of continual progress and improvement alive. If there were to be a temporal or spatial end, according to these concepts, it would be merely a brief pause or way-station between the termination of one mission and the commencement of another. That is, until the end of history. Progress, a key word for both America and the twentieth century, presupposes a certain kind of narrative, wherein the situation at the beginning is inferior to that at the end. *Pilgrim's Progress* (1678), John

Bunyan's allegory that was a staple of American home libraries, follows the character Christian from the City of Destiny through a series
of obstacles to the Celestial City. Any believer in Christianity, of whatever nationality, would find herein a familiar eschatology. Christian's
travails, the journey of the faithful toward heavenly reward, while in
no way a new literary form, must nevertheless have seemed peculiarly
appropriate to settlers of a New World who were pushing westward.
The habit of "reading" the land as evidence of a divine plan encourages a view of life in which progression and progress bring one closer
to a promised end; movement implies teleology.

In *The American Jeremiad*, Sacvan Bercovitch argues that the relationship between Christian narrative and the New World became
literal in the minds of the Puritan settlers: "What for others was an
ideational structure – the *New World* of regeneration, the *promised land*
of heaven, the *wilderness* of temptation, the *garden* of the spirit was . . . a
political reality, the civic, religious, and economic structures of a cov-
enanted New World society."[14] This fusing of worldly and otherworldly
makes for Bercovitch all the difference in the meaning of the form
called "the jeremiad." Whereas the formidable historian Perry Miller
had seen the "fire and brimstone" sermon as indicative of the failure
of the spiritual errand and its eventual replacement by a secular one,
Bercovitch argues that the jeremiad was designed to underscore the
inseparability of secular and spiritual and to hearten those committed
to that conception of life's purpose.[15] Threatened punishment signals,
according to this view, not damnation but love and belief that the
sinner can turn away from the sin.

The possibility of reward nevertheless implies the possibility of punishment; the possibility of success, failure. Arrival, as anyone who has
ever anticipated it knows, may evoke joy, sorrow, or even exhausted
indifference. The epic narrative of a traveler's adventures is nearly
always more compelling during the mid-story crises and temptations
than it is at the end – hence Turner's insistence that Americans must
seek new frontiers to replace the old, continually moving the goal. But
the edge of the continent is a physical reality that has had a powerful
grip on American imaginings of the end of something. Travel westward
functions as a trope for leaving behind one's troubles, for seeking
adventure or fame or wealth. Sunshine spills gold on the landscape.
The power of this image, precisely because it beckons and seduces, has
also provided rich material for visions of apocalypse.

The land of milk and honey in John Steinbeck's *The Grapes of Wrath*
(1939) is California, the US equivalent of the Celestial City. The Joad

family are forced to give up tenant farming in Oklahoma; agricultural corporations with tractors can do the job more efficiently and turn a profit. Their impoverished state is also a result of the 1930s "Dust Bowl," a period of drought and dust storms so relentless that it forced thousands of families to leave their homesteads. Most of them headed West. In his innocence, Grampa Joad anticipates the pleasures that await him out there: "Just let me get out to California where I can pick me an orange when I want it. Or grapes. There's a thing I ain't never had enough of. Gonna get me a whole big bunch of grapes off a bush, or whatever, an' I'm gonna squash 'em on my face an' let 'em run offen my chin" (chapter 8). Once the Joad family reaches this promised land, however, they face a near-biblical level of famine and flood, along with conditions for work different from, but no less brutal than, the arid fields they had left behind in Oklahoma. There are many more workers to do the picking of crops than there are jobs to go around, and owners can thus give work to the lowest bidder. The wages are not even at subsistence level. The Joad son, Tom, recently returned from prison, kills a man in self-defense and must go into hiding; the pregnant daughter Rose of Sharon is abandoned by her husband and her child is stillborn. Ma Joad is an icon of endurance amid the troubles.

Were it not for the final Pietà-like image of Rose of Sharon nursing a starving old man, the story of the Joad family's pilgrimage would be devastating: after so much suffering, no reward, no improvement, no change at all. But spiritual change is forecast, and Steinbeck strains credibility to embody that change in Rose of Sharon's selfless act. There is a modicum of hope on offer, if only humanity can change itself. "'I got to figure,'" a tenant farmer says at the beginning of the novel, "'We've all got to figure. There's some way to stop this. It's not like lightning or earthquakes. We've got a bad thing made by men, and by God that's something we can change'" (chapter 5). The heavy use of Christian iconography and other religious allusions in the novel along with a number of moving scenes of effective communal activity suggest that the change must include a radical shift away from individualistic, capitalistic practices. In an especially famous speech in the novel – a kind of set-piece later made indelible by the actor Henry Fonda in director John Ford's 1940 film version – Tom tries to explain to his mother, who fears he will be killed for standing up to the bosses, that his single life is inconsequential: "'a fella ain't got a soul of his own, but on'y a piece of a big one.'" Thus, even if he dies, he will still be present:

"Then I'll be aroun' in the dark. I'll be ever'where, wherever you look. Wherever they's a fight so hungry people can eat, I'll be there. Wherever they's a cop beating up a guy, I'll be there. . . . I'll be in the way guys yell when they're angry an' – I'll be in the way kids laugh when they're hungry an' they know supper's ready. An' when our folks eat the stuff they raise an' live in the houses they build – why I'll be there." (chapter 27)

Tom's belief in the "big" soul – an Emersonian Oversoul – gives him purpose, a long view of history, and belief in the power of concerted action. Steinbeck prepares the reader for this movement from "I" to "we" from the beginning of the novel, where chapters focused on the particular struggles of the Joads alternate with interchapters that narrate the trials of all those who migrated in search of work. In these sections, the pronouns are plural, the dialogue unpunctuated with quotation marks, and the quotations unattributed, all stylistic choices dictated by the decision to make the novel a representation of something larger than a single family. Every act of kindness and self-sacrifice in the novel builds toward a vision of a renewed nation capable of reform: what mankind has ruined, mankind can salvage – but a change of heart must first occur. The novel is a form of jeremiad and a view of the end times: Steinbeck describes the moral decline of a nation that has permitted the drive for profit and efficiency to displace all other values. Like the turtle that plods along the highway for the entirety of chapter 3, the "people" as a collective are slow and unprepossessing, but unstoppable. They embody a life-force with a will to survive. In that will, Steinbeck discerns a collective strength – a big soul – that can reshape the country's direction. The horrors of the novel, human cruelty and natural disasters, suggest that, without that change, the nation will become hell on earth.

It must be said, however, that Steinbeck's view of the people as a force for good, though it may still have vitality in political rhetoric, is not ubiquitous in American fiction. Just as often, "the people" are portrayed as an unthinking and therefore dangerous mob. In the darker view of such novels as Nathanael West's *The Day of the Locust* (1933), the state of California, and specifically the city of Hollywood, is a repository of failures. Sunshine and movie stars lure people to Hollywood; the "dream machine," as the film industry has often been called, creates but cannot satisfy the desire for lives that, like the images on the "silver screen," are larger than life. Because Hollywood is the source of most American movies, and because, especially in the early days of film, most filming was done on constructed sets, rather than on "location," West's setting exposes the tawdry artificiality of at least some American dreams.

The Hollywood novel, both pulp and high-toned, is a significant sub-genre in American writing. The stories nearly always take a dark turn. Jacqueline Susann's *Valley of the Dolls*, a massive bestseller in 1966 and still one of the three bestselling novels written by a female author, traces lives destroyed by alcohol, pills, and sex. More recently, the British writer Jackie Collins has offered a Hollywood title every few years: *Hollywood Wives, Hollywood Husbands, Hollywood Kids*. It is a premise of these formulaic novels that the rich, beautiful, and successful are, if we but wipe away the Vaseline from the camera lens, miserable, ordinary, and corrupt; these books detail the outrages of Hollywood lives with the same ferocity that jeremiads enumerate the pains of hell. Hollywood corruption has appealed to a variety of writers over the years: F. Scott Fitzgerald's *The Last Tycoon* (published posthumously, 1941), Bud Schulberg's *What Makes Sammy Run?* (1941), Joan Didion's *Play It As It Lays* (1971). And, as happens in any art that has become highly self-conscious, the Hollywood movie about Hollywood is a standard offering as well. Preston Sturges's *Sullivan's Travels* (1942) follows the journey of a Hollywood producer who wants to get in touch with "real" people and tell real stories, only to discover that people don't *want* reality from the movies. The producer has a falsely elevated sense of his mission. The money side of the movie business is a favorite target of Hollywood satire, and the approach is evident in some recent titles: Robert Altman's *The Player* and George Huang's *Swimming with Sharks*. Perhaps because the film industry deals in fantasy, perhaps because publicity always carries a whiff of untruth, perhaps even because movies are accessible to all classes of people, Hollywood symbolizes fraudulence, greed, hedonism, and meretriciousness – the seamier side of American optimism and prosperity.

The Hollywood hack writer symbolizes "selling out" artistic talent to mere entertainment. In *The Catcher in the Rye* one cause of Holden Caulfield's *contemptus mundi* is his belief that his writer brother is wasting his gifts. " 'Now he's out in Hollywood, D. B., being a prostitute' " (chapter 1). D.B.'s career is a synecdoche for the "phoniness" Holden sees everywhere in America. Todd Hackett, the artist-figure in *The Day of the Locust*, is named like a character in an allegory, combining two kinds of death, the German *Tod* with the spiritual death of hackwork. West's novel makes explicit what is always implicit in the horrors of Hollywood fiction: those who worship false idols (fame, money, glamour) will be spectacularly punished. Here is the meeting ground of jeremiad and apocalypse. The final scene of the novel is set at a Hollywood movie première, where a large crowd has gathered to see the stars go into Kahn's Persian Palace Theater (alluding both to the real Graumann's Chinese Theater and to Coleridge's *Kubla Khan*). Following a series of small incidents, none the true cause of the riot, the mob becomes violent; people are trampled; Todd is carried away screaming, laughing, imitating the wail of an ambulance. The painting he has worked on throughout the novel, *The Burning of Los Angeles*, has come to life.

More awful than the actual crush of the mob is West's explanation of the cause: boredom. Having worked in dull jobs to save money and move on to something better, the people have high expectations: "Where else should they go but California, the land of sunshine and oranges?" But these natural pleasures prove insufficient: "Once there they discover that sunshine isn't enough. They get tired of oranges, even of avocado pears and passion fruit."

> Their boredom becomes more and more terrible. They realize they've been tricked and burn with resentment. Every day of their lives they read the newspapers and went to the movies. Both fed them on lynchings, murder, sex crimes, explosions, wrecks, love nests, fires, miracles, revolutions, war . . . Nothing can be violent enough to make taut their slack minds and bodies. They have been cheated and betrayed. They have slaved and saved for nothing. (chapter 27)

Who or what is to blame? Some of West's rhetoric suggests that the people themselves are to blame (they have "slack minds and bodies"), but what or who has cheated and betrayed them? The corruption is so pervasive that the responsibility for it cannot be traced to immediate sources even in the syntax of his sentences. Rather, and this is the suggestion of apocalyptic fiction more generally, it is the society as a whole that is wayward. Material successes feed an insatiable desire for more; novelty is a perpetual-motion machine that destroys its own products even as it spits out new ones; violence begets violence. A nihilist novel like *The Day of the Locust* is predicated on unfulfilled promises: we imagine luscious oranges and then we imagine ourselves unsatisfied by them.

The Sense of Place

Most of this chapter has addressed possible ways of comprehending the sheer size of America. Attention to the continent as a land mass, however, tends to emphasize the idea of the US as a nation and global power. In the daily lives of people of any country, attention is more likely to be directed to immediate spaces – the home, the neighborhood, the state, the region. Although the particularities of a region can be – often have been – eclipsed by corporations and conglomerates, attachment to the food, speech patterns, habits, landscape, and history of specific places continues to matter. The American Way of Life has not entirely replaced specific American *ways* of life. In 1962 Flannery O'Connor, a writer who spent most of her life in rural Georgia, offered a way of thinking about region:

> The best American fiction has always been regional. The ascendancy passed roughly from New England to the Midwest to the South; it has passed to and stayed longest wherever there has been a shared past, a sense of alikeness, and the possibility of reading a small history in a universal light. In these things the South still has a degree of advantage. It is a slight degree and getting slighter, but it is a degree of kind as well as of intensity, and it is enough to feed great literature if our people – whether they be newcomers or have roots here – are enough aware of it to foster its growth in themselves.[16]

Two words from this passage, "feed" and "roots," point to the relationship between the rural and the regional. As in France, where the word "terroir" means "soil" but also refers broadly to the products of a region (as, for example, Provence or Normandy), so in O'Connor's definition of regional writing, there is a lingering association with the land itself.

The surge of interest in reading and writing about specific locations, known as the "local color" movement, occurred just after the Civil War, a period marked by the proliferation and increased circulation of magazines. Writing about the West was popular; Bret Harte's often humorous short stories were typical of the fare. Mark Twain (Samuel Clemens) was at first perceived as a local colorist because of his tales of life on the Mississippi River, though his reputation soon exceeded its regional beginnings. Regional writing functioned as virtual travel, a way of experiencing other parts of the United States. And the more specific the dialect, customs, and peculiarities of behavior, the better. Thus readers of Kate Chopin's *The Awakening* would have been interested not only in the progress of Edna Pontellier, but also in the manners of Creole life, the setting of New Orleans, and the smatterings of French in the characters' dialogue. Dialects signaled authenticity, an insider's view of the observed community.

In the witty preface to *The Adventures of Huckleberry Finn* (1885), Twain connects the transcription of dialect to the representation of the diversity of speakers even within a circumscribed region.

EXPLANATORY
In this book a number of dialects are used, to wit: the Missouri negro dialect; the extremest form of the backwoods Southwestern dialect; the ordinary "Pike County" dialect; and four modified varieties of this last. The shadings have not been done in a haphazard fashion, or by guess-work; but painstakingly, and with the trustworthy guidance and support of personal familiarity with these several forms of speech.

I make this explanation for the reason that without it many readers would suppose that all these characters were trying to talk alike and not succeeding.

THE AUTHOR.

Published post-war, the novel's events take place in the pre-war South. Twain is elegiac about Huck's and America's childhood even as he excoriates the South's dependence on the "peculiar institution" of slavery. The suggestion is of a time and place that will soon pass away. The insistence on specificity may be read, at least in part, as evading a national definition of Americanness. Huck announces he will "light out for the Territory" as the novel concludes, an area still not "sivilized" and thus not yet eroded of its distinctiveness. Desiring to feel free and easy, as he did on the river, Huck resists homogenization.

Readers in the North had a special interest in works set in the South, and both Southerners and Northerners preferred fictions depicting the ante-bellum South, works that often romanticized life on the plantation. An example of the genre called the plantation novel is Thomas Nelson Page's *In Ole Virginia* (1887), its title signaling the good old days before the war disrupted what Page depicts as a harmonious way of life. Most of these books are now merely curiosities, but they formed a significant part of the popular taste for sentimental historical fiction after the war. Some form of nostalgia about the ante-bellum US helped create the market for dialect poetry, as well. Following is a brief excerpt from Paul Laurence Dunbar's "When Malindy Sings":

> Easy 'nough fu' folks to hollah,
> Lookin' at de lines an' dots,

When dey ain't no one kin sence it,
An' de chune comes in, in spots;
But fu' real malojous music,
Dat jes' strikes yo' hea't and clings,
Jes' you stan' an' listen wif me
When Malindy sings.

Ain't you nevah hyeahd Malindy?
Blessed soul, tek up de cross!
Look hyeah, ain't you jokin', honey?
Well, you don't know whut you los'.
Y' ought to hyeah dat gal a-wa'blin',
Robins, la'ks, an' all dem things,
Heish dey moufs an' hides dey face.
When Malindy sings.

                    (*Lyrics of Lowly Life,* 1896)

Dunbar had, in fact, never visited the South when he wrote this poem, but he had heard stories from his parents, both of whom had been slaves. This poem, thought to be a tribute to his mother, is gently ironic, proposing as it does that no amount of training in music theory can create the sound that Malindy's natural ability and life experience make possible. That experience, we learn from the poem, has been hard, the singer has suffered, and she has been sustained by religious faith. Dunbar's dialect poetry far exceeded in popularity his other, more conventional poetry, which was mostly ignored; further, Dunbar himself was uncomfortably aware that his voice bore comparison with that of white writers like Thomas Nelson Page and Joel Chandler Harris, who had written the "Br'er Rabbit" tales. Dialect alone was not enough to distinguish the voice of Dunbar's speakers from those of writers who were not of the race they depicted. Dialect alone could not suggest the deep divide between the races.

Southern dialect, because of its soft sounds, coheres nicely with the "moonlight and magnolias" picture of the South, which emphasizes the gentility of plantation owners, the beauty of Southern belles, the ethos of Southern hospitality, and the contentment of slaves singing at their work. Implicit in this view, too, is the concept of the Lost Cause, the notion that the men of the South fought nobly to protect a way of life that ran counter to the forces of modernization. The Lost Cause undergirds Margaret Mitchell's bestselling novel *Gone With the Wind* (1936) and the Oscar-winning film based on it (1939). If we may judge by sales figures and the frequent airing of the film, this Civil

War novel retains its hold on the American imagination. Although written decades after the conflict, it draws heavily on the distinction between nostalgia and practicality in characterizing the two male protagonists, Ashley Wilkes and Rhett Butler. Scarlett O'Hara's inability to relinquish her attachment to the genteel but ineffectual Ashley in favor of the newly rich and rakishly cynical Rhett is an allegory of the South's reluctance to leave behind the ideal of the agrarian aristocrat.

The South has not, of course, furnished the only regional literature of consequence. Looked at in one way, the work of Transcendentalists like Emerson, Thoreau, or Margaret Fuller could be categorized as New England regional literature. Each of the nation's areas – the Northwest, the Southwest, the far West, and so on – has at one time or another amassed a body of writing. Southern literature has, however, received by far the most scholarly attention of any regional American literature. The University of North Carolina Press had by the 1950s already published 200 studies of the South. Southern universities routinely offer courses in Southern literature, and there are several journals of note that specifically focus on the South. Fred Hobson, a distinguished scholar of Southern literature, has labeled this phenomenon "The Rage to Explain." A work like *The Mind of the South* (1941) by the journalist W. J. Cash assumes that there is a particularly Southern mind and that its genesis needs explaining. In Cash's argument, frontier individualism, Protestantism, the climate, and a confluence of other conditions created the combination of romanticism and hedonism that eventuated in violence and racism. He was not sanguine about the ability of the South to transcend this heritage. The reasons for the compulsion to analyze the South are numerous, but a partial list would include the South's defeat in the war, its association with slavery, its resistance to incursions of commerce and other modernizing forces during the period called Reconstruction, its reputation for pockets of poverty and ignorance, its designation as a "Bible Belt," its insularity, its odd or charming speech (the *y'all* drawl), and its foodways (hush puppies, GooGoo Clusters, Moon Pies, gumbos). Asked to define what makes Southern literature distinctive, Southerners themselves name the sense of place, the uses of oral tradition, the prominence of stories of families, the emphasis on talk in general – in short, various means of maintaining a sense of community.

One way to approach a regional literature is, as indicated earlier, via the landscape, an approach especially important for the South, which made a difficult transition from a largely agrarian landscape to one of highways, suburban tracts of houses, strip malls, and sizeable cities.

The attachment to the land is the defining principle of Agrarianism, a term that refers broadly to the virtues of the farming life. Pastoral panegyric has ancient roots and so there is nothing inherently new about the basic tenets of Agrarian thought. Briefly, the principles are outlined in the *Encyclopedia of Southern Culture* as follows:

> cultivation of the soil is an occupation blessed by God; an economic system should be judged not by the prosperity it produces but by the degree to which it encourages independence and morality; the life of the farmer is harmonious, orderly, and whole, and it counteracts the tendencies toward abstraction, alienation and fragmentation; since nature is the primary source of inspiration, all the arts are better fostered in agrarian society; cities destroy independence, encourage crimes and corruption; farm communities encourage cooperation and neighborliness.[17]

What makes these ideas significant is not their novelty but their use in particular places at particular times. Adopted by groups like the Fugitives in the early 1920s, these ideas already seemed to mainstream intellectuals retrogressive, aggressively anti-modern. The Fugitives included a number of important writers, all loosely connected to Vanderbilt University in Tennessee, among them Allen Tate, John Crowe Ransom, Donald Davidson, and Robert Penn Warren. The manifesto of the group, *I'll Take My Stand: The South and the Agrarian Tradition* (1930), is a collection of a dozen essays by these four and others who argue for values they view as imperiled by the ruinous "progress" of modern life. As such, the manifesto is by definition conservative about social mores and, implicitly, about politics. In general, however, the Fugitives were most interested in writing and reading poetry and in fostering a culture in which they believed those activities would matter.

The Fugitives, named after their short-lived journal (1922–5), are also strongly associated with New Criticism. Robert Penn Warren co-authored with Cleanth Brooks (another Southerner and a student of Ransom), the influential and widely used textbook *Understanding Poetry* (1938). The book is perhaps now best known for what it says not to do. In the prefatory "Letter to Teachers," the following practices were discouraged:

1. Paraphrase of logical and narrative content;
2. Study of biographical and historical materials;
3. Inspirational and didactic interpretation.

Instead the student was to concentrate entirely upon the words on the page and poetry as poetry, i.e. not as a story accompanied by a moral and not merely as evidence of a writer's life and times. The joke used to be that New Criticism originated in the South because, lacking libraries, its residents were lucky even to have copies of poems. This witticism is in keeping with H. L. Mencken's remark in 1917 that the South was "the Sahara of the Bozart." (The pun is on *beaux arts*, but with a suggestion of Ozark and Bozo – both derogatory terms for deep ignorance and foolishness.) The view of the South as benighted has a long history that includes events from the ante-bellum period to the present time. The Fugitives, fully aware of this stereotype, were motivated, at least in part, by the desire to demonstrate that Southerners were intellectually able. Ransom claimed in a letter to Randall Jarrell that the professors of American universities were confused and directionless; he believed that his group could provide the necessary guidance. And, indeed, until at least the mid-1960s (and in some places well beyond), New Criticism was the dominant approach in the American classroom. Ransom and company made their mark.

Apart from the alleged absence of libraries, what drew these Southerners to New Criticism? Turning to Cleanth Brooks's *The Well-Wrought Urn* (1947), a highly influential book of criticism, one finds even in the title the beginnings of an explanation. Brooks concludes his essay on "The Language of Paradox" with a comparison of poems to urns:

> there is a sense in which all such well-wrought urns contain the ashes of a phoenix. The phoenix rises from its ashes; or ought to rise; but it will not arise from all our mere sifting and measuring of ashes, or testing them for their chemical content. We must be prepared to accept the paradox of the imagination itself.

The wholeness of the poem will not be reduced to its component parts, nor subjected to mathematical or scientific analysis – vital components of modern industrialization and technology. Furthermore, as Brooks points out, poetic language is like religious language; it depends upon paradoxical statements (for example, "the last shall be first") and in this regard encompasses what is not logical but is nevertheless meaningful. The organic structure of the poem – holding in tension all its conflicting energies, paradoxical, but finally harmonious and whole – resembles the imaginary society of the Agrarian philosopher. The attachment of the Fugitives to an idea of the agrarian South should not, however, be taken too literally: not expecting the return of the

Old South, they expressed instead misgivings about the direction of the nation as a whole toward progress for progress's sake, toward a shallow materialism, and toward the anomie that arises from rootlessness and impersonality. The Southern porch, which enables people to sit at home and still converse with neighbors, is one of the icons of Southern writing because the idea of the simple life in a neighborly neighborhood has not lost its appeal.

This is not to say that Southern writers assume a stable or peaceable land. On the contrary, much of the most memorable Southern writing derives its material from those contrary people and things that will not blend nicely into the landscape. The works of Flannery O'Connor are crowded with misfits, not only the man who calls himself The Misfit in "A Good Man is Hard to Find," but one-legged Hulga in "Good Country People," acne-ridden, Wellesley-educated Mary Grace in "Revelation," and deaf Lucynell in "The Life You Save May Be Your Own." For O'Connor, the woman who is well-dressed, respectable, church-going, and fiscally responsible is the favored symbol of moral depravity. Writing from a specifically Roman Catholic point of view, O'Connor upsets the comfort and complacency of a woman like Mrs. Turpin who seems justified in her pride: she takes care of herself and those around her; she is, by her own lights, a good Christian. "Revelation," the story in which she appears, ends with Mrs. Turpin's mystical vision of souls on their way to heaven:

> [A] vast horde of souls were rumbling toward heaven. There were whole companies of white-trash, clean for the first time in their lives, and bands of black niggers in white robes, and battalions of freaks and lunatics shouting and clapping and leaping like frogs. And bringing up the end of the procession was a tribe of people whom she recognized at once as those who, like herself and Claud, had always had a little of everything and the God-given wit to use it right. . . . They were marching behind the others with great dignity, accountable as they had always been for good order and common sense and respectable behavior. They alone were on key. Yet she could see by their shocked and altered faces that even their virtues were being burned away.

Stunned, Mrs. Turpin sees that the hierarchy she had taken for granted – and indeed assumed as a birthright – has been upended. Her vision of just deserts has been fundamentally altered. The other world beyond, or as O'Connor elsewhere names it, the "true country," must always be spoken of metaphorically: like the metaphysical poets of the seventeenth century, O'Connor draws her metaphors from nature and ordinary life: fires, rivers, bulls, peacocks. But the exultation of an "elsewhere" these images mean to capture is comprehensible largely because of O'Connor's precise depiction of the rural South where "place" refers as much to one's status as one's location.

Writing about "Place in Fiction," Eudora Welty praised fellow-Mississippian William Faulkner for his creation of Yoknapatawpha County, the setting of many of his stories and novels. "I am not sure . . . how widely it is realized and appreciated that these works of such marvelous imaginative power can also stand as works of the carefulest and purest representation. Heightened, of course: their specialty is that they are twice as true as life." Of the story "Spotted Horses," she writes, "it could happen today or tomorrow at any little crossroads hamlet in Mississippi; the whole combination of irresistibility is there." Welty, who herself had one of the most acute ears for local speech among the Southern writers, is praising more than Faulkner's accuracy; "irresist-ibility" arises from the confluence of physical detail and feeling: "Location is the ground conductor of all the currents of emotion and belief and moral conviction that charge out from the story in its course."[18]

Faulkner's Yoknapatawpha County is so thoroughly imagined that the Vintage paperback edition includes a map based on the fiction. Acknowledged as one of the great American novelists, Faulkner offers perhaps the best evidence that "regional" should not be confused with "provincial." His fictional county resembles the real Lafayette County; the terrain is recognizably like that of north-central Mississippi, and yet there is no attempt at documentary realism. The speech of his characters manages to sound at once like the speech of the types he depicts and yet like Faulkner himself. The stories he tells are saturated with the history of the South but entirely contemporary in the style of their telling, employing the whole repertoire of modernist tricks, from multiple points of view to stream of consciousness to un-punctuated prose. Like Quentin Compson, who appears in *The Sound and the Fury* (1929) and *Absalom! Absalom!*, Faulkner can be a roman-tic idealist about the South, but he articulates with equal persuasion the exhausted cynicism of Quentin's alcoholic father. The divisions observable in Faulkner's work mirror the contradictions the South faced as it gave up one way of life for another.

"Tell about the South. What's it like there. What do they do there. Why do they live there. Why do they live at all." Quentin has heard those questions since he arrived at Harvard. Shreve, a Canadian who is Quentin's roommate at Harvard, spends a night listening to Quentin try to reconstruct Southern history from the ante-bellum period up to the present moment. In *Absalom! Absalom!* the story that emerges is a collage; Quentin pieces together letters from home, conversations with his father, conversations his father had with his grandfather, conversations with the elderly woman who is the only articulate survivor of the Sutpen legacy. This tale of "garrulous outraged baffled ghosts" is so lurid and compelling that Shreve himself gets caught up in the telling: " 'No,' Shreve said; 'you wait. Let me play a while now.' " The two young men merge as narrators: "it might have been either of them and was in a sense both" (chapter 8).

As is customary for Faulkner, he draws plot elements from both popular genres (detective fiction's red herrings, bits of initially inscrutable evidence, questions that stay unresolved until the narrative concludes), from Gothic romance, from the Bible, and from Greek tragedy. *Absalom! Absalom!* is the Fall of the House of Sutpen, just as *The Sound and the Fury* is the Fall of the House of Compson. Like an audience member listening to a Greek tragedy, the reader is encouraged to see the fate of a family as a synecdoche for the fate of a country. In recounting the saga of Thomas Sutpen, Faulkner is also "telling about" the South, as Quentin's classmates had requested. Further, he is telling about the national history, not only in the sense that the biblical story to which he alludes involves inter-family conflict (the story of Absalom, Amnon, and Tamar), but also in the more indirect way that the novel refers to Matthew 12: 25 and thus to Abraham Lincoln's famous statement in 1858 that "a house divided against itself cannot stand."[19]

The references to the Civil War, textual and intertextual, enable Faulkner to present the relationship between two half-brothers, Henry and Bon, and their sister/half-sister Judith, as pointedly analogous to the relationship between the North and the South; this sibling relationship is, in turn, echoed by that of the Canadian and the Mississippian, Shreve and Quentin, in the novel's present time, 1910. In addition, the bodies of female characters as mothers and potential mothers express the novel's central themes of land and dynasty: Bon's West Indian mother, Sutpen's wife Ellen and her sister Rosa, Judith, the octoroon mother of Charles Bon's son, that son's black wife, Millie Jones, and her unnamed daughter, and finally the half-sister of Judith and Henry, Clytie. Here it is useful to recall that the land is often figured as a woman's body and has been so since the earliest colonial writings. Through the representation of these bodies, two forms of ownership converge: the land and the people on it. Thomas Sutpen's "design," as he calls it, must have both elements in order to be complete: he must own the acreage and he must be able to pass it on to a son, if his name is to be continued. The suggestions of miscegenation in the genealogy sketched above point to Sutpen's desire to control the bloodline by controlling the bodies of women and men; it points also to his failure to accomplish his design. He ruthlessly discards every person who is not "adjunctive to the forwarding of the design." But what is repressed returns in other forms; human beings refuse to fit in to the pattern. Sutpen first imagines his design when, as a boy, he is turned away from a plantation home's front door by a black servant. The concept of ownership is at this time foreign to him:

> Because where he lived the land belonged to anybody and everybody and so the man who would go to the trouble and work to fence off a piece of it and say "This is mine" was crazy. . . . So he didn't even know there was a country all divided and fixed and neat with a people living on it all divided and fixed and neat because of what color their skins happened to be and what they happened to own. (chapter 7)

Sutpen's plan, then, is to avenge himself for the humiliation he has experienced; he decides that "to combat them you have to have what they have." Eventually, he is able to buy 100 square miles of land from the Chickasaws. Sutpen's Hundred is the canvas for his design.

Racism is unquestionably an essential element of the South's history, and Faulkner makes the legacy of slavery and bigotry central to his novel. But it is not only the black slaves Sutpen seeks to oppress. *Absalom! Absalom!* makes a more comprehensive argument: attempts to own and control people, whether blacks, "white-trash" young girls, spinster aunts, or one's own daughters and sons, infect both the owner and the owned. The devastated land of Sutpen's plantation registers his personal corruption and the more inclusive corruption of the South's commitment to slavery. That corruption, it must be remembered, is linked to land ownership itself.

Faulkner's entire corpus examines the relationship between a people and their land. The Compsons of *The Sound and the Fury* have sold land to golf-course developers so that Quentin may attend Harvard. The Bundrens of *As I Lay Dying* (1930) embark on their mad journey because Addie, the mother, wishes to be buried in a particular graveyard in Jefferson. The stories of *Go Down, Moses* (1942) chronicle the growth of a child to manhood through his indoctrination in wilderness ways; the respect for wilderness that Sam Fathers inculcates in Ike McCaslin is the literal and figurative ground upon which Ike erects his ascetic stance. He will not accept a patrimony knowing that one whole line of his family (the Beauchamps) has been excluded from inheritance because it descends from a black mother. Faulkner's works repeatedly pose the question: what does it cost us to own the land?

Faulkner's repeated references to the symbolic and real uses of land in his works mark them as Southern, insofar as Agrarian principles do appear to have special resonance in the South. The principle of the sacredness of private property is, however, fundamental not only to the South but to the United States as a whole: it is perhaps the one belief that Americans of all classes and kinds can agree on. Faulkner's work challenges a number of the assumptions that make that belief viable. A topography "all divided and fixed and neat" charts property lines, color lines, class lines, battle lines, bloodlines. Both stylistically and thematically, Faulkner refuses the straight line. His prose is marked by recursion and entanglement. Scenes are repeated with variations, speakers shift in mid-sentence, characters obsessively review and reconstruct the past; readers come to the end of a sentence and find they must reread, but it is difficult to know how far back to go. Where did that sentence begin? Faulkner's style is a heuristic. The notorious difficulties of his modernist prose, akin to what we see in James Joyce's *Ulysses* or Virginia Woolf's *To the Lighthouse* or Djuna Barnes's *Nightwood*, enact the impossibility of straight lines on maps or family trees.

Emerson was right in observing that America's "ample geography dazzles the imagination." On the whole, however, its inhabitants have not been so dazzled as to be paralyzed by its breadth. Builders, farmers, painters, poets, miners, film-makers, photographers, city planners – all its citizens have exploited its resources, been inspired by its beauties, and fashioned identities from association with the particulars of its topography. At John F. Kennedy's inauguration in 1964, Robert Frost recited from memory a poem written two decades earlier, "The Gift Outright," in which he explores the paradox of owning and being owned, possessing and being possessed by the land: "The land was ours before we were the land's." The people, he claims, had to "surrender" to the country "vaguely realizing westward / . . . Such as she was, such as she would become." It is this continual *becoming* that prohibits final statements about the meanings of America's physical and symbolic out-sized identity. Each avenue suggested in this chapter curves beyond sight.

CHAPTER 2

Rich

FIGURE 4   *Gold Diggers of 1933*
Photograph Warner Bros / The Kobal Collection
Ginger Rogers is literally "in the money" as she defies "Old Man
Depression."

The love of wealth is therefore to be traced, as either a principal or accessory motive, at the bottom of all that the Americans do.
Alexis de Tocqueville, Democracy in America, II. 17, 1840

We might as well urge the destruction of the highest existing type of man because he failed to reach our ideal as to favor the destruction of Individualism, Private Property, the law of Accumulation of Wealth, and the Law of Competition; for these are the highest result of human experience, the soil in which society, so far, has produced the best fruit.
Andrew Carnegie, "The Gospel of Wealth," 1889

We're in the money, we're in the money;
We've got a lot of what it takes to get along!
We're in the money, that sky is sunny,
Old Man Depression you are through, you done us wrong.
We never see a headline about breadlines today.
And when we see the landlord, we can look that guy right in the eye.
We're in the money, come on, my honey,
Let's lend it, spend it, send it rolling along!
Gold Diggers of 1933 *(lyrics by Al Dubin)*

You know, Mr. Bernstein, if I hadn't been very rich, I might have been a really great man.
Charles Foster Kane in Citizen Kane, 1941

Goddam money. It always ends up making you blue as hell.
J. D. Salinger, The Catcher in the Rye, 1951

all right we are two nations
John Dos Passos The Big Money, 1936

America's prodigious size is of a piece with America's prodigality. For European explorers and settlers there appeared to be an abundance of everything in the "New World" – timber, water, soil for farming, grazing lands – and the native peoples seemed, despite their often fierce resistance to the colonist presence, to hold no conception of private property, or, more precisely, to hold no deeds or other written contracts white settlers felt obligated to honor. So, as Milton said of Adam and Eve, "the world was all before them." Unlike Adam and Eve, however, the first of these settlers, the Puritans, saw themselves not as leaving Eden but as setting about to build a new Eden. Other settlers, less spiritually driven, came for the money to be made from exploitation of the rich natural resources. There can be no question that for some settlers the religious motive remained all-consuming, but with the passage of time, those striving for earthly success would outnumber those motivated by a view of the world to come. The two threads of religious quest and profit motive quickly intertwined. In *Of Plymouth Plantation*, William Bradford mournfully predicts that the "pilgrim" community he governed for most of the period 1621 to 1657 will disband, as it has already begun to do, in the pursuit of material goods: "no man now thought he could live except he had cattle and a great deal of ground to keep them" (book II, chapter 23). Material considerations will, he concludes, lead to a different sort of poverty: "And thus was this poor church left, like an ancient mother grown old and forsaken of her children. . . . Thus, she that had made many rich became herself poor" (book II, chapter 34).

By 1839 Tocqueville could confidently declare the "love of wealth" as foundational to all American behavior. His assessment has had wide acceptance now for well over a century: the overfed, overdressed, overloud American with a big wad of cash is a staple of satire. It is a commonplace that America's wealth accounts in great part for its powerful presence in the world, a power sometimes welcomed and sometimes resented. America both produces and consumes more than any other country in the world, though its people represent only 5 percent of the world's population. A startling comparison gives some sense of the scale of difference between the United States and the rest of the world, both in size and wealth: in 1963, a year just beyond the decades discussed in this book, American adolescents spent $22 million – double the GNP (gross national product) of Austria. Comparison with a less productive, more impoverished nation would be more startling still.

The usual quality-of-life indicators – home ownership, education, wages, leisure spending, employment levels, life expectancy, literacy, and others – tell, *in the main*, a story of improvement and progress. By 1960, 60 percent of working men and women owned their own homes. The number of university graduates rose steadily. Real wages, more or less constant in the period 1890–1915, increased 40 percent from the beginning of World War I to the stock market crash in 1929. They rose again by the same amount between 1945 and 1960. Unemployment, except during the Great Depression, normally stayed in the single digits. The average length of life in 1900 was 47.8 years; by 1960, 69.7 years. Literacy was nearly universal. *Prima facie* and in comparison to global conditions, twentieth-century life in the United States was good.

These quality indicators, however, mask a persistent and serious gap between rich and poor, a division linked to the multi-racial, multi-ethnic composition of the nation. Consideration of American riches, therefore, must reckon not only with total wealth but with the distribution of wealth. The titles of two influential books whose dates of publication are just outside the opening and closing years of the period considered here, Jacob Riis's *How the Other Half Lives* (1890) and Michael Harrington's *The Other America* (1962), suggest how easily American poverty drops out of the narrative of American wealth, how persistently it is the overlooked subplot of the "other." Nor has literature always managed to tell the story of these others without condescension. From turn-of-the-century fiction like Stephen Crane's "An Experiment in Misery" or Theodore Dreiser's "Curious Shifts of the Poor" to Walker Evans and James Agee's photographic essay *Let Us Now Praise Famous Men* (1941), attention to the plight of the "have nots" runs the risk, whatever the authorial intentions may be, of framing and categorizing poverty as an aesthetic or sociological exhibit. Of the three titles just cited, Evans and Agee's ironizes the word "famous" by its focus on women, men, and children living in squalor and yet exhibiting a calm dignity to the camera's eye; Crane's "Experiment" depicts a narrator who, like an undercover agent, purposely "slums" it in order to see derelict men in their native habitats; and Dreiser's story, while written in sympathetic tones, expresses a narratorial recognition that, for the reader, this vignette will be a matter of curiosity, both in the sense of "interest" and in the sense of "oddity."

By contrast, the dominant narrative of mainstream success is founded upon premises more relevant to and more readily accepted by the "haves" than the "have nots." These principles may be derived from the Puritan inheritance, the biographies of eminent entrepreneurs, advertising, and political rhetoric, to name only a few rich sources. The tenets, broadly speaking, are those associated with liberal individualism: people who work hard deserve material success. Competition fosters effort, improvement, and invention. The person who is most able and who exerts the most effort wins the competition. Parents may reasonably expect that their children's lives will be more comfortable than their own. Some people do have more money than others, but America does not have "classes" or castes as other countries do; in any case, social mobility is common and people do improve their economic position. Consumption is good for the economy. Strikes are sometimes necessary but should be kept to a minimum. Inequalities are often the effect of a natural distribution of talent. Over time, democracy and capitalism will help to correct inequalities; the political and economic system is fundamentally sound. In the "gospel" according to Andrew Carnegie, cited at the beginning of this chapter, property, wealth, and competition are components of a system that is the best yet evolved.

Expressed so baldly, these principles seem astonishingly naive. For every citizen who believes his or her position in life is a function of individual effort, there is surely another who can prove that just rewards have been withheld. Thus there is a corollary set of propositions also fundamental to American conceptions of wealth: barring a crash or other catastrophe, rich people get richer. Although the rich apparently have everything anyone could want, they are never happy. E. A. Robinson's Richard Cory, envied by all for his wealth and position, "went home and put a bullet through his head." Jay Gatsby stands alone and lonely on his blue lawn in West Egg. Charles Foster ("Citizen") Kane, Orson Welles's thinly disguised (1941) film portrait of the newspaper magnate Charles Randolph Hearst, surrounds himself with priceless possessions but yearns at the end of his life only for Rosebud, the sled he had loved as a child. Indeed there may be an inverse relationship between wealth and contentment, a consoling equation for those who have little. True wealth is a function not of money but of romantic or familial love. Look to the working classes for virtue: people at the top of corporations and government are self-serving and overpaid, not to be trusted; furthermore, they often got where they are not by merit but by advances based on croneyism or chicanery. Ida Tarbell's muckraking *The History of the Standard Oil Company* (1904), indeed the work of all those journalists with a mission at the start of the last century, assumed and often demonstrated that the most fertile ground for the cultivation of wealth was that polluted by corruption.[1]

Implicit in this line of thought is the belief that, having achieved economic superiority, people at the top of the heap want to keep the rest of the population down: this assumption was crucial to the labor movements discussed later in this chapter. Rich people can "work the system" in ways that poor people cannot. Rich people don't go to jail; the cells are full of the poor. Because money corrupts, wealth makes it hard to be a person of integrity. Money lures people away from their true calling or vocation. In *Citizen Kane*, Orson Welles tracks the inverse relationship between idealism and wealth. The father James Tyrone in Eugene O'Neill's *Long Day's Journey Into Night* (1940) is miserly and terrified of poverty despite his financial security. He describes to his son Edmund the abjection of his immigrant Irish family: evictions from their "miserable hovel," a childhood spent working ten-hour days, "never . . . clothes enough to wear, nor enough food to eat." Having known the indignities of want, he turns away from roles in Shakespeare and opts instead, in the name of financial security, to play repeatedly a melodramatic and crowd-pleasing role. (O'Neill's own father had made his living acting the Count of Monte Cristo and almost nothing else). "The God damned play I bought for a song and made such a great success in – a great money success – it ruined me with its promise of an easy fortune," Tyrone declares in Act IV. "Yes, maybe life overdid the lesson for me, and made a dollar worth too much. . . . What the hell was it I wanted to buy, I wonder, that was worth – Well, no matter. It's a late day for regrets." Artists and inventors, indeed people of talent generally, these examples suggest, must guard themselves against such corruption if they are to be original and disinterested. As Holden Caulfield complains in *The Catcher in the Rye*, money "always ends up making you blue."

The divided view of material wealth is not a simple matter of either the rich or the poor cheering themselves up with bromides. Ambivalence about riches has existed since before the nation constituted itself as a nation. If the inviolability of private property is a point on which Americans largely agree, the moral value of possessions is not so clear-cut. On the one hand, is not wealth a sign that one's efforts are smiled upon by God? On the other, is not wealth the surest temptation away from God? Polls routinely confirm that Americans are a nation of believers in God, and therefore such questions are central. However, even if religious considerations are put entirely aside, ethical and psychological issues remain. Is it right for one nation to have such abundance? Should Americans not feel guilty that they have so much when others have so little? And so on. The exuberant joy of "We're in the money," quoted from the *Gold Diggers* film, verges on hysteria – a wild sense of release and relief in imagining a day when the Great Depression and its privations will end. Tap-dancing women dressed as coins, women who are "through" with Old Man Depression, while potent symbols of wealth, are not without irony. Fabulous wealth in American literature and the other arts is rarely untainted by suspicion, disapproval – even tragedy. The title of William Dean Howell's novel *A Hazard of New Fortunes* (1890) captures the double sense of "hazard" – as both a gamble and a danger.

Two theoretical views will provide scaffolding for this discussion of wealth: Max Weber's *The Protestant Ethic and the Spirit of Capitalism* (1904–5) and Thorstein Veblen's *The Theory of the Leisure Class* (1899). Both books have been influential, both are controversial, and both have provided a vocabulary that readers of American literature and students of American culture will find familiar – phrases like "work ethic" and "conspicuous consumption." Having considered the premises of these two studies, we will turn to a trilogy of novels that dramatizes the quest for "big money," John Dos Passos's *USA* (1930–6). Dos Passos's panoramic view of the American terrain of wealth, power, poverty, and failure will organize a discussion of the changing relationship between work and self, efforts at labor reform, and attitudes toward consumerism (including both enthusiasm and rejection) as they appear in a range of examples from twentieth-century American texts. The desire for or the envy of wealth is hardly limited to Americans, but views of the United States have historically, as in Tocqueville's assessment, seen material goods as central to national identity, one of the foundational myths about America.

Weber and Veblen: Reasons to Work and Reasons to Spend

Work has not always been viewed as elevating. In the Judeo-Christian tradition, part of Adam's punishment when he is expelled from the Garden of Eden is that he must earn his bread by the sweat of his brow. Hellenic tradition saw labor as inimical to self-cultivation: leisure was the *summum bonum*, and work only the means to that desired end. A Christian idea of stewardship (seen, for example, in St. Thomas Aquinas) provides a moral rationale for work: one is duty bound to make the most of one's abilities. Alongside the more somber view of work as punishment, sacrifice, and duty, exists another tradition, the idea of work as pleasure, a vehicle for exercising and taking delight in one's abilities. For an exuberant Renaissance figure like Leonardo da Vinci, or indeed a polymath like Benjamin Franklin, work and play were inseparable. But it is fair to say that, in the main, work has been viewed not as an end in itself but as a means to an end, whether subsistence, power, comfort, security, status, or salvation.

Given Benjamin Franklin's "Poor Richard" persona and his identification with numerous aphorisms on the subject of money – making it, saving it, and increasing it – the German sociologist Max Weber aptly begins his exploration of "the spirit of capitalism" with an analysis of a dozen of Franklin's admonitions about time, credit, character, and wealth. Weber argues that Franklin's advice amounts not just to a "how to" for aspiring capitalists, but to an ethical system. Franklin's views were based on utility (for example, that it is good to look busy if you expect people to bring you their business), but Weber believes that "something more is involved here than simply an embellishing of purely self-interested egocentric maxims." Franklin's ethic, he argues, is that "the acquisition of money, and more and more money, takes place . . . simultaneously with the strictest avoidance of all spontaneous enjoyment of it." In Franklin's *Autobiography* (part 4), he reports coming in to breakfast one morning to find "a China bowl, with a spoon of silver!" Although he is staggered by the cost, he is flattered that his wife has made this purchase because she believes "her husband deserv'd a silver spoon and China bowl as well as any of his neighbors!" With his typical mixture of pride and self-deprecation Franklin himself explains his success by quoting the biblical passage cited repeatedly by his Calvinist father: "See thou a man vigorous in his vocational calling? He shall stand before kings" (Proverbs 22: 29). Upon this premise of vocation, Weber builds his story of the relationship between Calvinism and the spirit of modern capitalism: work is not merely a means of acquiring the necessities for survival; work is a calling to which a believer is duty bound. Thus sanctified, one's labors acquire spiritual meaning.

For the Calvinist, continual introspection and effort accompanied the doctrine of election: God having foreordained who was saved and who not, the devout looked for signs that they were among the happy elect. While the Calvinist could not save herself, she could create the circumstances of salvation: leading a systematically controlled and productive life in service to the glory of God was understood as a sign of election. How? Unstinting dedication to the work to which one is called requires firm belief and a suppression of human weaknesses; such belief could come only from God. Thus one's dedication to and ability to perform one's work became itself a sign of God's blessing.

If this dedication to work leads to profit and if profit is re-dedicated to increasing still more the fruits of one's work, the next step in this circular logic is that wealth itself becomes a sign of salvation. Weber cites the Presbyterian minister Richard Baxter (1615–91), who insisted that competition and profit were requirements of stewardship: "If God show you a way in which you may, in accord with His laws, acquire *more profit* than in another way . . . choosing the less profitable course, *you then cross one of the purposes of your calling. You are refusing to be God's steward and to accept his gifts*" (emphasis in original). Puritan asceticism, however, required that wealth be re-dedicated in some fashion to God; thus, the acquisition of possessions for their own sake, beyond a reasonable level of comfort, was not the goal. To live lavishly would be to undermine the very motive of work, which, in Weber's view, was the psychological relief attendant upon the proposition that one's labors are evidence of election.

If Weber's analysis is right, it would be hard to imagine a more perfect blueprint for building a capitalist workforce: people who are hard-working, reliable, productive, frugal, and committed to reinvestment. If, however, the self-abnegating impulse is removed from this "Puritan ethic," then the spiritual motive for work dissipates as well. Set aside the notion that one is working for God (and thus for the kingdom, earthly or heavenly) and for the redemption of one's soul, and the question naturally arises: assuming one's subsistence needs are met, why work so hard? For whom or what am I working? And what do I forfeit in devoting most of my time to work? As Henry David Thoreau calculated his economies in *Walden*, he judged that "the cost of a thing is the amount of what I will call life which is required to be exchanged for it, immediately or in the long run." Here Thoreau indicates a respect for the Greek view alluded to earlier: self-cultivation is the superior employment. Further, he believes that objects too easily master their users. Bradford's seventeenth-century concern about the direction of his flock points to one way in which work pushes other considerations aside. Work breeds more work; material success fosters acquisition; more cows require more land. We work to retain what we have, or to extend what we have, or to have what others have. Or we work for the future: we work so that we can work differently or elsewhere or so that someone else does not have to. Whatever the motive, work remains fundamental to American life: at this writing, Americans work longer hours and take fewer holidays than workers in any of the developed nations of the West.

Thorstein Veblen's *The Theory of the Leisure Class* (1899) formulates another answer to the question, why work?[2] An eccentric and influential American social scientist of the Progressive era, Veblen offered a scathing assessment of many aspects of the nation's life, from its system of higher education to its preferences in consumer goods. In his judgment, the "instinct of workmanship" had been eclipsed by "a straining to excel others in pecuniary achievement" (p. 40). For Veblen, "Man is an agent . . . seeking in every act the accomplishment of some concrete, objective, impersonal end. By force of his being such an agent he is possessed of a taste for effective work, and a distaste for futile effort" (p. 29). This taste for effective work, that is, work that produces a usable object or provides a useful service, he labels "teleological." It is work, in other words, with a clear end in view. His indictment of the leisure class is based upon this fairly narrow conception of the nature of work. In his reading, "the archaic differentiation into noble and ignoble classes is based on an invidious distinction between employments as honorific or debasing." Some forms of labor, those that in the United States are referred to as "manual" or "blue-collar," are on this basis deemed inferior to "white-collar" work. The less one is seen to perform physical labor, the more one is understood to be of a higher economic class. Visible forms of labor are thus devalued, even derided as odious and undignified, associated as they are with women, slaves, and "lower" orders of men.

In his imaginative (and imaginary) rendition of the transition from primitive to modern societies, Veblen seeks to account for the way in which waste has become a sign of wealth. In the transition from the subsistence labor of "peaceable savagery" to "predation," he theorizes, booty taken in battle becomes a sign of a man's potency. Predation leads in turn to what he takes to be the present age of "pecuniary emulation" wherein "the incentive to accumulation" is driven not by the urgencies of subsistence but by desire for status. The instinct for workmanship Veblen finds praiseworthy is thus transmuted into competition to make the most money and "the failure to consume in due quantity and quality becomes a mark of inferiority and demerit" (p. 40). Conspicuous consumption and conspicuous leisure, even "vicarious leisure" experienced through a wife whose days are entirely leisurely, measure the degree to which one has succeeded in the race. In his discussion of "Dress as an Expression of the Pecuniary Culture," for example, he argues that elegant bonnets, French heels, skirt drapery and excessively long hair are prized because they "hamper the wearer at every turn and incapacitate her for all useful exertion" (p. 171).

Evidence of *waste* conveys high status. Defining "waste" is difficult, even for Veblen himself, who finds it "unfortunate" that the term is normally taken in "an odious sense" (p. 78). He plows on, however, describing "waste" as that which does not conduce to the "enhancement and well-being" of human life as a whole. Slippery as his definition is, Veblen recognizes that one person's waste is another's necessity. But what he has in mind is the sort of life pictured in the endless social calls among the women of Edith Wharton's New York or in the piles of shirts in Jay Gatsby's dressing room, that is, "make-believe accomplishments" (p. 76) and acquisition for the sake of what acquisition symbolizes. A bumper sticker popular in the 1980s read, "He who dies with the most toys wins." Having the most toys is a simple definition of Veblen's most famous formulation – "conspicuous consumption." It is not enough to have more than one needs, one must *be seen* to have more than one needs. The religious dimension of labor as a sign of election is absent, replaced by signs of status demonstrating one need not work at all. Veblen's work has long since been revised and complicated by economists and social scientists. It is generally agreed that his definition of what constitutes work in an industrialized society is over-simplified. But his conception of American wealth has had enormous staying power in the United States and elsewhere.

Henry James's tale of American innocence abroad, *Daisy Miller: A Study*, offers, to humorous effect, an especially conspicuous example of wealth as a badge of American honor. Daisy's little brother Randolph opens his conversation with the protagonist Winterbourne by making invidious comparisons between Europe and America, much to Europe's disadvantage. The chief exhibit in his brief is money:

> "My father's name is Ezra B. Miller," he announced. "My father ain't in Europe; my father's in a better place than Europe."

Winterbourne assumes the child euphemistically refers to his father's removal to "celestial rewards." But no:

> "My father's in Schenectady. He's got a big business. My father's rich, you bet."

The Miller family is, in effect, a traveling advertisement for Mr. Miller's success. His absence, because he must attend to business, is entirely in keeping with his self-representation through his family. Too busy with the real work of the world to tour, he nevertheless foots the bill for what are clearly extravagant (and largely pointless) travels through Europe. His spoiled boy's constant ingestion of candy, his expensively dressed daughter's flounces, even his wife's dyspepsia proclaim his success, and in precisely the terms that Veblen saw as the fruits of "pecuniary emulation."

The imagery of highly visible forms of wastefulness pervades American writing in the first half of the twentieth century. The books of the so-called Lost Generation of the 1920s (Fitzgerald, Hemingway, and others) are especially littered with the evidence of squandered time, talent, and money. Consider, for example, the number of hours lost to aimless drinking in works like *The Sun Also Rises* (1926), Hemingway's depiction of gifted, monied, and aimless people wandering around Europe in the aftermath of World War I; the desperate and unsatisfying night-time sexual adventures of Robin Vote and Dr. Matthew Grain-o-Salt Dante O'Connor in Djuna Barnes's *Nightwood* (1937); the easy wealth that corrodes Dick and Nicole Diver's marriage in Fitzgerald's *Tender Is the Night* (1933).

In Dos Passos's *USA*, the topic of the next section, Veblen is likened to Socrates; he drank "the bitter drink" and "suffered from a constitutional inability to say yes." A "masterless man," the eccentric sociologist has identified the dark heart of wealth and consumption. His status as "truth-teller" makes him for Dos Passos an exemplary man in the novelist's rendition of modern America.

USA

Dos Passos's *USA* trilogy, published under a single title in 1937, first appeared as separate novels between 1930 and 1936: *The 42nd Parallel, 1919,* and *The Big Money.* The novels comprise multiple kinds of storytelling: conventional narration, "Camera Eye," "Newsreels," and biographies. The most conventionally novelistic component is a series of intersecting plots that follow the lives of eleven characters from just before World War I to the Great Depression. The trilogy's most experimental writing appears in the numbered sections Dos Passos designates as the "Camera Eye." These "stream-of-consciousness" passages employ various techniques of modernist writing: absence of punctuation and capitalization, juxtaposition of incomplete sentences, and an intense and sometimes impenetrable subjectivity. "Newsreels" are another component, a verbal equivalent of what an inattentive viewer might gather from the short news presentations that usually preceded a movie in that era. These montages of contemporary culture – snatches of popular song lyrics, paragraphs and phrases from books and speeches, headlines – contribute to both the sense of history and the complex tonal texture. The last component is biography. These are brief lives of famous and notorious Americans, including scientists, politicians, businessmen, and artists. The first novel of the trilogy, for example, includes portraits of politicians Eugene Debs, William Jennings Bryan, and Robert La Follette, botanist Luther Burbank, inventors Charles Proteus Steinmetz and Thomas Edison, labor organizer Bill Haywood, and capitalists Minor Keith and Andrew Carnegie. These portraits function as exempla, lives to admire and lives to despise. While the biographies are for the most part factual, there is no attempt to be "objective." The narrative judge is always on the bench, expressing approval or disapproval. The variety of narrative means in the novels effectively signals the breadth and multiplicity of the nation and the ambition of the novelist to survey a panorama of American lives.

Dos Passos's portrait of Thorstein Veblen, "The Bitter Drink," is the third biography in the third novel of the trilogy, *The Big Money*. As is his custom in most of these portraits, Dos Passos selects personal details that capture essential facts of upbringing, education, achievement, and character; his placement of the biographies within the novel's structure comments obliquely on the action the biography interrupts. Thus, in an unusually direct connection, Veblen's biography appears shortly before we see the character Mary French reading *The Theory of the Leisure Class* and deciding that she will quit college and go directly to work at Hull House, one of the settlement houses discussed in chapter 1. Often the connections between the biographical portraits and plot points are much more generalized – for example, the lives of actual labor leaders juxtaposed with the story of Mac, a young man involved with the Industrial Workers of the World (the IWW or Wobblies), or the dovetailing of inventors' biographies with the story of Charley Anderson, a handy mechanic whose wealth eventually ruins him.

The trajectory of Charley Anderson's rise and fall charts the boom-and-bust economy of the period between the end of World War I and the Great Depression, and exposes the tension between Veblen's teleological and pecuniary cultures. Introduced at the end of the first novel, *The 42nd Parallel*, as a teenager in Fargo, North Dakota, Charley grows up along with the technology of transportation, as the surrey and horse are replaced by the automobile and the airplane. Bored by his work as a car mechanic in a "hick town," he daydreams over copies of *Popular Mechanics* and *The Scientific American*, planning to build a boat and travel down the Mississippi, "shooting ducks and fishing for catfish." His dream would make him, in Veblen's terms, a "peaceable savage." This Huckleberry Finn fantasy of self-sufficiency does not materialize. Instead, after a mishap in a car he shouldn't have been driving – an image that will recur throughout the narrative – Charley moves to Minneapolis, goes to night school, becomes involved with a young woman, travels, works as a mechanic, considers the merits of organized labor, and generally spins his wheels until the US enters World War I. He joins the ambulance corps and, at the conclusion of the first novel, is on his way to European front. He returns to the United States at the beginning of *The Big Money*, having invented an airplane starter with a friend named Joe Askew. The two take their idea to investor Andy Merritt, who sets up the Askew–Merritt company, furnishes capital, and handles financial and legal arrangements. So baffled is Charley by all but the mechanical side of his invention that he wonders, "Say, for crissake, Joe, are we rooking those guys or are they rookin' us?" Some version of this question will continue to trouble him – and to provide a theme – throughout the novel.

The starter is an enormous success, and Charley becomes extremely rich, but he squanders his wealth pursuing unsatisfactory sexual and business ventures and persistently acting against his own most deeply felt principles. Charley sees himself as what Americans call "a regular guy": good with his hands and clever, he thinks of himself as a member of the laboring class and sympathizes with ordinary workers. His fall results from his betrayal of that simpler self. In Veblen's terms, his career dramatizes the shift from teleology (useful work) to pecuniary emulation, and Charley enters the predatory phase. When an opportunity arises to make still more money by speeding up production – regardless of the effect on his employees or quality control – Charley grabs it. His recklessness causes the death of his friend and business partner, and his life spirals into chaos and self-destruction. Throughout the novel, he is unable to resist the corrupting forces of his culture: he cannot defend himself against big business; he fraternizes with but is often outfoxed by corrupt politicians; he cannot discipline himself to do without readily available drink and sex. He meets a predictably undignified end. And yet Dos Passos has created in Charley Anderson a likeable character for whom the reader can retain sympathy even as his life unravels. The novel suggests that had it not been for the power of a culture that valued only "the big money," Charley would have lived a simpler and happier life.

The biographies interspersed with Charley's narrative document a shift from the self-made and self-reliant man to the corporate man, a shift for which Charley is unprepared. Dos Passos presents the lives of Veblen, the efficiency expert Frederick Winslow Taylor, and the inventors Henry Ford and the Wright brothers as commentary on Charley's development and, simultaneously, on modern America. Veblen, as we have seen, is described in admiring prose that styles eccentric independence as a virtue. The Taylor biography does the opposite. F. W. Taylor's efficiency studies set standards for the assembly line and his name was eventually adopted for any process that had been standardized for efficiency (Taylorization). The biographer admires his ingenuity, but the emphasis of the portrait is on the way that Taylor's good ideas produce bad results. What begins as a labor-saving process evolves into the mechanization of human beings. The laborer who repeats the deadening tasks of the assembly line ("reachunderadjustscrewdownreachunderadjust," we read in the Ford biography) is little different from the machine he builds. Even on his deathbed, Taylor winds a watch.

Biographies of Henry Ford and the Wright brothers highlight two of the most important inventions of modern life, the automobile and the airplane, both of which play significant roles in Charley's story. Once again the juxtaposed biographies emphasize innocent curiosity and the pleasures of discovery and hands-on invention. This ethos may be likened to the idea of work as pleasure discussed above. Like Charley, Henry Ford is fascinated by engines and works as a mechanic; like Taylor and Charley, he favors efficient output, economical production, quick turnover, and cheap, interchangeable parts. He introduces the assembly line into his plant in 1913. "The American Plan; automotive prosperity seeping down from above; it turned out there were strings to it," the narrator comments. Ford pays well but seeks to control the lives of his employees, forbidding drinking and smoking. With success comes overreaching. Henry Ford, the biographer reports wryly, "was full of ideas." He buys a newspaper to spread the ideas. So great is his self-regard that he hires a ship to convey pacifists to Europe to end the war "and get the boys out of the trenches by Christmas." In his declining years, an ardent anti-Semite and a man fearful of change, Ford becomes a reclusive "passionate antiquarian." In Dos Passos's America, self-reliance easily declines into self-regard, self-delusion, and selfishness. The biography of Wilbur and Orville Wright follows a similar pattern, but with a saving difference. Bright, hard-working, clean-living, and curious, the brothers clearly relish their efforts to become airborne. They, too, are tantalized by worldly pleasures after their success, but unlike the prideful Ford they forsake neither their independence nor their commitment to their project as an end in itself. The conclusion of the biography appropriately soars. It is a measure of Dos Passos's idealism that the flight at Kitty Hawk is presented as a moment that cannot be sullied by the interests of big money:

> but not even the headlines or the bitter smear of newsprint or the
> choke of smokescreen and gas or chatter of brokers on the stockmarket
> or barking of phantom millions or oratory of brasshats laying wreaths
> on new monuments
> can blur the memory
> of the chilly December day

two shivering bicycle mechanics from Dayton, Ohio,
first felt their homemade contraption . . .
soar into the air
above the dunes and the wide beach
at Kitty Hawk.

Every fictional character of the *USA* trilogy begins in the spirit of this passage, with elevated hopes and ideals, and each is pictured in the final scenes as having compromised, abandoned, or destroyed those ideals. J. Ward Morehouse, by some measures the most successful man in the novel, not only wealthy but famous and well respected, is not who he wants to be. "I'm a lonely man," he admits to Richard Savage. "And to think that once upon a time I was planning to be a songwriter." Savage responds, "Shake hands, J. W. . . . with the ruins of a minor poet." The poet has become a public relations man. Eveline Hutchins and Eleanor Stoddard build their youthful friendship upon shared love for the paintings in the Chicago Art Institute but find their artistic aspirations revised downwards to interior decorating and party-giving. Mac, the Wobbly who wants to assist a workers' revolution, is drawn from his aspirations by the pull of family life. Mary French, the social worker, though badly mistreated by her communist co-workers, resists the comforts of home and family, but we see her grow increasingly weary and unwell, battling forces she cannot defeat and doing work that is usually futile. The corrupt figures, like G. H. Barrow the labor organizer, Senator Planet, and E. R. Bingham the patent medicine con man, all thrive.

Summarized so briefly, the novels may appear simple and schematic – good guys versus bad – but reading them is a more complicated experience, often evoking admiration and disdain simultaneously. Dos Passos is devoted to a romantic conception of America that is at odds with the unlovely reality he depicts in detail. The novels are long, dense, teeming with elements of popular culture – movies, slang, nightclubs, cocktails – and the close observation often associated with the French naturalist tradition of Émile Zola. The characters typify a carefully chosen variety of occupations, geographical locations, educational histories, sexual inclinations, and class. (Race is the novel's blind spot: African Americans, for example, appear only as porters or denizens of Harlem nightclubs.) Dos Passos documents representative American lives at the point when the energies of individualism are being redirected to corporate conformity. The pervasive irony of the book's structures, the sadness of its tone, arise from Dos Passos's nostalgia for a nation once devoted to higher aims than getting and spending. *USA* is an elegy for individualism.

The last two biographies of the trilogy dramatize the uneven applicability of the so-called American Dream, whereby a person can, through hard work, discipline, and clean living, not only pursue happiness and wealth but actually get them. The first depicts energy magnate Samuel L. Insull ("Power Superpower"), the second an unnamed transient or vagabond ("Vag"). The latter was added when Dos Passos consolidated the three novels into a trilogy, thus creating an ending that balances the first novel's focus on Mac. The Insull biography records the rags-to-riches narrative that has been fundamental to the American Dream or, in Dos Passos's terms, the American Plan. Starting as a secretary to Thomas Edison, Insull works his way to the presidency of the Chicago Edison Company. Devising monopolies on both electricity and gas, "With the delicate lever of a voting trust controlling the stock of the two top holding companies he controlled a twelfth of the power output of America." Eventually put on trial for corrupt management of his stockholders' funds, a $10 million accounting "error," he tearfully recounts his rise from "officeboy to powermagnate" and is found not guilty. Insull's trade is "Power Superpower" both as material energy – in the form of electricity, gas, and coal – and as power over the lives of stockholders, businessmen, bankers, and the public who sympathize with him at trial.

The portrait of Vag, the last in the novel, is in dramatic contrast to Insull's success story. A hitch-hiker, Vag sees a plane in the sky. The narrator imagines the airplane's transcontinental flight and the wealthy passenger who thinks about "contracts, profits, vacationtrips." Hungry and exhausted, the hitch-hiker thinks of unkept promises: "went to school, books said opportunity, ads promised speed, own your home, shine bigger than your neighbor." Meanwhile his hands are idle, his head swimming, his belly aching with hunger.

Just before "Power Superpower" comes one of the stream-of-consciousness sections called "Camera Eye." Camera Eye 51 ends with the phrase, "we have only words against." This is an ambiguous statement, depending on whether or not one believes words are sufficiently powerful to change people or institutions. Elsewhere in the novels, Dos Passos writes, "But mostly USA is the speech of the people." How powerful is speech against the big money? The novel offers contradictory responses. The chief evidence of the novelist's investment in the power of language is of course the existence of the trilogy itself. And yet most of the novel's wordsmiths, Moorehouse and Savage, for example, are hirelings whose success is a function of their ability to manipulate words for suspect ends.

One of the most eloquent sections of *The Big Money* is Camera Eye 50. It begins, "they have clubbed us off the streets they are stronger they are rich." The immediate setting is the aftermath of the famous case of Sacco and Vanzetti. Tried and found guilty of having murdered a paymaster and his guard during the robbery of a truck carrying a factory payroll, Nicola Sacco and Bartolomeo Vanzetti were immigrant Italian anarchists who, it was believed by many, had been falsely accused. They were electrocuted in August 1927; the form of their execution is perhaps another reason that Dos Passos focuses next on the power magnate, Insull. Theirs was a *cause célèbre*, particularly among artists and intellectuals. The trial and its outcome were significant motivations for Dos Passos's writing of *USA*

The tone of Camera Eye 50 is largely despairing. But not wholly. Admitting that "all right we are two nations" the speaker of this section indicts those who "have turned our language inside out who have taken the clean words our fathers spoke and made them slimy and foul." But he predicts that these injustices will be the spur to renewal of the language: "the old words of the immigrants are being renewed in blood and agony tonight." The preponderance of the evidence presented in *USA* is that the ideals of America – including self-determination and justice – have been trampled and are unlikely to rise again. Nevertheless, the strength of the novelist's respect and admiration for these ideals cannot, even on the most cynical reading, be dismissed. One source of the emotional power of *USA* is the sense of loss, the sense of a falling off from laudable principles.

For Dos Passos, the energies of the nation have been misdirected, aimed toward amassing wealth for its own sake – Veblen's predatory phase writ large. The purposes of work have been divorced from either survival or service. Except in a few cases singled out for praise, characters do not work for the love of what they are doing. Rather, the fruits of work become less and less tangible: a palpable product is exchanged for abstract stocks, public relations subsume public service, status outranks achievement, workers are as interchangeable as the parts they assemble. Dos Passos represents the inevitable rise of interdependent networks of business and personal relations in a large and complex capitalist economy. The intermeshing of plot lines in the novels is one means of conveying the characters' reliance on one another. Indeed, reliance on others, whether in the form of sexual liaisons, business partnerships, corporations, or labor unions, dominates the personal arrangements of the novel. Characters rarely escape their entanglements. The American Adam discussed in the last chapter is an increasingly obsolete model. The newsreels, too, record sights and sounds that impinge on privacy: the media's message here is that one is connected, like it or not, to a larger world. Acknowledging the interconnectedness of humankind, however, Dos Passos finds that what might have been the formidable energies of concerted effort have been wasted on venal aims.

The diminished meaning of self-reliance informs another memorable depiction of American aspiration, F. Scott Fitzgerald's *The Great Gatsby*. James Gatz has become the rich and somehow larger-than-life Jay Gatsby. As a boy, Gatz modeled himself on Benjamin Franklin by scheduling his self-improvements. We learn near the end of the novel that young James had written on the fly-leaf of *Hopalong Cassidy*, a Western, his "SCHEDULE: Rise from bed . . . 6.00 a.m.; Dumbbell exercise and wall-scaling . . . 6.15–6.30; Study electricity . . . 7.15–8.15 . . ." Gatsby is "self-made" in the sense that he has discarded his birth identity and created another. He has been willing to do whatever it takes to succeed: the rumors of bootlegging, baseball game-fixing, and other unsavory activities that taint his reputation also mark him as a man of his time, that heady period that included the speakeasy, a fixed 1919 World Series, a boom economy, and a lucrative climate for racketeers. His quest for success has found an object in Daisy Buchanan, a Southern girl whose "voice is full of money."

Fitzgerald thus traces a decline in the quality of dreams. Unlike earlier Americans, he suggests, the hero dreams not of a republic but of a woman who represents what is meretricious in American values. Gatsby's ideal woman is corrupt, his ideals perishable. Often mentioned as a contender for the Great American Novel, Fitzgerald's book owes its esteem partly to its having captured so memorably the contradictory nature of American aspiration – both the most idealistic and the most debased quests of the nation. Like his contemporary Dos Passos, he decries America's failure to meet its own highest expectations. For Nick Carraway, the narrator, Gatsby is "great" because he alone is capable of passionate devotion to an ideal, a devotion Nick sees nowhere else in a society where objects and people are used, damaged, and discarded with insouciance. Because Fitzgerald presents Gatsby as a man apart – a self-made man, a near-heroic figure, but finally a failure – his novel concedes the implausibility of Gatsby himself: how can this throwback to a more idealistic time find a home in Jazz Age America? Both *USA* and *The Great Gatsby* interrogate the meaning of self-reliant manhood, and both find it an obsolescent model for the world of twentieth-century work.

Work and Identity

The tenets of liberal individualism have been crucial to the shaping of American attitudes toward work, wealth, and property. The term "individualism" did not come into frequent use in the language until the 1820s, though the foundations for the political and economic significance of the single person were laid by the early modern period. As a democratic and capitalist nation, the US is an important exhibit in the history of this idea. In *Democracy in America*, a work cited at the start of this chapter. the French commentator Tocqueville predicted that the country's emphasis on the significance of the individual would eventually lead to an egocentric disregard for the good of the community. As we have seen, Dos Passos and Fitzgerald recognize a potential for monstrous selfishness as inherent to the autonomy of the self-made man.

Nevertheless, one of the favored figures of American culture over many decades has been the loner whose solitude is a sign of moral stature. This particular form of heroism is clearly on display in Hollywood movies of the 1930s and 1940s. Typical "heroes" include the man or woman who defies convention in favor of conscience, who is willing to go it alone: Jimmy Stewart's tireless filibustering against political chicanery in *Mr. Smith Goes to Washington* (1939) or Rosalind Russell's crusading journalist and sole woman in the newsroom in *His Girl Friday* (1940). Alan Ladd as *Shane* (1953) and Humphrey Bogart as Philip Marlowe in *The Big Sleep* (1946) are the cowboy and private detective who prefer solitude to the entanglements of civilization; Joan Crawford is *Mildred Pierce*, the tough, successful woman who can be touched by no one but her ungrateful daughter. Despite the appeal of independence, however, the Hollywood plot usually traces the loner's gradual recognition of the necessity and even the joy of connection to others. A fixture of the Christmas season on American television is the showing of Frank Capra's film *It's a Wonderful Life* (1946), in which a suicidal man (Jimmy Stewart as George Bailey) is awakened to the value of community. George is led round his town by an avuncular angel who shows him how his absence would affect his family, friends, co-workers, and neighbors. When a greedy lender tries to close a bank and deny depositors their cash, George discovers that he and other decent folk can "fight the system" through cooperative effort. The film is a kind of fairy tale or Dickensian fable about the essential goodness of humankind and the force of communal effort in the defeat of corruption. For all that American movie heroes are, in the public mind, built along the lines of laconic men like Humphrey Bogart or John Wayne and feisty women like Rosalind Russell, Joan Crawford, or Katharine Hepburn, a happy and shapely ending to a narrative often dictates that the loner be reincorporated into society. Thus the erstwhile suicide is tearfully reunited with his family and friends around a Christmas tree; the tough-talking dame is finally able to admit her vulnerability and marry a man who is even tougher. The classic expression of this view is the final moments of Michael Curtiz's *Casablanca* (1942). In a thrilling act of self-denial, Rick Blaine (Bogart) sends the woman he loves off with her husband, who does important work resisting the Nazis. He consoles himself and her with this speech, known to movie-goers everywhere: "Ilsa, I'm no good at being noble. But it doesn't take much to see that the problems of three little people don't amount to a hill of beans in this crazy world." At the film's close, Rick prepares to emerge from his retreat, a smoky bar in an exotic land, and will join the French resistance.

The expression of tension between individual and community values is of course hardly limited to American works; this fundamental conflict shapes plots from Sophocles to Shakespeare to Tolstoy. It is not therefore an inherently American plot. But when one thinks of the American hero, he is far more likely to be a cowboy than a co-worker. Yet the real world of work in the twentieth century far more often required an ability to fit in than to stand out. Most forms of labor are done in groups – why then this special praise of and pressure on the individual in American culture? Some answers come readily to mind, of course. The first public expression of nationhood was a Declaration of Independence; thus a break with traditional society is fundamental to the nation's history and image. The size of the country, as discussed in the last chapter, invites free movement. Democracy is defined by its valuing of the single voice as equal to every other single voice. And capitalism is fundamentally connected to free enterprise, competition, and private property – all of which assume the rights of individuals to better their lot, make what they can, and keep what they make.

A major document in the definition of the proper relationship between the self and the world is Ralph Waldo Emerson's 1841 essay "Self-Reliance," with its famous sentences known even to people who have never read the essay. "Imitation is suicide." "Trust thyself: every heart vibrates to that iron string." "Whoso would be a man must be a nonconformist." "No law can be sacred to me but that of my own nature." "But do your work and I shall know you." The ease with which aphorisms and greeting-card sentiments may be extracted from Emerson's essays has led to an over-simplification of his multiple views of the self. His essays are in fact densely argued, ambivalent, self-contradictory, and subject to multiple readings. But it is the brave "isolato" that has been labeled "Emersonian" by all but specialists. The appeal of the aphoristic Emerson is that he seems to prize (and does praise) nonconformity as an expression of courage, virility, and self-respect. Gaining a reputation as a homegrown sage, Emerson was adopted as a kind of household god in the late nineteenth and early twentieth centuries, his portrait hanging in American classrooms as inspiration to follow one's conscience, to hear and heed, as his contemporary Henry David Thoreau expressed it, "the beat of a different drummer."

But Emerson recognized, more than this reduced rendition captures, that the powers urging conformity were potent and definable in economic terms:

> Society everywhere is in conspiracy against the manhood of every one of its members. Society is a joint-stock company, in which the members agree, for the better securing of his bread to each shareholder, to surrender the liberty and culture of the eater. The virtue in most request is conformity. Self-reliance is its aversion. It loves not realities and creators, but names and customs. ("Self-Reliance")

Emerson's views were shaped by his own experiences, as he had been lambasted for opinions expressed in an earlier essay (the "Divinity School Address") and had suffered under the criticism. Beyond this personal dimension, he is reacting to the economic structures of an increasingly corporate culture and its implications for the concept of selfhood. A joint-stock company is an apt metaphor for the interdependence that arises when a society moves from an agricultural to an industrial model, from a system in which the necessities of life are mostly produced in the family unit to one in which the provenance of goods is often unknown. Imagine the difference between eating the pig you raised and slaughtered and eating the plastic-encased, processed bacon purchased at a Safeway. It is, then, not hard to see how the definitions of work and self connect.

How, then, to reconcile the solitary entrepreneur with the corporate system? In *The Work Ethic and Industrial America*, Daniel Rodgers argues that, in the United States, the ideal of self-sufficiency and the ideal of cooperative work existed simultaneously (if illogically) into the early twentieth century:

> As the self-sufficient worker disappeared in fact, nineteenth-century ideals of self-sufficiency slowly gave way to ideals of teamwork more suited to an industrial and bureaucratic society. By the same token, success writing grew more involuted in the face of narrower opportunities, retreating from the domain of work and habits to the less pregnable citadels of mental attitude and self-confidence.[3]

Thus social Darwinism, with its praise for unfettered economic enterprise, coexisted with cooperative ventures like the Knights of Labor. Even as the labor movement gained strength in the early decades of the century, the fascination with "captains of industry" was undiminished. Theodore Dreiser presented a series of interviews with business tycoons. In 1906, the magazine *Success* had as high a circulation as the popular muckraking magazine *McClure's*. Hugely successful businessmen like Andrew Carnegie and Cornelius Vanderbilt were held up as models of the rewards of diligence, discipline, and thriftiness even as they were maligned as "robber barons." With titles like "Work and Win," the dime novels and cheap weeklies of the Progressive era promulgated the view that good things happen to the deserving; at the same time, Dreiser, Stephen Crane, and Frank Norris, writers of naturalist and realist fiction, exposed such a narrative as a cruel myth. In *Individualism Old and New* (1930), John Dewey noted "the tendency to combination in all phases of life,"[4] and sought ways to educate children to enter a world of work in which a "combination" rather than a competition of individual wills would be the expectation. Meanwhile adventure stories encouraged boys to be self-sufficient. The Boy Scouts taught survival skills and self-reliance even as it inculcated loyalty to the "troop." To point out these apparent contradictions is not to fault them; it is impossible to think of a complex modern society without contradictory values, especially given the enormous changes in social and economic patterns. As Rodgers expresses it, "the striking phenomenon of the age was not change but persistence amid change" (p. 136).

The odd coupling of individualism with corporate culture illustrates the staying power and appeal of the solitary achiever. One particularly long-running example of this link was E. I. du Pont de Nemours and Company's sponsorship of *The Cavalcade of America*; first introduced as a radio program in 1935, this ran for nearly two decades and then became a television program that aired from 1952 to 1957. *Cavalcade* was the company's means of aligning itself with the attributes of American heroes (and a few heroines). Begun in the early nineteenth century as a manufacturer of gunpowder and, later, dynamite, DuPont went on to create in its chemical laboratories such products as celluloid shirt collars, artificial leather, nylon, rayon, Teflon, and other widely marketed and successful products. During World War I, DuPont was heavily involved in the manufacture of munitions. A series of plant explosions in January 1916 and consequent rough handling by the press made clear to the president, Pierre S. du Pont, that the firm needed better control of information reaching the public: he established an advertising division. By the 1930s, sentiment against big business having gathered force throughout the Great Depression, DuPont came under investigation by the US Senate as one of the manufacturers labeled "Merchants of Death."

Clearly, DuPont had an image problem beyond what could be handled in-house. The public relations firm Batten, Barton, Durstine & Osborne devised the radio program *Cavalcade* to shift the public perception of DuPont from that of death merchant to provider of life-enhancing consumables for a peacetime economy and, hence, contributor to the American way of life. Functioning in much the same way as the biographies of *USA*, *Cavalcade* presented exemplary lives. As was to be expected, the lives chosen for dramatization were those illustrating the virtues of the work ethic: initiative, drive, tenacity, self-reliance, and inventiveness. First-season telecasts included dramas about Benjamin Franklin, Samuel Morse (inventor of the telegraph), and Eli Whitney (inventor of the cotton gin). Even when the programs became more various, focusing on such contemporary figures as Olympic medalists, the traits celebrated remained identifiable with free enterprise. Those enlisted to help with the project in the 1950s were also achievers: among the scriptwriters was the playwright Arthur Miller; among the historians, Arthur Schlesinger, Jr. Thus icons of individual achievement were enlisted in projecting a corporate image: the great American corporation, the public was given to understand, was simply a magnified version of the individual achiever. The DuPont slogan to reassure America's consumers of its good intentions was "Better Things for Better Living – Through Chemistry." The phrase would be ironically adopted by the drug culture of the 1960s, signaling disdain for what was by then known as the "military-industrial complex," but the success of *Cavalcade of America* suggests that for over two decades many accepted an equation of personal with corporate success.

However, despite the ritual praise of individual initiative, rugged individualism, nonconformist behavior, and other forms of self-making, by the late nineteenth and early twentieth centuries people recognized that freedom of action was not simply there for the having. Certainly the Civil War contributed to the sense of a complexity beyond individual control. And as the country became increasingly industrialized and urbanized, the sensation of being merely one of a mass of individuals was bound to intensify. The Great Depression that lasted from 1929 through the 1930s would also have made self-sufficiency seem more and more impracticable. Dos Passos, as we have seen, ends *USA* with the rise of the corporate man. By the period after World War II, this new breed of person became a familiar figure in public discourse: the cavalcade of heroes was replaced by corporate man, the man on the street, Gregory Peck as *The Man in the Gray Flannel Suit* (1956).

The American sociologist David Riesman saw this "other-directed" figure as the man appropriate to the consumer and service economy of postwar America, a type that had been in development throughout the first half of the century. Riesman's study *The Lonely Crowd* (1950) argues that changes in Western society over time have caused a shift in the locus of selfhood; in particular, he sees a new "type" emerging in the upper-middle-class urban population. He contrasts this type with an earlier one:

> If we wanted to cast our social character types into social class molds, we could say that inner-direction is the typical character of the "old" middle class – the banker, the tradesman, the small entrepreneur, the technically oriented engineer, etc. – while other-direction is becoming the typical character of the "new" middle class – the bureaucrat, the salaried employee in business, etc. Many of the economic factors associated with the recent growth of the "new" middle class are well known. . . . There is a decline in the numbers and in the proportion of the working population engaged in production and extraction – agriculture, heavy industry, heavy transport – and an increase in the numbers and the proportion engaged in white-collar work and the service trades.[5]

The inner-directed worker, according to Riesman, is at home in a society "characterized by increased personal mobility, by a rapid accumulation of capital . . . and by an almost constant expansion: intensive expansion in the production of goods and people, and extensive expansion in exploration, colonization, and imperialism" (p. 15).

These characteristics answer the requirements of a young and expanding nation. In a later phase, however, this self-starting and adventurous spirit is no longer needed: instead, "the frontiers for the other-directed man are people" (p. 131); "*their contemporaries are the source of direction for the individual – either those known to him or those with whom he is indirectly acquainted, through friends and through the mass media*" (p. 22, emphasis in original). In short, the other-directed person must be attuned to the responses of others and able to gain their approval. Similarly, William Whyte's *The Organization Man* (1956) observes a shift away from the Puritan work ethic toward what he terms a "social ethic," in which the community's claims take precedence over those of any individual. Whyte sees a "tyranny of the majority," necessitating a drive to be "normal," acquiescent, adaptable, a team player.[6] The apotheosis of this ethos is the conformity of appearance and behavior in the American middle-class suburb. In 1956, for the first time in American history, white-collar workers outnumbered blue. Rising wages meant that home ownership was increasingly a reasonable expectation.

Arthur Miller's *Death of a Salesman* gives dramatic life to Riesman's and Whyte's abstractions. In the play, the aptly named Willy Loman is in crisis: his company no longer needs his skills as a salesman and, in any case, he is no longer able to do the job well. His son Biff, a high school football star, has returned home after another failed attempt to make a life for himself; his son Happy is a low-level clerk who womanizes and drinks excessively; his long-suffering wife Linda anxiously watches his moods and tries to keep the peace between her husband and her sons. Having spent his working life "riding on a smile and a shoeshine," Willy dimly realizes that he has almost nothing to show for his labors. He cannot get ahead; he cannot even catch up. Miller's aim, at least in part, is to chronicle an unchronicled life, one that will not appear in a cavalcade of American heroes. As Linda expresses it to her sons in Act I, "A small man can be just as exhausted as a great man." While the playwright clearly sympathizes with Willy and his family (and invites his audience to do so), he wants also to investigate why and how Willy "had the wrong dreams." The values of good salesmanship – contacts, charm, an ability to project self-confidence or to tell a good joke, in short to be not only "liked, but well liked" – have proved unsatisfactory both emotionally and financially.

Miller's stage directions prescribe imaginary wall lines that enable scenes to change seamlessly from present to past and from reality to dream. This fluidity of presentation generates contrasts that, in turn, help to explain the family's inability to be truthful to one another. Further, the easy shifts in time and space contribute to the play's rhythms, in which disputes begin slowly, increase in pace, rise to the level of crisis, and then "melt" into earlier dreams. Against the "wrong dreams" Miller offers some sturdier alternatives in the representation of his neighbor Charley and his son Bernard. Not a popular high school hero, Bernard was an excellent, diligent student and is now a lawyer about to make an argument before the Supreme Court. Unwilling to exaggerate or brag, both of which the Loman men do, Bernard does not report this information but leaves it to his father. Although Willy hasn't done so consciously, he has inculcated in his sons the notion that the only thing they need to "make" is an impression. This selling of the self is a form of Riesman's "other-directedness." The alternative is embodied in the character of Willy's brother Ben, a fantastical adventurer who claims to have "walked into a jungle" and come out a rich man. Clearly Ben is meant to symbolize the entrepreneurial, adventurous (and of course imperialist) conqueror. He asks Willy, "What are you building? Lay your hands on it. Where is it?" The exoticism of Ben's adventures suggests that this mode of achievement is not readily available to men of Willy's generation. Willy, we learn from other characters, is good with his hands, can put up a ceiling, "was a happy man with a batch of concrete"; we are here reminded of Veblen's instinct of craftsmanship. Similarly, Biff has sought to find himself in manual labor, working on a ranch in the West. Miller implies that these forms of labor are substantial, valuable, and a fit occupation for manly men. Charm and gab, white lies and incidents of petty theft and cheating, exemplified by the younger son Happy, are the lot of the man in the service economy, which apparently has little need of virility. The undermining of masculinity that Miller puts into the foreground also matches Riesman's description of other-directedness. Stereotypically, conventionally, and historically, it is women who have found it necessary to please, to be sensitive to small nuances of behavior, to assess their self-worth in terms of their impression on others. Miller's characters dramatize nostalgia for a time in which the products of male labor were tangible. In his final appearance, Willy is plotting out a garden, expressing a desire to "get something into the ground." Biff, in his final confrontation with his father, cries, "Why am I trying to become what I don't want to be?" His complaint resembles Emerson's: "Society everywhere is in conspiracy against the manhood of every one of its members."

The plight of the white male has been examined at great length in American writing, literary, historical, and critical. However, as the critic Nina Baym asserts, such "melodramas of beset manhood" have a way of obscuring and even deforming the histories of other groups.[7] Her concern is primarily with the way that attention to men in American literary criticism has pushed aside stories of women's lives, thus distorting the conception of American authorship. A similar argument can be made about a number of other groups, those who, usually because of color or ethnic background, have been poorly paid, neglected, and exploited. The discussion of immigration in the last chapter offers evidence that Carnegie's "Gospel of Wealth" is a satisfying set of tenets for the powerful and successful but not one that describes the world as it appears to those living a hand-to-mouth existence. For these groups neither the work ethic nor other-directedness adequately accounts for the necessity motivating their working lives.

Feminist analyses of women's work would not enter the mainstream of American thought until after 1960, a period beyond the scope of this text. Betty Friedan's *The Feminine Mystique* (1963) marks a dramatic shift in the American perception of women and their work. This is not to say that women were not working throughout the early to mid twentieth century, particularly in the lower economic strata. Paid domestic work, factory work, secretarial work, sales, teaching, nursing, and other labor was regularly performed by women, particularly unmarried women. And, during World War II, some 35 percent of the female population entered work outside the home. With this exception, however, the tendency throughout the period was for a woman to leave work in favor of child-rearing and home-making when it was financially possible for her to do so. And the view that women belonged in the home was rarely contested. Even among the most radical women calling for suffrage before the granting of the vote in 1920, employment outside the home was not a high priority in the revision of women's rights. There were, of course, notable exceptions. In New England, Emerson's contemporary Margaret Fuller, in both her life and her publication of such works as *Woman in the Nineteenth Century* (1845) provided a corollary to his view of self-determination. The Woman Question, discussed as such throughout the late nineteenth and early twentieth centuries, included concerns about the dependence of women on their "providers." One of the most articulate of these inquiries was *Women and Economics* (1906) by Charlotte Perkins Gilman, who argued that the next important step in "social evolution" must be to separate the "sex relation" from the "economic relation." "The girl must marry: else how live? The prospective husband prefers the girl to know nothing. He is the market, the demand. She is the supply."[8] The result, Gilman concluded, was an unhealthy emphasis on the personal to the detriment of the larger society, an imbalance that harmed both men and women. "Only as we live, think, feel, and work outside the home do we become humanly developed, civilized, socialized" (p. 222). Generally speaking, Gilman's aims were of a piece with utopian fiction. Edward Bellamy's *Looking Backward*, a bestseller in 1899, also envisaged a society in which space outside the home was most valued, and social commitment the highest commitment. Gilman's views would be echoed again and again throughout the next five decades. Edna St. Vincent Millay's poetic expressions of the free spirit, Emma Goldman's campaign for free love, Dorothy Parker's wry view of feminine dependence, Margaret Sanger's efforts to make methods of birth control accessible – all these alternative views of women's place in the society found an audience. But the role of women as workers comparable to men and the recognition of domestic work as real (though unpaid) labor would not gain currency until the social and political events of the 1960s – and in some parts of the country even later.

For African Americans, the momentous events occurring between 1865 and 1919 also necessitated a revision of the relationship between work and identity. The abolition of slavery as a result of the Civil War, the participation of African Americans in World War I, and mass migration to northern cities following the war all altered the position of the African American, but in ways not yet clearly defined. The terms of the debate emerge in the different views of Booker T. Washington and W. E. B. Du Bois, two spokesmen for the advancement of what came to be called "the New Negro." Washington favored small increments of progress. His strategy was to make the black worker useful to the economy through agricultural and mechanical skills; his vision found expression in his direction of the Tuskegee Institute in Alabama, where students were instructed in practical employments and urged to lead disciplined lives patterned after the Puritan work ethic. Washington's speech at the Atlanta Exposition in 1895, which came to be known as the Atlanta Compromise, expressed the Tuskegee philosophy on a national scale: not asking too much too soon, the rhetoric is humble and diplomatic. If allowed to go about its business peacefully, he promises, the race will become educated in useful work that will be an economic asset to the nation. He assures white Americans that they will then be surrounded by "the most patient, faithful, law-abiding, and unresentful people that the world has ever seen." The chief "compromise" of his address is the often-cited metaphor of the hand: "In all things that are purely social we can be as separate as the fingers, yet one as the hand in all things essential to mutual progress." This image of simultaneous separation and unity would be adopted to justify "separate but equal" practices that in fact were separate and unequal: separate and inferior schools, separate and inferior jobs, and separate and inferior status under the law. But the historical context of Washington's conciliatory remarks is necessary to understanding the address's seemingly excessive humility. Between 1885 and 1910, some 3,500 lynchings occurred in the United States. Washington's first goal is cessation of violence, a soothing of white America's fears. Without a truce, education and productive labor on non-servile terms could not go forward.

The "compromise" inevitably seemed to some African Americans to give too much away. Notable among the dissenters was W. E. B. Du Bois, who passionately criticized Washington's strategy in a 1902 essay "Of Mr. Booker T. Washington and Others" (in *The Souls of Black Folk*). Du Bois argues that Washington's willingness to set aside principles of enfranchisement, civil rights, and higher (that is, liberal, non-vocational) education concedes rights and privileges fundamental to equality. He revises Washington's hand metaphor:

> His doctrine has tended to make the whites, North and South, shift the burden of the Negro problem to the Negro's shoulders and stand aside as critical and rather pessimistic spectators; when in fact the burden belongs to the nation, and the hands of none of us are clean if we bend not our energies to righting these great wrongs.

Du Bois, in contrast to Washington, frames his demands as fundamental to the national interest not on the basis of progress but on the basis of fidelity to its own founding principles. He ends the essay by quoting from the Declaration of Independence, reminding the country of its professed commitment to the self-evident truth: "That all men are created equal." Working as a writer, editor, organizer, and reformer over the next half-century, and increasingly focused not just on the nation but on racial inequality world-wide, Du Bois was ultimately disappointed by his country's response to the challenge.

This brief episode in the debate over the meaning and value of labor in one racial group typifies the ways in which self-reliance, self-determination, self-making, and self-respect – all principles related to the national work ethic and the achievement of American dreams – resonate differently to different Americans. Ralph Ellison's 1952 novel *Invisible Man* explores several avenues of self-making as it traces the growth and development of one African American from youth to self-realized man. He develops in symbolic stages. First, as a student at the college of the Founder (clearly modeled on Tuskegee) he practices the disciplined and humble behavior recommended by Washington. Later, he accommodates himself to the more radical approaches of the Communist Party and Black Nationalism movements, exemplified in his involvement with the characters Brother Jack and Ras the Destroyer. An idealistic striver, the Invisible Man repeatedly does what he is told, whether it is driving a college benefactor to view abject poverty as if it were scenery or making a rousing speech to a huge gathering on behalf of the Brotherhood. Able and intelligent, he finds that, despite his gifts, he is continually made a pawn in someone else's game. Throughout the novel, the Invisible Man follows rather than leads. He cannot choose because the choices offered are equally negative, though in diametrically opposed ways. Dominating every institution or organization with which he has to deal are traitors, self-servers, and megalomaniacs. He learns through repeated disillusionment that the Founder had had an insufficiently sophisticated view, that "free" enterprise is not free to all. By the novel's end, the Invisible Man has fallen through a manhole and decided to stay underground, making a fact of the metaphor of invisibility.

The novel opens in a vague underground space, with a prologue and the announcement: "I am an invisible man." The prologue is in part devoted to defining the nature of this invisibility. Neither an Edgar Allan Poe "spook" nor a "Hollywood-movie ectoplasm," he is invisible because "people refuse to see me." The narrator makes literal the sensation of not being seen, that is, not recognized for what one is, and he has come to accept invisibility as an asset. He has, for example, managed to tap into the Monopolated Light and Power for the energy to light 1,369 light bulbs in his subterranean home. The novel bears comparison to Fyodor Dostoyevsky's *Notes from the Underground* in that both offer the sur- or perhaps *sub*-realistic perspective of the dispossessed and disempowered. Here, as Dos Passos does with his portrait of "Power Superpower" in *The Big Money*, Ellison employs power and light both as tangible utilities and as symbols. Indeed this emblem-heavy novel, with its Sambo dolls, yams, and shackles, invites readers to think analogically about the visible and invisible forms of slavery for black Americans. *Invisible Man* is an inversion of *Pilgrim's Progress*. The protagonist regresses to a womb-like environment to become reborn, but can offer no certainty about what the new identity will be nor imitate Christian's faith in ultimate salvation, the goal of *Pilgrim's Progress*. He is in the dark but in the light, free and yet confined, certain that he is uncertain. The paradoxes that shape the novel are potent reminders that, for some, the route to self-determination is circuitous, hazardous, or blocked.

Labor Reform

A substantial portion of Dos Passos's *USA*, as we have seen, centers on the activities of the IWW (Industrial Workers of the World) and the work of labor organizers, both sincere and corrupt; the novel evokes compassion for the workers much more often than for the owners and managers. However, in 1934, after a socialist rally in New York's Madison Square Garden was broken up by members of the Communist Party, Dos Passos became increasingly convinced that group effort was not the most effective way to create a just society. Inevitably, he believed, corruption led to suppression of individual rights. His support and subsequent rejection of collective action tell a typically American story of conflicting allegiances. On the one hand, a sense of justice or fair play has motivated, and continues to motivate, Americans to support reasonable efforts to improve the worker's life. On the other hand, the culture's preference for explanations that look to individual responsibility rather than to systems or groups has meant that, on the whole, Americans have often been wary of labor unions and political philosophies favoring the group over the individual. While there have been periods of intense and often bloody disputes aimed at resisting overweening or greedy management, it is notable that the United States has never experienced a national general strike like that of Great Britain in 1926. America's writers, intellectuals, and artists have been more sympathetic to labor reform and left-leaning political thought than have the majority of their compatriots.

A text of this kind cannot undertake a detailed history of labor reform. Readers who wish to know more about the US labor movement may turn to the bibliography at the end of the book for more information.[9] Because the American Dream, the work ethic, and other dominant cultural ideals are firmly linked to the world of work and the cycles of prosperity and poverty in the first half of the twentieth century, it may be helpful to extract some general principles from labor history, particularly as they may apply to the literary representation of work. The chief incentives for strike actions and other organized activity are, first, the belief that owners and managers, driven by the profit motive, will not make concessions to workers unless pressed, and, second, that it is harder to ignore a group than an individual. Yet even the massed forces of workers could not always gain their objectives. As names of strikes, such as the "Ludlow Massacre," indicate, confrontations between workers and management were often violent and fatal. Lost lives were not only an outcome but also a cause of strike actions, unionization, and legislation. The 1911 fire at the Triangle Shirtwaist Factory in New York's garment district is a particularly horrific instance of working conditions that galvanized labor reform.[10] Exits in the factory were kept locked so as to prevent workers from stealing; when fire erupted, 146 workers, the majority female immigrants, were burned to death or died attempting to jump from the building. Fire ladders did not reach to the ninth floor, where the exit was locked. The scale and drama of the incident directed public attention to the unsafe and squalid conditions in the so-called sweatshops. Unions like the International Ladies Garment Workers (ILGWU) assisted in the relief of the survivors. The governor of New York formed the Factory Investigation Commission, which affirmed findings long known to labor organizers: the sweatshops were dangerous places and the working conditions execrable. As a result of their findings, new legislation made it considerably more difficult for owners and managers to ignore minimum standards. Versions of this episode – conditions exposed and legislation mandated – occurred throughout the first half of the twentieth century.

During this period, labor leaders sought wage increases, safer working conditions, shorter working hours, holidays, medical insurance, and other improvements directly affecting the quality of workers' daily lives. By the 1960s, federal statutes outlawed discrimination in employment on the basis of gender or race. The perilous working conditions that had caused the illness and even death of workers in the first decades of the century had been improved dramatically. Child labor had been prohibited. A minimum wage had been established. The eight-hour workday and two-week vacation had become standard. Taking the long view, then, it appears that many of the goals sought by labor reformers in the period 1900–1960 have, in principle if not always in practice, been met.

The eddies of power between labor and management have followed fairly predictable patterns. When the supply of workers outstrips the demand for them, wages fall; scarcity of workers raises wages. At the turn of the century, waves of immigrants made labor plentiful and permitted owners to offer very low pay. In periods of war, workers not in the military, including groups that normally do not work, are fully employed and their value is higher because of need. War is good for business generally. The years immediately following large-scale wars usually see a significant upsurge in labor activity, as was the case in 1919 and in 1946. Grievances held in abeyance during wartime demand attention. In recessions and depressions, when jobs are scarce, labor initiates strikes with some regularity, often as a means of protecting jobs as employers try to reduce expenses. Consider these numbers for the Ford Motor Company: in March 1929, 128,000 people were on the company payroll; in August 1931, 37,000. During and just after the Great Depression, between 1929 and 1939, the number of union members tripled nationwide.

The USA celebrates "Labor Day" on the first Monday of September. And yet it would not be accurate to say that Americans manifest a strongly developed working-class consciousness, even in the lowest economic brackets. Given the accomplishments of organized labor, the weak attachment to or identification with collective effort is surprising. Why is there no greater sense of unity? General prosperity and low rates of joblessness may in part account for the lack of fervor. Furthermore, group affiliation in the US is complex: the ethnic and racial diversity of the country means that many people identify more readily with their language group or race, country of origin, or even geographical region than with others in their socio-economic stratum. Sometimes, as has historically been the case for recently arrived immigrants and African Americans, ethnic and racial definition overlaps substantially with economic level to create a particularly strong sense of solidarity. Racial and ethnic prejudice has also been economically divisive. Established male workers throughout the century resented the "intrusion" of immigrants who might undermine work practices and wages, an exclusionary attitude that worked against combining forces for economic ends. The labor movement itself has been torn by competition among the various organizations, not only on the basis of occupation (whether miners, teamsters, or steelworkers) but also because of differences in skilled and unskilled labor, degrees of conservatism or radicalism in politics, size and clout, willingness to compromise, and so forth. And of course, as in any organization, differences of principle and practice arise within particular unions. In the twentieth century the labor movement usually shared basic goals, but often not much else.

Union members have not always trusted their leaders, and leaders have not always warranted their trust. In a 1941 poll conducted by the Gallup organization, 74 percent of respondents expressed the view that "many" union leaders were racketeers. The taint of gangsterism and violence once made unions a source of fear not only to employers but to the general population. Another counterweight to the unions' effectiveness throughout the century was near-constant suspicion of conspiracy with the communists: labor unions became a significant target in the "Red Scare" of 1919 and the subsequent Palmer raids in 1920, when an entire division of the US Justice Department was given extraordinarily wide powers to roust out suspected radicals and communists. The "witch hunts" of the McCarthy era discussed in the previous chapter were another instance in which the fear of "Reds" made radical thinking suspect. A number of unions were eventually ousted from the largest of US labor unions, the AFL-CIO, on the grounds of their demonstrated sympathies with communism.

In fictional representations of the conflict of labor and management, it is rarely the "rank and file" or ordinary workers who are demonized. Rather, accusations of corruption and "un-American" beliefs are more frequently directed at the organizers and leaders of unions, who are presented as lining their own pockets by being in the pay of the owners. The 1954 film *On the Waterfront* portrays this moral division between the workers and their union representatives. The screenplay by Budd Schulberg was based on a series of news articles about long-shoremen published in the *New York Sun* newspaper that won the Pulitzer prize for local reporting in 1949. The articles described the forms of criminality that had festered among the officials whose purported job was to protect the dockworkers. In the pay of gangsters, racket-eers, and an unseen high-level owner (referred to as "Mr. Upstairs"), the leaders make no pretense of looking out for worker interests but manage the apportionment of work and wages to increase their own kickbacks and bribes. There is little to choose between the perfidy of the owners and that of the labor "bosses." In an atmosphere of phys-ical violence and psychological intimidation, the workers have settled upon "D and D" as their mode of operation: it is best to be "Deaf and Dumb." To be a "cheese-eater" (rat) or "stool pigeon" (whistleblower) is not only disloyal to the system but potentially fatal. Better to be silent and keep one's head down. No one is inclined to talk to the Waterfront Crime Commission investigating dockside practices.

The film's protagonist, Terry Malloy (played by Marlon Brando), is a failed boxer who has become an errand boy for the biggest of the union bosses. Indeed, he has purposely failed as a boxer, allowing himself to lose so that the boss and his friends could profit from betting against him. He is, at best, a pawn – not heroic, not articulate, and not a natural leader. Schulberg underscores Malloy's low status and threatened manhood by making his primary associates a priest and a woman. They appeal repeatedly to his sense of fairness. Having himself played the victim in unfairly determined competition, he finds his conscience awakened, first by the courage of the priest who attempts to rouse the workers and then by the tenderness of the woman who teaches him compassion. Father Barry preaches to the men about their apathy:

> Every time the mob puts the crusher on a good man – tries to stop him from doing his duty as a citizen – it's a crucifixion. Anybody who sits around and lets it happen – keeps silent about something he knows has happened – shares the guilt of it just as much as the Roman soldier who pierced the flesh of Our Lord to see if He was dead.

This way of looking at the world is not what experience has taught Terry. In his philosophy, "it's every man for himself. It's keeping alive." It's "do it to him before he does it to you." He calls the woman Edie "a fruitcake" when she asks, "Isn't everybody a part of everybody else?" Circumstances work to change Terry's view and he chooses to speak to the Commission. He not only testifies but fights the union boss hand-to-hand. The men refuse to go back to work unless Terry works, too, and the boss, thrown into the water, screams empty threats as the workers follow Terry in triumph.

The optimism of the ending is darkened by the film's acknowledgment that Terry's victory is primarily a personal one. While the current boss is vanquished, the real power (Mr. Upstairs) is still in place, lying low until the Commission finishes its work. The solidarity of the racketeers may prove more powerful than that of the dockworkers. The film is dark and gritty in appearance, the acting highly naturalistic; though the plot offers a romantic vision of the hero who defies the power-structure, these other elements suggest a darker reality. Terry's own brother has been a willing participant in the corruption, even at the expense of Terry's self-respect. It is he who has engineered Terry's "throwing" of boxing matches. This distortion of biological brotherhood undermines the likely success of a brotherhood of workers. Terry Malloy has set an example that will be difficult to emulate once the temporary enthusiasm for his actions abates.[11]

The drama of fraternal betrayal also animates the 1935 Clifford Odets play *Waiting for Lefty*. Odets was a member of New York's Group Theatre, a project begun by Harold Clurman, Cheryl Crawford, and Lee Strasberg (the revered teacher of Method acting, of which Brando was a star student). Their objective was to reduce the artifice of theatrical presentation and to make the stage relevant to, even formative of, current affairs offstage. Odets wrote *Waiting for Lefty* as an incitement to worker rebellion, drawing material from a 1934 strike of "hacks" or taxi drivers. Presented as a series of vignettes or "episodes," the frame of the piece is a union meeting at which the leaders attempt to talk the rank and file out of striking. But the union members are "waiting for Lefty," whom they trust. The scenes that follow work backward in time. Edna berates her husband Joe for not being manly enough to fight for his rights. A lab assistant refuses to assist a manufacturer of poison gas by spying on a co-worker, despite the temptation of a big raise in pay. A young hack and his girlfriend realize that "the cards are stacked" against them, and they lack the money to marry. In the play's central episode, which returns to the setting of the meeting, brother turns against brother. Tom Clayton argues that the time isn't right for a strike, but his brother, shouting from the crowd, calls Tom an imposter. Tom Clayton is, in fact, Tom Clancy, the mouthpiece of the bosses. Following this climax of betrayal, two more episodes about a young actor and a medical intern dramatize their growing recognition that their virility and integrity are compromised when they placidly take things as they find them. In the concluding scene, a union member, Agate Keller (played by Elia Kazan, who would go on to direct *On the Waterfront*), attempts to rouse his co-workers, noting that his union button is so ashamed that "it has blushed itself to death." A man rushes in to say that Lefty has been found murdered, and the men, led by Agate, begin to chant: "Working class, unite and fight! Strike! Strike! Strike!" They are enacting the advice of Edna in the earlier scene. When Joe argues that "one man can't –" Edna cries, "I don't say one man! I say a hundred, a thousand, a whole million, I say." The audience on the first night took up the chant and headed into the streets. "Agit-prop" drama – plays designed to create this kind of political fervor – has usually been short-lived in the American theater, and idealistic enterprises like the Group Theatre have struggled to survive. So the play may be less significant for its artistry than for the ways in which it offers scenic summaries of many of the issues we can trace from Emerson forward: the relationship between self-respecting male identity and work; the ways in which greed, corruption, and capitalism obstruct the formation of a group ethos, even turning brother against brother; the deleterious effect of poverty on families; disillusionment about the possibility of true self-reliance; tension between the dream of success and the desire for a clear conscience; and in general an emerging sense that the game is fixed, the deck stacked against the weaker players.

Throughout the first half of the twentieth century, a general disinclination to stifle individual enterprise and competition often undermined the urge to organize. Attachment to private property and the exercise of self-interest have usually trumped the ideal of worker unity. This tendency cannot be blamed on a lack of idealism but rather on the preference for one set of ideals over another. Communities organized along socialist lines, those in actual practice and those existing only as thought-experiments, have always been marginal in the United States. The ideal attractive to the mainstream is that individuals, left free to make the most of their abilities and to avail themselves of opportunity, are the source of national strength and progress toward equality for all. Even people who would seem least likely to have those opportunities and least likely to have the chance to develop and employ their abilities subscribe to this principle, as we have seen in the example of Booker T. Washington.

On the questions of self-determination and equal opportunity, American writers, artists, and intellectuals have often been contrarians, asking hard questions, posing alternatives, and actively pursuing unpopular social and political ends. Naturalist writers – Theodore Dreiser, Stephen Crane, Frank Norris – of the late nineteenth and early twentieth centuries focused on the poorest and least powerful city dwellers, and muckraking journalists exposed ugly truths about corruption in high places. Realist and regionalist writers (Samuel Clemens, Sarah Orne Jewett, Henry James, Edith Wharton, and others) took pains to document status details in their fiction: clothing, furnishings, etiquette, regional foods, and speech patterns. They thereby kept wealth, poverty, and the overt and subtle signifiers of class at the center of American fiction. High modernist writers, on whom we will focus in the next chapter, energetically sought to *épater les bourgeois*, to disturb smugness and complacency, to create new ways of looking and thinking. Writers of the late 1920s and the 1930s were especially sensitive to the economic devastation of the Great Depression; many of them called for radical change and involved themselves directly in political and legal events such as the Sacco and Vanzetti trial. Some, like Hemingway, went to Europe to fight in the Spanish Civil War. They edited and wrote for radical journals, signed petitions, raised money. Hemingway's *For Whom the Bell Tolls* (1940) and Steinbeck's *The Grapes of Wrath*, discussed in the last chapter, represent much of the fiction of this period in expressing a clear political aim. And we can look to the poetry of Edna St. Vincent Millay ("Say That We Saw Spain Die"), Genevieve Taggard ("Mill Town"), and Muriel Rukeyser ("The Trial") for direct commentary on specific events like wars, strikes, and trials.

The 1930s also saw a reconsideration of the role art could play in society: what were the political obligations of the artist? was political art always bad art? was the notion of art for art's sake merely an excuse for maintaining the status quo? Throughout the 1930s, 1940s, and 1950s, writers and artists were susceptible to accusations of sympathy with and overt support of communism. Indeed main-stream journals and newspapers played up a simplistic equation of the "bohemianism" of artists with anti-American sentiments. Especially in the minds of Americans who lived outside urban centers like New York, enclaves of artists in places like Greenwich Village were under-stood to be morally dubious territory. While there was a truce of sorts in these cultural skirmishes during World War II, the postwar period again saw writers and other artists chafing at the restrictions of con-vention and celebrating heroes of nonconformity. The Beat poets' diatribes against materialism and hypocrisy typify this resistance to homogenization. By the 1960s, this resistance was both louder and more widespread, even fashionable. The 1960s in general saw a kind of saturnalia, in which hierarchies were reversed and home truths exploded. Satirical novels like Joseph Heller's *Catch-22* (1963) dis-mantled, through grotesque humor, the structures of military authority, patriotism, and rationality. The phenomenon of "confessional" poetry, for example that of Anne Sexton, made even the most intimate details of the poet's life public, thus erasing the line between the private and the public and revising the standards of poetic decorum.

This sketch of the political climate over several decades is drawn with very broad strokes and is subject to corrections and exceptions. Dur-ing these same decades some writers and artists were accused of sup-porting fascism. Others, disillusioned by the dictatorial behavior of Joseph Stalin in the Soviet Union, turned away from the promises of a communal society. And, of course, neither the writers on the left nor those who held opposite views were motivated solely by considerations of wealth and poverty. Nevertheless, these broad strokes – major events, trends, dominant ideas – create a backdrop against which the details of American literature and culture become visible.

Consumption and Identity

In 1666 the Puritan poet Anne Bradstreet saw her house burn down. The "Lines upon the Burning of Our House" register her horror and then her acceptance, "Farewell my Pelf, farewell my Store":

> And when I could no longer look,
> I blest his name that gave and took,
> That layd my goods now in the dust:
> Yea so it was, and so 'twas just.
> It was his own: it was not mine;
> Far be it that I should repine.

For Bradstreet, the acceptance that her "store" is not "mine," but "his," that is, a loan from God, is consistent with the religious commitments that enabled her to follow her husband to the New World. Her mission is never hers alone.

In 1956 the Beat poet Allen Ginsberg published a fantasy about grocery shopping with Walt Whitman, "A Supermarket in California."

> I saw you, Walt Whitman, childless, lonely old grubber, poking
> among the meats in the refrigerator and eyeing the boys . . .
>
> I wandered in and out of the brilliant stacks of cans following
> you, and followed in my imagination by the store detective.
> We strode down the open corridors together in our solitary
> fancy tasting artichokes, possessing every frozen delicacy,
> and never passing the cashier.
>
> Where are we going, Walt Whitman? The doors close in
> an hour. Which way does your beard point tonight?
> (I touch your book and dream of our odyssey in the
> supermarket and feel absurd.) . . .
> Will we stroll dreaming of the lost America of love past blue
> automobiles in driveways, home to our silent cottage?
> Ah, dear father, graybeard, lonely old courage-teacher
> what America did you have when Charon quit poling his ferry
> and you got out on a smoking bank and stood watching the
> boat disappear on the black waters of Lethe?

Three centuries of change and cultural difference separate Bradstreet and Ginsberg; ostensibly the poems seem to have little in common besides the word "store." But both these poets have written meditations on the meaning of possessions, both poets experience loss, and both poets perceive spiritual significance in their experiences. Further, Ginsberg (overtly) and Bradstreet (implicitly) see their encounter with commodities as meaning something about America. Bradstreet considers herself a caretaker but not an owner, in keeping with the Puritan ethos of stewardship. For Ginsberg the abundance of choice – the frozen artichokes and the blue automobiles – are evidence that "the America of love" is lost. His invocation of Whitman calls to mind the Transcendentalist conception of objects as symbols of something larger – an ideal, a belief, a god of love. With the demystification of goods, supermarket shopping, as he is reminded by touching Whitman's book, is "absurd."

The preceding discussions of work and identity and of labor reform outline a narrative that historians, sociologists, politicians, artists, and indeed all who lived though it have perceived as epoch-making. One way to define twentieth-century modernity is to connect the simultaneous emergence of new forms of work (industrialization, assembly-line work) to new conceptions of self and other. As we have seen, in the first fifty years of the century, the model of self-sufficiency – the self-made man – became if not obsolete then at least questionable. Further, the equation of work and morality, outlined by Weber as fundamental to the Puritan work ethic, gave way to other formulas. The professionalization of many forms of work would supply new codes of conduct and a sense of affiliation with one's peers. For many, corporate culture came to substitute for other forms of belonging. Owners could of course remain invested in what they did since they owned the products of their labor. For workers, Veblen's instinct of craftsmanship diminished. Suppose you had to explain to yourself why you should go each day to a job that is routine and tedious but that pays a living wage. You no longer believe that idleness is a sin. You know that you are easily replaceable since your work involves no special skill. You don't own the company or have a profit-sharing arrangement, nor is there likelihood of advancement. Apart from the admittedly powerful argument for avoiding starvation, how do you find the motivation to work?

Daniel Rodgers offers four early twentieth-century responses to the realization that work is not always fulfilling: handicraft, vocational education, industrial psychology, and less work. Handicraft as an antidote to mechanization has surfaced repeatedly since the Industrial Revolution. Whether as a hobby or as a profession, handicraft functions not only to provide the satisfaction of full engagement in the making of an object but also to mount a critique of mass manufacturing. Similar values motivated the various artisans of America's Arts and Crafts movement, visible in such structures as California's Gamble House, designed by Greene and Greene, who supervised the making of not only every structural element but every light switch, or in the simple and sturdy "Mission" furniture designed by Gustav Stickley, or in pottery made by the Roycroft colony. We may also look to modernist experiments in painting, sculpture, decorative arts, and architecture for projects that attempt to revise the meaning of modern media like concrete and modern techniques like the use of interchangeable parts. These experiments will be discussed in the next chapter.

A second antidote to worker alienation might be education: vocational education, championed by Progressives like Jane Addams, was designed to help workers understand their jobs as part of a much larger project. In Edward Bellamy's *Looking Backward*, each worker is considered a member of an "industrial army," contributing to a large cooperative venture. Understood as promoting the collective good, any job, whatever its form, should be a source of pride, or so the reasoning went. But as Rodgers explains, there was a "fragile" line "between education to help workers see the full dimension of their work and education to adapt them, unthinkingly, to it" (p. 87). In other words, "knowing one's place" can be understood either as integration or as oppression by other means.

A third strategy to counter tedious work is to address the worker's mental and emotional health. Industrial psychology emerged as an effort to understand workplace dynamics and the effect of personality on job performance. Its aims were to match the mind to a suitable form of work or, alternatively, to find means of distracting laborers from monotony in the interest of workplace harmony. If the job itself could not be made pleasant, then perhaps the environment could be made so. Fourth, and most practically, the solution to tedium was to work fewer hours. The eight-hour day, vacations, days off – all these helped to ease the problem of worker discontent.

Once the worker has free time, how is it to be spent? Veblen was admonishing the nation about conspicuous leisure as early as the turn of the century. By the 1920s leisure had emerged as a centerpiece of American life: dancing, listening to music, going to movies and amusement parks, participating in roller derbies, competing in football and baseball, beauty pageants, stunts, and so forth were pleasures readily available to all strata of society. Hours of leisure became something to be managed, and thus a leisure industry emerged to direct the use of spare time. For all but the poorest of Americans there was also the perennial favorite: buying things.

Between 1860 and 1920, the population of the nation a little more than tripled, while the volume of manufactured goods increased somewhere between twelve- and fourteen fold. Once the products of manufacturing outstripped need, once the economy moved from one of scarcity to one of abundance, the national emphasis shifted from production to consumption. The United States became and remains the largest consumer in the world. It is a long way from the principles underlying Anne Bradstreet's "Lines on the Burning of My House" to those of the dissatisfied housewife drifting down the aisles of a supermarket in Randall Jarrell's poem "Next Day." She moves "from Cheer to Joy to All" as she surveys the labels on laundry detergents. Veblen's theory of "pecuniary emulation" seems an inadequate explanation for this seismic change. Self-expression and self-realization may be signified through the loss or gain of worldly goods, and it is in this signification that we may detect a link between the self-abnegation that fulfills the Puritan poet and the self-furnishing that fulfills the modern shopper. Profound differences shape the nature of those desires. For Bradstreet, desires should be subject to discipline, acknowledged but held in check. But in the modern world, consumer desire, abetted by the messages of advertising, is by definition insatiable. We want something. We work for it. We buy it. We use it and use it up. We want something to replace it. Or we want something not for its usability, but for its beauty or for what it signifies. Tastes change, and so do standards of what is beautiful or meaningful. Thus new desire is created and fulfilled and the cycle begins again. Producers must not only fulfill existing needs but produce new ones.

Three aspects of getting and spending will reveal the contours of commodity culture and prepare for an analysis of its representation in fiction: the marketing of one product as an example of the relationship between advertising and consumerism; the psychological effects of department store shopping, and the implications of "shopping" for conceptions of selfhood.

But first, to borrow a phrase from American radio and television, a word from our sponsor. First appearing in 1911, Crisco was – and still is – an unglamorous but useful product with a price low enough to be within most Americans' reach. A shortening used in cooking, the product has been a mainstay of the company Procter & Gamble. The story of its marketing illustrates the ways in which advertising creates a "relationship" between a product and a consumer, one based not just on the utility of a product but on its appeal to the personal. William Procter and James Gamble first formed their partnership in 1837; a candlemaker and a soapmaker respectively, they were led to collaborate on the basis of shared ingredients – tallow, lard stearin, and cottonseed oil. By 1870 Procter & Gamble included "Refined Family Lard" in its product list. "Crisco" was the company's improvement on lard. Hydrogenation catalysts were first patented in 1902, and the process of hydrogenation allowed P&G to solidify vegetable oil and keep it stable on shelves regardless of temperature. Money, not health, was the selling point: vegetable oil was an inexpensive alternative to lard for both producer and consumer. Here, then, scientific progress, profit motives, and market demand met.

The Procter & Gamble company spent $3 million in a carefully planned, step-by-step introduction and promotion of Crisco. Over the first half of the twentieth century, P&G employed every new medium with alacrity: producing a free cookbook to accompany the product in 1912; airing its first radio advertisement in 1923; producing its first television commercial in 1949. It stayed current with sociological and historical developments, shifting from vegetable oil to corn oil to canola oil as the most recent medical advice dictated, substituting glass containers for metal cans during wartime, repackaging the product as butter-like sticks for convenient use. American middle-class consumption patterns are reflected in the evolution of its marketing: fat phobia, cleanliness, and efficiency. P&G's practices exemplify clearly certain modes of product presentation designed to create a bond between maker and user:

Branding. It is the unsurprising philosophy of P&G's marketing division that consumers buy brands, not just products. Establishing the trustworthiness of the product and the company from which it comes, the logo, packaging, color, and slogan become over time the symbol of both the product and the buyer's relationship to it. A brand may even become the generic name for a product of which it is a single specimen: Kleenex, Coca-Cola, Jello. In many parts of the United States, Crisco is a household name. The initial challenge for Crisco advertising was to dissociate the product from lard and to emphasize the purity of its contents. The first cans were wrapped in white paper and carried the product name in simple blue letters, employing an oversized "C" for the first letter. The color blue and the enlarged C have remained constant even as packaging has changed. As the producers succeeded over time in distancing Crisco from the unpleasant connotations of animal processing associated with lard, purity became a less urgent selling point and the white packaging gave way to blue, a more vivid color for supermarket shelves. The solid shortening itself has remained glacially white. The insistence on purity and wholesomeness makes sense for a food product of this period. In the first decades of the twentieth century fears about the adulteration of food were widespread in the United States. Not coincidentally, publication of Upton Sinclair's muckraking novel about meat-processing (*The Jungle*) and the founding of the Food and Drug Administration occurred in the same year, 1906.

Education. Among the most effective strategies for selling Crisco was the introduction of the cookbook, available free by mail once the product was purchased, and the enlisting of home economists, a then new profession espousing the "science" of cooking and home-making. The second edition of the cookbook ran to 615 recipes, all of which incorporated Crisco. Traveling home economists acted as missionaries to the cooking-impaired, offering instruction in how to be a modern cook and, by extension, a modern woman. As with other food products of the early twentieth century, the instruction was frequently teamed with an explanation of how the product represented progress. The aura of science and professionalism in home economics, and of course the introduction of the subject in schools, did a great deal to spread the message of modern convenience. Similar patterns held for canned foods (as opposed to home preserves), for pressure-cooking, and for frozen foods. As new products and techniques became available, a "need" was created, often emphasizing time- and labor-saving techniques. The thrust of the message was that the product was better for health, more economical, and, especially, more convenient. In all cases, the presentation sought to make the product "user-friendly." The product is unsullied, dependable, accessible – the virtues of a good friend.

Service. Business also signals its relationship to a community by "giving back": building arts centers, sponsoring educational programs, creating foundations. Since tax laws often drive these donations, the motives are not entirely philanthropic. Charitable donations may be profitable, if only in "symbolic capital," as a product acquires patina by association with a prestigious or admirable endeavor: a conglomerate like P&G is expected to do a certain amount of good works. Throughout its history Crisco's marketing persistently conveys the message that the company wishes to be of service to its customers: as a friend concerned for their health, as a teacher who helps one to use the product, as a neighbor who cares about the community. These representations attempt to give the corporation a human face. Even in a thoroughly commercialized culture, attention is paid to values that are not pecuniary, even if this is done for pecuniary purposes.

Advertising existed much earlier than the twentieth century, of course, but advertising as an industry in the United States dates from about 1920. The career of the publicist J. Ward Moorehouse in *USA* flourishes between the two world wars. Chiding, reminding, seducing, enticing, promising – the advertising industry has played a major role in creating willing buyers. And, as the story of Crisco illustrates, that advertising also responds to market research. Buyers, in this sense, can affect product development. But advertising, for all its appeals to the personal – "Because I'm worth it," "You deserve a break today," and so forth – is directed not at individuals but at aggregates of buyers. Thus its effectiveness depends upon its ability to spread the message widely and to target the right groups of potential customers. The key word here is "group." Until about 1880, the conception of the American public was primarily a political construction. As urban centers grew in the early twentieth century, civic leaders increasingly viewed the public as a physical mass whose movements and behaviors required management. This same way of thinking informs advertising, which, like politics, is often thought of in terms of campaigns.

At roughly the same point in history that urban planning charted and studied the movements of crowds, the department store emerged as a major commercial center, a machine designed to manage the movement of customers and merchandise. Paris's Au Bon Marché, completed in 1876, furnished a model for the major emporiums of Chicago, New York, and Philadelphia, grand edifices Émile Zola described as "cathédrale[s] de commerce moderne." These temples of consumer goods were arranged in such a way as to stimulate and manage feelings of attraction and desire, invite spectatorship, and induce fluidity of movement. The great stores – Wanamaker's of Philadelphia, Marshall Field's of Chicago – were fashioned as palaces in which the customer was a special guest. The shopper is drawn in by attractive window displays and then eased through a revolving door. Strategically placed at the corners of busy intersections, the doors pull in pedestrian traffic from two directions. Inside the scale and decoration are magnificent: the floor plan is open, the galleries are visible overhead, the stairs and escalators aim heavenward. On the upper floors are dining rooms,

FIGURE 5   Interior of John Wanamaker Store, Philadelphia, 1979
Photograph by Walter Smalling Jr., Library of Congress, Prints and
Photographs Division, Washington, DC
The soaring spaces of Wanamaker's recall Zola's description of department
stores as "cathedrals of commerce."

writing rooms, luxurious toilets. At its most ambitious, the department store could act as a club or restaurant in which to meet friends, a school in which to learn good taste, a pleasant spot in which to idle.

Similar principles informed the design of large public spaces like New York's Grand Central Station, where design facilitated the rail transport of masses of people in and out of the city and, at the same time, catered to the desire for privacy and comfort by providing hairdressing parlors, kissing galleries, restaurants, and post offices. The success of spaces like the department store and Grand Central required a fundamental shift in the conception of the individual: the design appears to increase a person's sense of importance; the logic underpinning the design, however, depends upon a standardization of humanity that undermines individuality. Clerks in department stores must be interchangeable, capable of serving in a variety of store areas; a store's buyers must be able to think of consumers as an aggregate if volume buying is to be profitable; sizes must be standardized in order to fit most bodies. Thus both sellers and buyers are, as it were, cogs in a large machine of getting and spending even though the semiotics of the grand building promise special treatment and attention to the personal.

The department store invites drift and malleability of purpose. The solid walls of smaller shops have been replaced by columns; the divisions between one department and the next are vague; wide aisles, like generous avenues, encourage movement along the lines of horizontal display cases and arouse *flâneur*-like observation of other shoppers; mirrored columns induce self-scrutiny and, at the same time, multiply one's focus and desire. Beyond the reflection of oneself in a hat appears an image of the next department and the next, promising accessories to accompany the hat. When Dreiser's Sister Carrie sets her heart on the "peculiar little tan jacket with large mother-of-pearl buttons," she is delighted not just with the jacket but with the charm she possesses in it, with her beauty measured against that of other shoppers. She also relishes the imagination of her future, which that beauty betokens. All shopping is, in this sense, shopping for possible selves.

A striking fictional expression of the polymorphous self is Madame Merle in Henry James's *The Portrait of a Lady* (1880): "There's no such thing as an isolated man or woman: we're each of us made up of some cluster of appurtenances. What shall we call our 'self'? Where does it begin? Where does it end? It overflows into everything that belongs to us – and then it flows back again" (chapter 19). This self, she asserts, is "one's expression of one's self" through, among other things, "one's house, one's furniture," that is, the things one has elected to buy. The drama of self-assertion is made problematic by this skeptical view of personhood. If Isabel Archer, the American heiress, is merely a cluster of appurtenances, what is the self she jealously protects from suitors, what is the self that wills to choose for itself? What has happened to the stability of the self-reliant man? A succinct answer may be expressed in terms provided by social historian Warren I. Susman: the difference between character and personality.[12] Whereas "character" deploys the language of morality – the unified self responsible for its own moral maintenance in accord with established, often religiously based principles – "personality" connotes a series of modalities, emphasizing self-expression, situational adjustment, reinvention, and adaptability. "Character" emphasizes stability; "personality," change. Commodity culture, the many behaviors and languages involved in producing, distributing, and consuming commodities, caters to and depends upon the malleability and continual transformation of "personality."

The temporary selves of "personality" coexist in American literature with the stable self of "character" as a tension between the "self" and the "made." The standard view of the self-made man (for it is usually a man) is of an individual who takes himself in hand, making a self that, husbanding its own abilities, becomes a better and more successful self, the self waiting to be discovered. The end product of this undertaking is a stable, self-reliant entity. What begins as an exercise of "personality" – reimagining and reshaping the self – ends as an expression of "character," that is, the uncovering of a true self, one that had been temporarily masked by accidents of birth or circumstance. Jay Gatsby becomes, in Fitzgerald's phrase, "a Platonic conception of himself," and for him this image, not the poor boy from North Dakota, is his true self. The question that haunts American literature is whether such a true, inviolate self exists or whether Madame Merle is right in believing we are what we buy or, at least, what we want to buy. A cavalcade of fictional people faces this question: is there a "republic of the spirit," as Lily Bart wishes to believe in Wharton's *The House of Mirth*, or is she a "product" of her dressmakers, milliners, and hairdressers – those "dull and ugly people" who, Lawrence Selden observes, "must . . . have been sacrificed to produce her." In Dreiser's *An American Tragedy* (1925), Clyde Griffith seems especially American and especially tragic because he pursues a life that almost everything in his surroundings has taught him to desire.

Materialism received several boosts in the twentieth century: at various points, Americans were told by economists and government leaders that it was acceptable, even patriotic, to be in debt; that waste could be "creative" insofar as what is discarded makes space for innovation; that physical, social, and spiritual ills are curable by generous application of the salve of more things; that deficit spending by government leads to economic growth; that the purpose of life is pleasure; that acquisition assists progress and progress is good for democracy. "The American Way of Life," a phrase popularized in the 1930s and employed as a rallying cry during World War II, signified material success and the freedom to pursue it. Between 1900 and 1960 those criticizing the growth of acquisitive behavior were a worried few. But these few were vocal: the criticism of materialism, smugness, and greed among Americans was vigorously articulated in sermons, in thoughtful journals like *Partisan Review*, and in novels and plays. Projects like the federally funded Works Progress Administration in the 1930s fostered an interest in the "simple" folk still living a rural and impoverished existence. In the 1940s, the Fugitives praised the agrarian life as an antidote to the corruptions and shallowness of modern urbanity. Youthful rebellion in the 1950s and 1960s was often directed at America's wealth. Commodity culture was, however, sufficiently flexible to absorb the protests and turn the signs of resistance, whether leather jackets or peace signs, into more things to buy. Some American commentators, influenced by European theorists, declared the culture of consumption an instrument of social control. What are we if not the products we consume? "In a sense," begins John Barth's novel *The End of the Road* (1958), "I am Jacob Horner." Jacob Horner is, in a sense, the advertising that echoes in his head: "Pepsi Cola hits the spot; 10 full ounces, that's a lot."

America's abundant wealth can be compared in useful ways to the abundant space discussed in the previous chapter. Both inspire a sense of possibility: "the sky's the limit." But just as endless space can be terrifying, so can endless wealth. Boundaries and limits can be comforting as well as oppressive; their absence can be dizzying. What do you give the man or woman who has everything? The question is still open.

CHAPTER 3

New

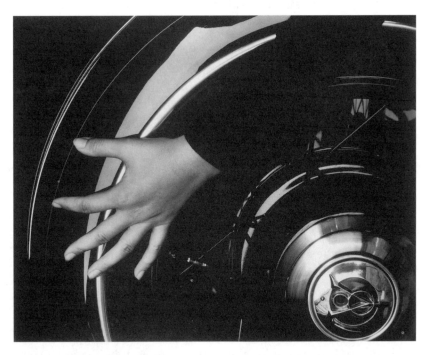

FIGURE 6   Alfred Stieglitz, *Georgia O'Keefe's Hand and Wheel*, 1933. Gelatin silver print, 24.2 × 19.2 cm
© The Cleveland Museum of Art, Gift of Cary Ross, Knoxville, Tennessee, 1935.99. © ARS, New York and DACS, London 2006
Two kinds of elegance: the human hand and what the hand can make.

What then is the American, this new man?
    J. Hector St. John de Crevecoeur Letters from an American Farmer, *1782*

"Begin all new."
    Hester Prynne, in Nathaniel Hawthorne, The Scarlet Letter, *1850*

*But there sits the old master, over in Europe. Like a parent. Somewhere deep in
every American heart lies a rebellion against the old parenthood of Europe.*
    D. H. Lawrence, "The Spirit of Place," Studies in
Classic American Literature, *1923*

*No one who understandingly faces the situation with its substantial accomplish-
ment or views the new scene with its still more abundant promise can be entirely
without hope. And certainly, if in our lifetime the Negro should not be able to
celebrate his full initiation into American democracy, he can at least, on the
warrant of these things, celebrate the attainment of a significant and satisfying
new phase of group development, and with it a spiritual Coming of Age.*
    Alain Locke, The New Negro, *1925*

*"I believe in the future of television. I wish to be ready to go up right along with
it. Therefore I'm planning to get in on the ground floor. In fact, I've already
made the right connections and all that remains is for the industry itself to get
underway. Full steam. Knowledge – Zzzzzp! Money – Zzzzzp! – Power! That's
the cycle democracy is built on!"*
    Jim O'Connor, in Tennessee Williams, The Glass Menagerie, *1945*

*The existing monuments form an ideal order among themselves, which is modi-
fied by the introduction of the new (the really new) work of art among them.
The existing order is complete before the new work arrives; for order to persist
after the supervention of novelty, the whole existing order must be, if ever so
slightly, altered; and so the relations, proportions, values of each work of art
towards the whole are readjusted; and this is conformity between the old and the
new. Whoever has approved this idea of order, of the form of European, of
English literature, will not find it preposterous that the past should be altered by
the present as much as the present is directed by the past.*
    T. S. Eliot, "Tradition and the Individual Talent," The Sacred Wood, *1920*

The perceived newness of the New World is recorded in American
place names: the states of New Jersey, New York, New Mexico, and New
Hampshire, the cities of New York and New Orleans, and hundreds
of other settlements, small and large. Names function as reminders of
the United States' former colonial status and its citizens' cultural backgrounds. Every New place presupposes an Old: New Rome, Wisconsin;
New Egypt, Ohio; New Bordeaux, South Carolina; New Sweden, Texas.

In addition, there are scores of towns in the United States called "New Hope" or "New Era." In the twentieth century, the language of the public sphere in America, as in most modernized countries, became crowded with claims of novelty. Advertising offered consumers "new and improved" products as an inducement to spend. Fashion magazines promoted a seasonal change of look. Historical shifts in the expectations of a gender or race were registered by titles like the New Negro, and the New Woman evolved into the flapper. The hunger for novelty created a cult of celebrity requiring constant verbal refurbishment, with revelations about the private lives of public figures, especially stars of the moving pictures, a significant new element in visual culture. Even academic disciplines like literary criticism and philosophy were refashioned: humanism was transformed into the New Humanism (1920s); New Criticism (1940–60) yielded to New Historicism (1980s); Americanists become the New Americanists (1990s). Schools of writing were christened New American Poetry, New Journalism, New Formalism, and even New New Formalism. And politics could not describe its workings without recourse to versions of the word: New Deal, New Frontier, New Left, Neo-Conservative. In future-focused politics, where promise of renewal and progress is fundamental to winning an election, it is perpetually morning in America. A designation of newness can encompass tones of both condemnation and praise, genres both satiric and romantic, attitudes both pessimistic and optimistic, and mixed connotations all along these spectra. But if the term is polymorphous, it is nevertheless essential to the study of American literature and culture, if only because it is ubiquitous.

One interpretation of America's newness is that the young country lacks tradition, is naive, is, in Ezra Pound's characterization in *Hugh Selwyn Mauberley*, a "half-savage" country. This perceived shortcoming has implications for Americans' views of themselves and for other nations' views of Americans. The stereotypical Innocent Abroad, like the stereotypical Ugly American, assumes that Americans are less sophisticated, less cosmopolitan, less mannerly, and less educated than citizens of other countries. As latecomers to art and literature (measured usually in relation to the cultures of Continental Europe and, in literature especially, of Great Britain), American artists have felt burdened by the past; in critic Harold Bloom's diagnostic vocabulary, they have suffered an acute "anxiety of influence." Prior to the twentieth century, American writers complained frequently of their secondary status, their sense of belatedness and inferiority. In the course of the century, this "stepchild" status changed.

In the first half of the twentieth century, American writers regularly left the US – some for good. Motivations varied: some wished to live cheaply; some sought an audience for their work; some fled what they saw as a prudish and narrow-minded nation. T. S. Eliot became an English citizen; Ezra Pound settled in Italy; Gertrude Stein set up in Paris. H. D. (Hilda Doolittle), Sherwood Anderson, F. Scott Fitzgerald, Ernest Hemingway, Djuna Barnes, John Dos Passos, and Langston Hughes are among the many writers who, for substantial periods of their lives, chose residence outside the United States. Gertrude Stein labeled the group who gathered in Europe between the first and second world wars the "lost generation." A comparable "expatriation" was common for musicians and painters. *Civilization in the United States: An Inquiry by Thirty Americans*, edited by Harold Stearns (1922), captures the mood of American intellectuals after World War I. In a series of essays by various hands, nearly every aspect of American culture is tested and found wanting. The aim of the project, Stearns explained, was "to speak the truth about American civilization as we [see] it, in order to do our share in making a real civilization possible" (p. iii). That the civilization was still in process, not achieved, is a fundamental proposition of these and similar critiques: Ezra Pound's *Patria Mia* (1912– 13); Randolph Bourne's *Youth and Life* (1913); Van Wyck Brooks's "On Creating a Usable Past" and "Young America" (1916 essays in *The Dial* and *Seven Arts* magazines); Waldo Frank's *Our America* (1919).

The narrative of expatriation reverses that of immigration – and not only in the direction of travel. Desire for a better life motivated both those who came to America and those who left. Insofar as the great waves of immigration discussed in chapter 1 were driven by a desire to escape poverty and political repression, the stories of immigration are largely about physical and political need: a quest to improve one's material life and to possess one's own body and property. Insofar as expatriation was driven by a desire to escape cultural mediocrity, provincialism, and closed-mindedness, it is a narrative of intellectual and emotional need. For example, Shari Benstock proposes, in *Women of the Left Bank*, that Paris functioned as a place of acceptance for lesbian writers and artists in ways not possible in the United States. African Americans, too, found they did not face the intolerance they experienced at home. Those artists, of whatever race, gender, or sexual orientation, who were inclined to leave often declared the exceptional person to be more welcomed in Europe than in America. Small-town (and even large-city) provincialism in America was a frequent topic: classic statements of this view are Sinclair Lewis's novels *Main Street*

(1920) and *Babbitt* (1922). The materialism of America, it was thought, its preoccupation with getting and spending, caused financial success to overshadow all other forms of achievement.

On the other hand, America has been perceived by influential thinkers and artists world-wide as untrammeled by tradition, courageously innovative, and enviably energetic. This view has been reinforced by the nation's size, wealth, and success and its achievements in business, science, and technology. Jim O'Connor, the "gentleman caller" who visits the Wingfield home in Tennessee Williams's play *The Glass Menagerie* (1945), exemplifies the "go-getter" American attitude that, if naive, is also exciting and conducive to progress. He stands in poignant contrast to the delicacy and nostalgia of the little glass animals collected by the fragile daughter of the family, Laura. Juxtaposition of raw force and refined sensitivities is a central conflict of Williams's plays, revisited again in *A Streetcar Named Desire* (1947) and *Cat on a Hot Tin Roof* (1954). It is significant that, in every instance, persons of sensitivity and culture are ridden down by physical and psychic vitality. Williams has clear sympathies for his more delicate characters, but the portraits of what we might think of as his "red-blooded" Americans also demand our attention and even respect.

Whether to engage in blame or praise, American artists and critics continued to pursue the goal of making a peculiarly American literature in the twentieth century. The poet William Carlos Williams, for example, was a lifelong campaigner for the cause: American poetry should be made of American speech, landscape, and history. "The old cultures cannot, can never without our history, our blood, our climate, our time of flowering in history – can never be the same as we. They cannot" ("The Pluralism of Experience" in *The Embodiment of Knowledge*). His long poem *Paterson* (issued in five volumes between 1946 and 1958) is centered on the physical features and history of Paterson, New Jersey. The focus on American landscape, history, and speech is an effort to follow his own dicta, elaborated in the prologue to *Kora in Hell* (1918) and his book of essays on American history, *In the American Grain* (1925). Marianne Moore, though not so programmatic as Williams, found, as she put it in her poem "England," that "plain American which cats and dogs can read" was more than adequate to her purposes. Robert Frost's most significant landscape, as we saw in chapter 1, is that of New England in autumn and winter: his poetry is unimaginable without the birds, the snow, the trees, the vistas of New Hampshire. Wallace Stevens, too, though deeply appreciative of European culture, lived his life and created his poetry on the eastern seaboard of the

USA – with Connecticut and Florida as his north and south poles. Willa Cather's major settings were Nebraska and New Mexico; William Faulkner's, Mississippi. Although the expatriate "lost generation" makes an excellent tale of American disillusionment, it is important to remember that as many significant writers stayed home and gave literary expression to the immediate surroundings of their native country.

The double view of America as naive and uncivilized and, simultaneously, as fearless and vital is explored with particular subtlety by Henry James in fictions of Americans abroad: *The Ambassadors* (1903), *The Wings of the Dove* (1902), and the earlier tale, *Daisy Miller*. The latter, discussed in chapter 2, dramatizes especially clearly the conflict between approbation and disapproval felt by a European observer of an American girl. Writers of the generation after James continued this investigation, with the additional perspective of postwar uncertainty about civilizations of any national brand. In works like Hemingway's *The Sun Also Rises* (1926) or Djuna Barnes's *Nightwood* (1937), the emphasis is not on the Old World view of Americans abroad but rather on their view of themselves as at home in neither Old World nor New.

Newness, then, is a thoroughly relative concept, understandable only in terms of what went before and soon eclipsed by what comes after. This chapter will explore some of the complexities and ambiguities of its applicability to the literature and culture of the United States in the twentieth century. In keeping with the need to define the "old" in order to understand the new, we begin with a backward glance before surveying some artistic meanings of newness in twentieth-century America. The first section, "Beginning Anew," examines two works considered "classics" of American literature, both of which depict the complexities of living as "the new man" or woman: *Letters from an American Farmer* and *The Scarlet Letter*. The struggles of conscience, the tensions between tradition and change, between old and new allegiances represented in these two texts serve to introduce the sections that follow: "Young America" (depictions of the nation as a youth; depictions of youth in literature and public policy) and "Making it New" (American culture between the world wars: part I focused on literature and part II on other arts and popular culture).

Beginning Anew: Crevecoeur and Hawthorne

The United States had yet to constitute itself as a nation when Hector St. John de Crevecoeur began writing *Letters from An American Farmer* in 1769. The fictional premise of *Letters* is that the learned "Mr. F. B." has requested the farmer "James" to correspond with him regarding the particulars of his life, work, and surroundings. James warns him to expect only the plain writing of "a simple citizen." He must rely upon the authenticity of his experience to make up for the lack of literary or scientific expertise to which Mr. F. B. is accustomed. The candor and wisdom of the man who works the land is itself, of course, a literary convention as old as Virgil's *Georgics*, and the farmer's disavowal of rhetorical skill is belied by each elegant turn of phrase. The authenticity of the letters derives not from the absence of literary convention, then (the epistolary form itself is such a convention), but from Crevecoeur's occupation as a farmer in New York's Hudson Valley from 1769 until the American Revolutionary War. Charting a portion of the history through which he lived, Crevecoeur's narrative registers the painful dilemma of a man who loves both his birth country and his adopted country and cannot choose between "these jarring contradictory parties." The final letter (XII) begins, "I wish for a change of place; the hour is come at last that I must fly from my house and abandon my farm!" At the conclusion of the letters, James plans to remove himself and his family to a Native American settlement until the war ends. In fact, however, Crevecoeur, anxious about establishing his children's right to inheritance, sailed to France in 1780. The letters were sold for publication in 1781; two years later, he returned to his American farm to find his house burned, his wife murdered, and his children missing.

The first letters in Crevecoeur's work present the American as a self-made man untouched by the past – the ahistorical American Adam discussed in chapter 1. "He is an American, who, leaving behind him his antient prejudices and manners, receives new ones from the new mode of life he has embraced, the new government he obeys, and the new rank he holds" (letter III). The character James appears to be the agrarian aristocrat Thomas Jefferson proposed as the model citizen in a democracy: educated and self-sufficient. But in the later letters James realizes how thoroughly the events of history and other people make the man, how fragile is his self-sufficiency. "What is man when no longer connected with society; or when he finds himself surrounded by a convulsed and a half-dissolved one?" (letter XII). Despite its distance in time from the twentieth century, *Letters from an American Farmer*, as a document of conflicting allegiances and violent change, is richly relevant to the study of twentieth-century America. The shift in self-representation – from a liberating sense of possibility to a sober recognition of the inescapability of the past and the human need for others – captures a paradox central to the mixed blessings of being a "new man."

Recognizing Crevecoeur's pertinence to his own life in the twentieth century, the poet John Berryman refers to him in his Dream Songs (i.5) as "Mr. New Man" and "Mr. Heartbreak." The tonal and emotional distance between these two names characterizes a pattern repeated often in American literature: the inextricability of old and new; the tension between moving forward and looking back; the disappointments shadowing the highest hopes. When Crevecoeur began writing his *Letters*, his notion of a new sort of human being might have been derived from any number of sources: in religion, the Protestant Reformation; in economics, a rising middle class; in the history of ideas, the legacies of early modern humanism and the Enlightenment. All of these historical developments promised, in differing ways, that human beings could think for themselves, rise above the circumstances of their birth, and use reason to manage and understand their environment. To be sure, for the great majority of Crevecoeur's contemporaries – penurious, illiterate, kept down by class, race, or gender – these were ideas only, with little relevance to their daily lives. Nevertheless, it is not too much to say that during this era the relationship between individuals and the institutions that dominated most lives in western Europe – the king, the church, the landowning master – evolved in ways that opened up the possibilities for self-determination. America as a place and as an idea became and has remained a symbolic site for the working out of those possibilities.

Is it possible or even desirable to "begin all new," as Hester Prynne counsels her lover? *The Scarlet Letter*, Nathaniel Hawthorne's romance of 1850, is agonizing for many readers because the narrator seems alternately to defend and prosecute those characters who have violated their community's norms. Hester Prynne, the adulteress forced to wear the scarlet letter as a mark of shame, is dignified and courageous, even using her skill at the needle to transform her shame into an ornament for public show. Hawthorne gives us much in her character to admire. Her lover and the father of her child, the Reverend Dimmesdale, is highly respected by his parishioners but lives with private, searing guilt. He is, in some ways, a coward. These chiasmic features, the "crossing" of public and private, disgrace and respect, truth and falsity, are designed to reveal the costs of exercising individual will in a strongly regulated community. In the central chapters of the novel, "The Pastor and his Parishioner" and "A Flood of Sunshine," Hester and Dimmesdale meet in the forest, itself a space signifying "wilderness" and, consequently "wildness" as opposed to civil order. Hester, removing her letter and her cap, emerges as a sensual woman. More startling still, she advises Dimmesdale to leave the village and return to the Old World, where it will be possible for him to forget the past and "Begin all new." "Let us not look back. The past is gone. Wherefore should we linger upon it now? See! With this symbol, I undo it all, and make it as it had never been."

In this arresting episode, Hawthorne presents the warring impulses that mark so many narratives of America, fictional and otherwise. That Dimmesdale is advised to go to the Old World to regain the freedom lost in the New is only the most obvious of the ironies. In the history of Puritanism Hawthorne draws upon, wasn't the journey to the New World embarked upon so that freedom – religious freedom – could be enjoyed? But here one set of freedoms clashes with another. Hester exults at convincing Dimmesdale to erase the past, but when her daughter Pearl refuses to acknowledge her until she refastens the scarlet letter to her bosom, she receives immediate proof that the past cannot be erased. The chapters here are heavily marked with images of light and shadow, contrasts that heighten the dialogue and the dialectic of this tale. The advice Hester offers and the fears Dimmesdale expresses, Hester's rejection of the scarlet letter and Pearl's rejection of her mother, Hester's later decision to reside near the village that has shunned her – the novel's plot and imagery schematize the inescapability of sin, the entanglements of community, and thus the foolishness of expecting that one can simply begin anew, burying the past and dissolving previous ties. So powerful is the wish to believe otherwise, however, that readers may yearn for a happy ending even as they admit its impossibility. The most recent Hollywood film of the tale gives in to that wish, undermining the moral sophistication of the novel by giving audiences the closing shot of the lovers' horseback escape to some happier future somewhere. For Hawthorne, the only escapee is Pearl, who, once married, moves to an unspecified European country. Hester receives letters from her "with armorial seals upon them, though of bearings unknown to English heraldry." Pearl has gone back across the ocean and joined the aristocracy, thus reversing the usual westward and democratizing trajectory of much American fiction.

These two letters from the past, Crevecoeur's and Hawthorne's, elucidate the bonds of history and community and the ambiguous status of newness. Self-determination is an essential principle of American institutions – one person, one vote; private property; religious tolerance; free enterprise. Equality under the law is one of those "self-evident" truths upon which Thomas Jefferson built his argument for a new regime in the Declaration of Independence. The American experiment was meant to prove the workability of this not-so-new idea. Absolute clarity of the sort implied in such myths as the city on the hill can exist only on paper, as a template, an ideal. In practice, it may not be possible to begin anew, but the dream dies hard.

Young America

The nation as youth

The colonists' declaration of independence from England in 1776 (and thus for would-be citizens, the relinquishing of fealty to any other nation) can be figured as a child's rebellion against a parent, a metaphor D. H. Lawrence exploits in *Studies in Classic American Literature*. Embedded also in Lawrence's trope are other connotations of generational and cultural power struggles. Europe is figured as having the strength and authority of a "master" but also the relative weakness of an "old," perhaps even infirm, culture. From this perspective, the rebellion of the young appears essential to the continuing vitality of a nation or, more generally, a culture and even civilization itself. This investment in youth as essential to progress and innovation is a significant theme of the twentieth century, particularly in the period of literary modernism, about 1900–1940. However, Lawrence's diction also suggests the childishness of rebellion – an insistence upon having one's own way, purely for the pleasure of self-assertion. Youthful rebellion can also engender chaos, disorder, even fear. And these effects, too, repeatedly surface in the first half of the twentieth century.

In *Studies*, Lawrence exploits both possibilities in his reading of works from James Fenimore Cooper to Walt Whitman. Note that, in the passage quoted, Lawrence does not limit his metaphor to writers; rather, he provides what we might call a psychology of Americanism. Every American heart, he asserts, rebels. Thus the nation, its literary culture, and the individual psychology of each citizen are figured analogically: the nation is to its past (as a dependent colony) as the grown-up is to his or her infancy and youth. This way of describing the development of nations became common in the Romantic era (a period in which the child, at least as a theoretical construct, had high status). Well into the twentieth century, in discourses ranging from anthropology to educational psychology, the growth and development of a civilization or nation was routinely compared to the growth and development of a human being. Thus some societies were said to be in their infancy, others fully mature. Often, imperial powers justified colonization on the grounds that less "advanced" cultures needed exposure to the superior practices of more advanced ones. According to this view, a "young" country like America lacks experience and thus wants wisdom. By the same logic, however, it is innocent, unspoiled, open-hearted, and sincere.

In the 1910s and 1920s, it became customary for American intellectuals to declare that the time had arrived when America should take its place at the table with the grown-ups. Van Wyck Brooks's *America's Coming-of-Age* (1915), a case in point, asserted there could be no "true revolution" until "a race of artists, profound and sincere, have brought us face to face with our own experience." Brooks assigned these artists the task of imagining a society in which "art" and "business" are not separate spheres. In Brooks's view it was time to put away childish things and to forge a culture not focused solely on material comforts. The sense of goals yet to be achieved was evident in the demands of women and African Americans as well. The female suffrage movement called for women to have full adult status, not dependent upon their fathers, brothers, and husbands to furnish them with opinions. Having begun the discussion of political equality at Seneca Falls, New York, in 1843, suffragists finally won the vote for women in 1920, with the 19th Amendment to the US Constitution. But the power of the "woman's vote" did not materialize as some of the leaders had hoped, and in many ways, the status of women as second-class citizens remained unchanged. In matters of race, as the epigraph from Alain Locke's *The New Negro* quoted at the opening of this chapter attests, African Americans, too, believed that the moment had arrived for "full initiation," Locke's metaphor connoting an overdue rite of passage into adulthood. Reassessment of status also informed James Weldon Johnson's ground-breaking anthology *The Book of American Negro Poetry* (1922). Johnson's preface surveys previous African American achievements in stories, poetry, song, and dance and challenges the black artist to find fresh ways to articulate the distinctive experience of life in the new century. In short, populations in America that had previously been infantilized demanded to be treated as adults.

Literary children

The depiction of children in American literature adds another dimension to the image of American culture as childlike or, at best, adolescent. The fictional children of nineteenth-century America were in most respects comparable to those of English literature. In *The Scarlet Letter*, Pearl is an oddly precocious child, sometimes seeming to embody her parents' transgression (she is thought an imp or demon by some in the community), and at other times, as in the scene recounted above, evincing a stern wisdom and a creepy knowingness. In seeming to understand more than her years and innocence warrant, she belongs in the company of Charles Dickens's Paul Dombey of *Dombey and Son* or Thomas Hardy's Little Father Time in *Jude the Obscure*. Harriet Beecher's Stowe's saintly child Evangeline, her unruly but loving Topsy in *Uncle Tom's Cabin*, and Louisa May Alcott's Amy in *Little Women* are types of the child-as-spiritual-guide who belong in the company of Eppie in George Eliot's *Silas Marner* or Dickens's Fanny Cleaver (or Jenny Wren) in *Our Mutual Friend*.

Mark Twain's tough adolescent in *The Adventures of Huckleberry Finn* might be compared to other boys who come of age in the Victorian novel – Oliver Twist and David Copperfield – though there is no mistaking the novel's special relevance to American history just before the Civil War. The peculiarly sexualized children of Henry James's *The Turn of the Screw* (1898) or the perceptive little Maisie in *What Maisie Knew* (1897), though created by an American, are not American children nor are they comparable to English Victorian children. Twain's and James's children seem to point toward a different view of childhood innocence, to be elaborated in the twentieth century.

In American autobiography, especially in the slave narratives of African Americans like Frederick Douglass and Harriet Jacobs, the journey of the slave-child to emancipated adulthood may be seen as a sophisticated and politically effective turn on the novel of growth and development or *Bildungsroman*. Poetry and fiction of the Harlem Renaissance, too, summoned up the experience of the child to represent the particularly painful passage to adulthood suffered by many African Americans. Here, for example, is Countee Cullen's "Incident" (1924).

> Once riding in old Baltimore,
> Heart-filled, head-filled with glee,
> I saw a Baltimorean
> Keep looking straight at me.

Now I was eight and very small,
And he was no whit bigger,
And so I smiled, but he poked out
His tongue, and called me, "Nigger."

I saw the whole of Baltimore
From May until December;
Of all the things that happened there.
That's all that I remember.

Langston Hughes also employed the voice or the memory of child-hood in some of his best-known poems: "Mother to Son," "Mulatto," and "Genius Child." This tradition is extended in the work of ethnic minorities well into the twenty-first century, in both fictional and nonfictional forms. After about 1960, when more and more previously marginalized voices enriched American literature, such stories were told with great frequency: Toni Morrison (*The Bluest Eye*, focused on an African American); Maxine Hong Kingston (*Woman Warrior*, focused on an Asian American); Louise Erdrich (*Love Medicine*, focused on a Native American) are a tiny sampling of writers who have rejuven-ated this narrative form.

Though without the frequency of their appearance in nineteenth-century works, then, children and adolescents do figure in twentieth-century American literature – one thinks for example of J. D. Salinger's Glass clan in *Franny and Zooey* or Holden Caulfield in *The Catcher in the Rye*; Flannery O'Connor's Beval eating his parents' cocktail party leavings in "The River" or June Star and John Wesley arguing with their grandmother and reading comic books in "A Good Man is Hard to Find"; Frankie Addams, the child at the center of Carson McCullers's play *The Member of the Wedding*; Scout, Jim, and Dill in Harper Lee's *To Kill a Mockingbird*. Popular culture also offers children aplenty. By the start of the twentieth century the resourceful, hard-working, good, and successful child had been established as an American type for some time: Horatio Alger's entrepreneurial boys went from "rags to riches" and Martha Finley's character Elsie Dinsmore exemplified Christian piety. Perhaps the most famous child characters of the century are the creations of juvenile fiction writers, such as the hugely popular and long-lived series of novels centered on Nancy Drew or the Hardy Boys, whose youthful perspicacity leads to the solving of crimes. In long-lived comic strips like Harold Gray's *Little Orphan Annie*, launched in 1925, entertaining depictions of children also offered arch com-mentary on contemporary events. Even adult characters like L'il Abner, the muscle-bound and yet childlike country boy of Al Capp's comic strip, furnished only a slight variation on the child as truth-teller.

However, children are conspicuous in their absence from the canonical literature of American modernism. Modernism, in the context of this chapter, refers to literary and other art forms created during the period just before World War I and continuing until World War II. The decade of the 1920s, especially, is strongly associated with artistic innovation in American literature. What might the disappearing child suggest about modernist American literature, the "newness" of the nation, and attitudes toward the future? What should we make of the dead, dismissed, and disheartened children? Might there be a relationship between demands of cultural critics that the US should grow up or come of age and the slackening attachment to the celebration of childhood?

A widening of permissible subject matter in literature contributed to the frequency with which abortion and infertility appear as plot devices or imagery in modernist writing. One of the most famous instances in which abortion is thematically tied to barren land and a barren culture is a scene in T. S. Eliot's *The Waste Land* (1922). In the second section of the poem, "A Game of Chess," a female speaker in a pub tells the story of Lil and Albert to a silent companion: she had, she reports, berated Lil for her failure to make herself attractive for her demobilized husband: "You ought to be ashamed I said, to look so antique." Lil's response, the speaker reports, is that she "can't help it. . . . It's them pills I took, to bring it off." The speaker concedes that the births of Lil's children have played havoc with her looks: "She's had five already and nearly died of young George." The scene, with its oblique reference to an abortifacient, gathers up a number of the imagistic, thematic, and allusive threads of Eliot's poem: the destruction of life in war, the battering of beauty, conflict and failed communication between the sexes – a depiction of postwar society as literally and figuratively drought-ridden, infertile, and damaged. Eliot's setting is not, of course, American, though he was born and grew up in St. Louis, Missouri; he presents an altered world that was most keenly experienced in Europe. Nevertheless, the emotional and intellectual import of *The Waste Land* was widely recognized by American readers, and the handsome monetary prize he won for the poem was awarded by an American "little" magazine, *The Dial*.

Abortion is used to similar effect in Theodore Dreiser's *An American Tragedy*. In Dreiser's novel, the unwanted pregnancy of Clyde Griffith's girlfriend Roberta poses an obstacle to his relationship with the socialite Sondra and his access to the glittering prizes she embodies. After an unsuccessful effort to obtain an abortion for Roberta, Clyde plans another means to rid himself of his encumbrances. The boating accident at the climax of the novel, presented with enough ambiguity to undermine certainty that it *is* in fact an accident, causes Roberta's death and that of her unborn child. It simultaneously destroys Clyde's hopes for success, love, and money, a version of the American Dream. In short, the novel's events signify what Dreiser perceived as a larger cultural tragedy: how America fostered a hunger for riches, success, and fulfillment that, for many, could not be satisfied.

The couple in Hemingway's elliptical short story "Hills Like White Elephants" have a related sort of problem, too much and too little: too much leisure, too much freedom, too much mobility, and too little purpose. As the woman says, "That's all we do is, isn't it . . . look at things and try new drinks." The impending abortion is never named directly and this style of circling round the unsaid invites the reader to see the decision the couple must make as a symptom of a more thoroughgoing malaise. Versions of this topic are fairly common in Hemingway's fiction: the wife in "Cat in the Rain" diverts her desire to nurture onto a cat; Jake Barnes, the protagonist of *The Sun Also Rises*, has a war wound that has made him incapable of fathering a child.

Dying or dead children in nineteenth-century fiction are meant to move readers; the child's peaceful acceptance of death chastens adult onlookers, reminding them that goodness, innocence, and humility are possible and adjuring them to change their lives accordingly. The death of fictional twentieth-century children is rarely so consoling. In "Home Burial," for example, Robert Frost confronts the most impossible of verbal tasks, speaking the unspeakable: how does one properly mourn a dead child? The wife berates her husband for lack of sensitivity; the husband is frustrated by his wife's inconsolability. Neither is right or wrong. Neither is to blame. And neither can comfort the other. His poem "Out, Out –", in which a boy severs his hand with a chainsaw and dies, is equally comfortless. Its final lines are devastating: "No more to build on there. And they, since they / Were not the one dead, turned to their affairs." William Carlos Williams's "The Dead Baby" employs a similarly matter-of-fact tone:

> Sweep the house clean
> here is one who has gone up
> (though problematically)
> to heaven, blindly

by force of the facts –
a clean sweep
is one way of expressing it –

Without the context of the complete poems, the lines from Frost and Williams may seem inexcusably cold, but in fact the poems create a powerful sense of loss precisely by refusing tears. Two further instances of this tone may be heard in poems by John Crowe Ransom, "Bells for John Whiteside's Daughter" and "Janet Waking." The first is an elegy, the latter a poem about a child's first experience of death in the loss of her pet hen, Chucky. Again, the two poems exhibit a flat and oddly witty style that might seem inappropriately distant given the subject matter: "we're vexed at her brown study, / Lying so primly propped" ("Bells"); Janet's Chucky has been killed by a "transmogrifying bee."

The absence of children in fiction and poetry was more than compensated for by their presence in other forms of public discourse. The "child-study" and educational reform movements advocating child-centered pedagogy powerfully influenced public policy in the first decades of the century. G. Stanley Hall, a psychologist who trained under William James and who taught the education reformer John Dewey, might be said to have "invented" adolescence as a developmental phase. The reception of his two-volume *Adolescence: Its Psychology and its Relations to Anthropology, Sociology, Sex Crime, Religion and Education* (1905) demonstrated that child-study had, along with other social sciences, become a respected professional field, generating theories and scholarship that had genuine impact on education and other public policies. The first White House Conference on Children was held in 1909. The Children's Bureau was established as part of the Department of Labor in 1912. One of its first efforts was publication of the widely disseminated pamphlet *Infant Care* (1914) which, until the publication of Benjamin Spock's *The Common Sense Book of Baby and Child Care* in 1946, was the most influential childcare manual in America. State mechanisms were put in place, ready to assist in the rearing of future citizens.

In *Exile's Return* (1933), a memoir of the 1920s, Malcolm Cowley contends that Greenwich Village, the bohemian sector of New York City, was in 1920 not only a place but a "doctrine." As we saw in chapter 1, imbuing landscape with symbolic meaning has a long history (the word "bohemian" itself is an example). Cowley interprets the Village as a set of ideas, the first of which is "salvation by the child." According to this line of thought, he explains, "each of us at birth has special potentialities that are slowly crushed and destroyed by a standardized society." Students of educational theory may recognize this principle as the basis for Rousseau's *Émile*, a memoir-cum-manual in which the French philosopher lays out a program for educating a child without eroding what is particular to him; the practices espoused by Rousseau formed a cornerstone of the child-study movement just discussed. Tongue firmly in cheek, Cowley parrots a guiding principle of that movement: "If a new educational system can be introduced . . . then the world will be saved by this new, free generation." Cowley includes in his description of Village "doctrine" several other ideas that derive from Romanticism: that self-expression is the central purpose of life; that the body is a thing of beauty, not shame; that "living for the moment" is superior to preparing for the future; that repression of any sort is likely to lead to psychological maladjustment; finally, that only by expatriation can the artist "break the puritan shackles, live freely, and be wholly creative." In short, in Cowley's satiric view, the doctrine of the Village was that adults should be children themselves.

Hemingway's *The Sun Also Rises* can be read as a repudiation of these enticing views of human freedom even as it depicts those who seem to have it. In the novel, a group of people, variously motivated, arrives in Pamplona, Spain, for the Fermin fiesta and the running of the bulls. They know one another from previous encounters either in Europe or America. Passing the time, they fish, argue, dance, work a little, and drink a lot. Like the characters in "Hills Like White Elephants," these are people with a kind of liberty. But the freedom is, for most of them, merely aimlessness. Jake Barnes, the protagonist, has an emasculating war wound. Lady Brett Ashley has lost her husband in the war and, though she loves Jake, appears to be incapable of forming a lasting attachment to any man. Robert Cohn's decisions are driven by chivalric fantasy. "He had been reading W. H. Hudson," Jake reports:

> "The Purple Land" is a very sinister book if read too late in life. . . . for a man to take it at thirty-four as a guide-book to what life holds is about as safe as it would be for a man of the same age to enter Wall Street direct from a French convent, equipped with a complete set of the more practical Alger books. (chapter 2)

Jake's swipes at sheltered girls and parables for children are in keeping with his hard-boiled persona. The world of men – significantly Wall Street, the symbolic center of American business – now requires the ability to live without consoling stories. Cohn projects his illusions onto Brett and, predictably, becomes disillusioned himself. Frances Clyne, a minor character who is the most recent of Cohn's lovers, confesses that "I never liked children much, but I don't want to think I'll never have them. I always thought I'd have them and then like them." Her attitude is that of a child who might like a puppy. At one point, another minor figure drunkenly accuses Robert Cohn of being "a case of arrested development" (chapter 6). His diagnosis applies to most of the novel's characters. The anomie, boredom, and disgust that pervade the novel are relieved by two things only: Spanish tradition (the religious festival, *corrida*, and bullfight) and the discipline of work well done, exemplified by Jake (who writes) and Romero (who fights bulls). The emphasis on religion, discipline, and work is familiar in American discourse; the discussion of Puritanism in chapter 2 is relevant here. Jack admires the rituals of Spanish life (he is an aficionado of the bullfight and he goes to mass), but the culture that sustains these practices is not truly his own. He can only borrow and imitate what he admires. The world Hemingway depicts – a glamorous homelessness – is not one in which to bring up children. Thus Jake's wound is a synecdoche for losses of many kinds, not only sexual, but emotional and social. Something, most tangibly the recent war, has halted progress toward adult responsibility.

There are several plausible explanations for the disparity between the anxious attention to children by progressive government and educational institutions, on the one hand, and the dispassionate treatment of children, when they appear at all, in modern American writing. The Romanticization of children and the Victorian glorification of the family in the preceding periods were distasteful to many modernists, especially male writers eager to distance themselves from a view of art as a feminized practice. Sentimentality was, if not forbidden, at least highly suspect. The overpowering actuality of war, the sense of a world dead or dying, may have seemed deeply incompatible with the notion of progeny to inherit the future. Changes in women's status continued to undermine the stature of "mother women," to use Kate Chopin's phrase, and the cult of domesticity was potentially stifling to those women who saw themselves as modern. Certainly, in the public mind, "mother" and "flapper" were contradictory terms. And, while the vast majority of American women married and cared for families, those who chose demanding careers – doctor, lawyer, college professor – often gave evidence of their seriousness by eschewing married life. In addition, Freudian theories of infant sexuality radically altered the view of childhood innocence. Conventionally, the literary child symbolizes hope, promise of a better future. In America in the 1920s the future was expressed in other kinds of symbols. Consumer culture promised better things to come in the form of products and services. And, as Cowley suggests, living for the moment – not the future – was the slogan of Jazz Age culture. The perceived childishness of American culture was precisely what irked the culture critics. How was America to come of age when its populace was largely caught in adolescence? The artists and culture analysts believed the job fell to them.

Making It New I: Literary Modernism

The question of canon

Because a major objective of this book is to consider manifestations of four foundational ideas about America, analysis of the content of literature has, in the two preceding chapters, tended to overshadow attention to style. In this chapter, however, the techniques of artistic experimentation and their relationship to certain ideas about modernity and America will be the primary concern. While "modernist" methods in the arts were not the only form of artistic innovation, a number of the techniques we will examine are, for most students of the period, highly significant practices of the first three decades of twentieth-century American writing. This is not to privilege experimentation in and of itself. As scholarship in the last three decades has abundantly demonstrated, "modernism" is a contested term; what it "was" or "is" includes dimensions that do not fall under the rubrics of internationalism or experimental style that once seemed best to define the movement. "Modernism" can describe works of conventional genre and straightforward style, as well, because of either the subject matter, the intended audience, or the authorship. The writing of the Harlem Renaissance, for example, was "new" and modern but not always as a result of experimentation. Although Jean Toomer, Langston Hughes, and Zora Neale Hurston employed experimental forms, their work would have been considered new even had they not done so; their poetry and fiction arose from the historical contexts of the Harlem Renaissance, that is, an educated and vocal gathering of African American writers who confronted, as Hughes expressed it, "the racial mountain" ("The Negro Artist and the Racial Mountain"). Depiction of other marginalized cultures also contributed to the making of a new

American literature. Mourning Dove's *Cogewea the Half-Blood* (1927) was innovative because of the people to whom she had access and the anthropological perspective she brought to her work. Carlos Bulosan or D'Arcy McNickle, writing memoirs and fiction depicting Filipino and Native American experience in the USA, were also innovators. The sense of renaissance, rebirth, and discovery emanated from these new perspectives and from the sound of new voices.

Defining a "canon" of American literature has been an interest of literary historians from the beginning of the nation. Early proponents of a national literature were concerned to establish American writing as serious art deserving recognition. In the 1920s and 1930s, as American writing gained attention in Europe and became an acceptable subject for academic study, literary critics sought to define the particular characteristics that made American literature American, and the work continued through the entire period covered by this text. Works like V. L. Parrington's *Main Currents in American Thought* (1927–30), F. O. Matthiesson's *American Renaissance* (1941), Alfred Kazin's *On Native Grounds* (1941), Constance Rourke's *American Humor* (1931) and *The Roots of American Culture* (1942), Richard Chase's *The American Novel and its Tradition* (1957) and Leslie Fiedler's *Love and Death in the American Novel* (1960) are examples of this effort. In the last four decades of the twentieth century, many scholars were dedicated to elucidating the diversity of American literature – its range of styles, settings, and representations of class, race, gender, and cultural background. This undertaking has been energized by many factors (intellectual, social, political, and institutional) with the result that the criteria by which readers approach and evaluate works of art have been revised – not altogether transformed but significantly expanded.

A simple way to begin thinking about literary criticism and its changes over time is to ask this question: to what aspect of a work does this approach pay special attention? *Formalist* approaches to a poem, for instance, consider meter and rhythm, rhyme schemes, diction, and the like, what we might think of as the poem's architecture. Or it may attend to matters of structure in fiction: openings, closings, parallels, plot structures. *Cultural studies* asks questions about the historical and material contexts of a work's production. *Reader-response criticism* focuses on the ways that readers "construct" a text and its meanings. And so forth. The text, the author, the reader, the world may each be attended to with greater or lesser intensity in a given set of critical practices. Normally, of course, approaches shade into one another, as in the overlapping circles of a Venn diagram. Attending to techniques of modernism in this chapter, therefore, does not and should not, preclude attention to other dimensions of the works' production and reception. As will be obvious even from this brief sketch of critical history, canon-making, dismantling, and re-making is always work in progress.

Defining American modernism

The year 1925 was a bonanza for American literature: Sherwood Anderson's *Dark Laughter*, Willa Cather's *The Professor's House*, Ellen Glasgow's *Barren Ground*, H. D.'s *Collected Poems*, John Dos Passos's *Manhattan Transfer*, Theodore Dreiser's *An American Tragedy*, T. S. Eliot's *Poems, 1909–1925*, F. Scott Fitzgerald's *The Great Gatsby*, Ernest Hemingway's *In Our Time*, Alain Locke's *The New Negro*, Ezra Pound's *Draft of XVI Cantos*, Gertrude Stein's *The Making of Americans*, William Carlos Williams's *In the American Grain*, and Anna Yezierska's *The Bread Givers*. These titles, all from writers who are staples of literature anthologies inside and outside the USA, signaled the "arrival" of American literature. Indeed, a similar list could be constructed for nearly every year of that decade. Of course, individual writers in earlier decades had achieved recognition at home and abroad, but by the 1920s American literature as a body of work, as an idea, had a currency of its own and, increasingly over the next decades, would attract world-wide attention. The first decades of the twentieth century were also the era in which the popular music of Tin Pan Alley, jazz, the Broadway musical, and the Hollywood movie became emblematic of American creativity, and, until the crash of 1929, the economy was booming. In the first of the two decades between world wars, the United States was on a roll. This burst of activity did not, however, silence the American critics of America. Some refused to see popular music or movies as "art" at all; others despaired of America's ever maturing into a culture of the depth and value of Europe's; still others believed that inherent in the American temperament were traits hostile to intellectual and artistic pursuits. Nor were these opinions expressed only by critics – each of these views of America also informed poetry, fiction, and drama. American writers have rarely been shy of criticizing America.

Is there a specifically American modernism? Or only American permutations of international modernism? And why do these questions matter? As we have seen, from Emerson to Williams, some American writers argued vigorously that the country required its own vocabulary, its own articulation in art; similarly, influential literary historians carried on the mission by identifying distinctive qualities of American literature. During the 1910s and 1920s, members of the group Russell Jacoby has labeled "public intellectuals," those who wrote for a readership beyond academic walls, spent their energies on either promoting the existence or encouraging the making of an American arts tradition. Van Wyck Brooks, Randolph Bourne, Waldo Frank, Paul Rosenfeld, Constance Rourke, and H. L. Mencken all wrote on the subject, and journals like the *New Republic*, *The Masses*, *The American Mercury*, and *The Seven Arts* were dedicated, in their individual ways, to the cultural health of America. There is an urgency about the essays of these writers that suggests crisis.

Shifting the frame of reference might clarify what is at stake in claiming a work of literature for a nation. An indisputably representative text of modernism is James Joyce's *Ulysses*. Is this work Irish literature? It takes place in a single day in 1904 in locations throughout Dublin. The speech and behavior of the characters are drawn from Joyce's experiences as a resident of the city, and they are unmistakably indigenous. By these measures, the novel is Irish literature, and Ireland can take pride in Joyce as one of its own. But when one reviews the publication and reception history of the novel, especially its printing by "Shakespeare and Co." – a bookshop named after an Englishman, owned by an American, and situated in Paris – it seems to belong to another sort of country, one made up of citizens from many places whose primary interest is not nationality. What we might think of as such dual, even multiple, citizenship similarly characterizes many works by American writers of this era. Eliot's *The Waste Land* alludes to London landmarks, but it draws upon materials as diverse as ragtime music, Dante, and the Upanishads. As far as William Carlos Williams and Hart Crane were concerned, the poem was not especially American. It lacked, from their point of view, not only the specificity of American speech and landscape but also the forward-looking, optimistic ethos they prized. Williams considered the poem a "catastrophe"; Crane worried that it might be "an impasse" unless one could "go *through* it to a different goal." Yet the poem was embraced by many in the American intelligentsia with the same fervor as it was by its European champions. That embrace, however, had little, if anything, to do with patriotic pride. Though the poem was written by an American, one proof of Eliot's having, as Ezra Pound put it, "modernized himself on his own" is that he did not give civilization's "waste" a local habitation.

American literary modernism, according to C. Barry Chabot in *Writers for the Nation*, arose from "shared dismay about the character of American social and cultural life in the early years of [the twentieth] century."[1] Continuing the work of the Progressive Era, it sought "to imagine conditions that would either restore to the national life the possibility that all citizens could enjoy access to functioning and supportive communities, or failing restoration, at least providing something by way of a substitute." By employing a range of strategies, some looking to the past, some to the future, these writers, he argues, wished to create a sense of the Americanness of America, to offer better models for its development, to chastise it for its failings; participants in this project included even writers who were no longer resident. Chabot's argument has the merit of recognizing the historical continuities between America at the start of the twentieth century and America in the 1910s and 1920s, and he rightly points out the evangelical tone in American artists' and intellectuals' demand for reform. A reasonable response to his argument, however, would be that the reformist impulse in modernism was in evidence in many other nations as well. Insofar as modernism sought to change minds by many means and to many ends, its manifestations knew no national boundaries.

"The art of Europe is finished – dead – and . . . America is the country of the art of the future," Marcel Duchamp declared in 1915. A striking number of non-Americans saw America as an especially suitable site for these changes to develop, among them the painters Pablo Picasso, Jean Cocteau, Francis Picabia, and Piet Mondrian. Duchamp's *Nude Descending a Staircase*, lampooned as "an explosion in a shingle factory" by a *New York Times* art critic, became an emblem of the joy, rage, confusion, and excitement created by America's first major exposure to modernist art at the 1913 Armory Show in New York. If Duchamp believed his art was especially right for America, many Americans viewed it as a foreign invasion. The twentieth century has been widely referred to as "the American Century" in recognition of the dramatic ways that the US came to dominate global politics and economics. The image of the USA as the country of the future was founded upon a notion of America as fertile territory for the discovery and application of modern methods in warfare, consumerism, productivity, medicine, and technology. And American appearances on the world stage (in business, politics, technology, and elsewhere) reinforced that association. Susan Hegeman makes an argument for the modernism of America and the Americanism of modernism in *Patterns for America*:

One place to bridge the gap between modernism's internationalism and the American context is with an account of modernism that takes seriously the centrality of the ideology of *Americanism* to modernist theory and practice. For intellectuals from Italy to Russia to Japan, "America" was taken to be synonymous with the massified modernity that presented such an object of combined horror and fascination.[2]

As evidence of America's influence on key practices of modernism, Hegeman lists such phenomena as the skyscraper, the assembly line, and jazz, and cites the view of architect Le Corbusier that modern architecture began with the American grain elevator. In these examples, we can discern altered thinking about the relationship between utility and beauty, between part and whole, between regularity and irregularity of measure, and between old crafts and new materials – all important dimensions of aesthetic experimentation in this era. If America lacked tradition in the usual sense of the word (as a legacy of centuries of social, religious, artistic, and other practices), it offered another sort of legacy – a tradition of innovation.

A counter-argument can be made that even this legacy has roots in older cultures, that most of the ideas and events we normally think of as giving rise to modernism in the arts germinated outside the USA. Nearly every history of modernism agrees on the following historical and intellectual influences: the theories of Sigmund Freud, Karl Marx, and Friedrich Nietzsche, the ideas of the Enlightenment and Romanticism, the events of the Industrial Revolution and the Great War (World War I), and increasing urbanization. None of these *originated* in America. In designating America the country for art of the future, then, Duchamp was pointing not to beginnings but to potential for developments, in expectation that the full effects of modernity were going to be seen most clearly in American art. Whether he was right in this prediction is debatable, but it is certainly clear that, in contributing to an emerging set of artistic practices, Americans began at this period not just to imitate but to create, not just to be open to influences but to be influential.

One of the most successful Americans on this score was, of course, T. S. Eliot. Born in 1888 in St. Louis, Missouri, to a family that included in its heritage Unitarian ministers, a Harvard president, and the founder of Washington University, Eliot was firmly rooted in America but chose to live most of his adult life in England. Like others of his generation, he was drawn during his undergraduate studies to the apparently greater sophistication and richer culture of

Europe. By 1916 he had married an Englishwoman, taken up work in London, and decided not to return to Harvard, though he had completed the work for a doctoral degree in philosophy. In 1922, *The Waste Land* established him as a member of the avant-garde, innovative to the point of near-incomprehensibility, and the poem became required reading for anyone who wished to be among the cognoscenti, including young men and women who saw the poem as specifically addressed to their generation. In 1927 Eliot became a British subject. With his journal *Criterion* and his editorial work at Faber & Faber, his essays on topics ranging from modern poetry to education to religion, and his uncanny ability to express ideas that spoke strongly to his contemporaries, Eliot exercised a power well beyond what might have been expected of a twentieth-century artist in any medium.

To the 13,000 people who attended his lecture in a Minnesota basketball arena, Eliot symbolized modernism. He was also, however, a spokesman for the value of tradition, and not, as might be expected, only when he was older. "Tradition and the Individual Talent," an early essay of his career quoted at the head of this chapter, is perhaps the most memorable of his many pronouncements on the coexistence of old and new. In it, he makes the case for the symbiosis of past and present. A "truly new" work of art, in his model, alters the previous order of valued works. This is the sort of forward-looking, experimental attitude normally associated with literary modernism; new art revitalizes old. But equally important in Eliot's formulation is the dependence of new work on that of the past. Innovation too has a history, a genealogy – what Eliot alludes to in the essay as "the mind of Europe." Eliot exemplifies the multiple allegiances common among those Americans associated with the "international" model of modernism. Arthur Symons's *The Symbolist Movement in Literature* drew his attention to French poets, who furnished models for his early poetry. He studied in Germany, heard Henri Bergson lecture at the Sorbonne, applauded Igor Stravinsky's *Rite of Spring*. *The Waste Land* is polyglot and allusive to both Eastern and Western literatures, and it evinces a world-weariness more clearly appropriate to an exhausted postwar Europe than to the bumptious American Jazz Age. Yet its author's commitment to innovation in the arts and to renovation in the world at large, and his audacious – one might say outrageous – ambitions, were diagnosed by George Santayana as an instance of "prophetic zeal and faith in the Advent of the Lord." For Santayana, Eliot was more American than he acted, more an heir of his preacher grandfather than he admitted. An American-Englishman, banker-poet, modernist-traditionalist, Eliot embodies the paradoxes of modernism itself. He also exemplifies one of the complex patterns by which Americans came to terms with European tradition.

Eliot's argument for the symbiosis of past and present counters the fiery rhetoric of many modernist manifestos, European and American. Famous examples of the incendiary style are the Vorticist journal *BLAST* (the work of American Ezra Pound and Englishman Wyndham Lewis) and the Italian Futurist declarations of F. T. Marinetti. Equally famous is the 1928 manifesto for the "little magazine" *transition*, "The Revolution of the Word":

We hereby declare that:

1. The revolution in the English Language is an accomplished fact.
2. The imagination in search of a fabulous world is autonomous and unconfined.
3. Pure poetry is a lyrical absolute that seeks an a priori reality within ourselves alone.
4. A narrative is not mere anecdote but the projection of a metamorphosis of reality.
5. The expression of these concepts can be achieved only through the rhythmic "hallucination of the world" (Rimbaud).
6. The literary creator has the right to disintegrate the primal matter of words imposed on him by text-books and dictionaries.
7. He has the right to use words of his own fashioning and to disregard existing grammatical and syntactical laws.
8. The "litany of words" is admitted as an independent unit.
9. We are not concerned with the propagation of sociological ideas, except to emancipate the creative elements from the present ideology.
10. Time is a tyranny to be abolished.
11. The writer expresses. He does not communicate.
12. The plain reader be damned.

The declarations are interspersed with quotations from Arthur Rimbaud and William Blake, thus allying the signers of the manifesto with the power of the unfettered imagination. We should note, too, the insistence on artistic autonomy and the proud disregard for the "plain reader." There is little here to suggest a commitment to the egalitarian premises of democracy. Among the signatories were the American writers and editors Kay Boyle, Hart Crane, Harry and Caresse Crosby, Martha Foley, and Elliot Paul. Published in Paris by the New Jersey-born Eugene Jolas, *transition* (1927–38) was yet another kind of hybrid enterprise, a small-circulation journal that published British, Continental, and American writers, but until 1933 translated all work into English. It typifies, in these ways, the cross-currents of international modernism.

There were also, however, many home-grown ventures of this kind, mostly based in New York or Chicago: *Poetry* (founded 1912), *The Little Review* (1914), *The Seven Arts* (1916), *The Dial* (1916), *Contact* (1920), *The Fugitive* (1922), *The Soil* (1922). The manifesto of *Contact*, edited by William Carlos Williams and Robert McAlmon, underscores the American orientation of their project: "We are here because of our faith in the existence of native artists who are capable of having, comprehending and recording extraordinary experiences." Despite the rhetoric of American-authored manifestos, it was a rare writer who truly expected to start from scratch, without reference to Emerson's "courtly muses of Europe." But then it is not in the nature of manifestos to make fine distinctions. The American little magazine of this period was committed, first, to educating its readers, by promoting work unlikely to appear in more commercial venues; second, to providing favored writers with a location for their work; third, to building a larger audience for new writing over time, including an audience of writers interested in the efforts of other writers; fourth, to furnishing a forum for the expression of opinions that might run counter to mainstream culture. In some cases, too, a kind of boosterism motivated the editors, a desire to show the Old World what Young America could do, and to show America itself what its artists felt it ought to see. Manifestations of American literary modernism are thus Janus-faced: the artists look to their peers for approval and thus belong to a coterie; they want their work to be in some way "good for America," and thus have democratic impulses; they aim to outstrip their European predecessors and yet yearn for their benighted compatriots to recognize the great achievements of those same predecessors; they want the shine of the new and the patina of the old.

Some techniques of modernism

Whether content dictates form or form content, or whether the two are inextricable – and all these arguments have been made repeatedly – we can assume a relationship of some kind connecting the two. There is a similarly tangled relationship between a moment in history and a moment in the arts. Common sense tells us that the two must be connected, even if we cannot unequivocally determine cause and effect. There can be no question that many writers in the early decades of the twentieth century, inside and outside the United States, believed in the occurrence of a rupture or break from what had gone before and felt that art must somehow recognize the change. The American poet John Gould Fletcher announced in 1915, "It is time to create something new." Willa Cather dated the world's breaking in two to "1922 or thereabouts." These and many comparable expressions of seismic change are echoes of Virginia Woolf's famous declaration that human nature changed "on or about December 1910." So the dating of the world's transformation varied, but not by very much. For some it felt like a breakdown, for others a breakthrough. The two perceptions are related. *The Crisis* (potential breakdown) and *Opportunity* (potential breakthrough) were the names of the two dominant journals of the Harlem Renaissance, both of them responses to the same sense of a new order. If there was general agreement that the world had reached a pivotal moment, there was no clarity about how people might live in this changed world, nor was there a uniform artistic strategy of response.

Nevertheless, at least within the arts, we can identify at least three key moves. The first is to imitate or reflect the chaos: put another way, modern life is hard; therefore, art should be hard, too. Here is Eliot's diagnosis of the situation:

> We can only say that it appears likely that poets in our civilization, as it exists at present, must be *difficult*. Our civilization comprehends great variety and complexity, and this variety and complexity, playing upon a refined sensibility, must produce various and complex results. ("Metaphysical Poets")

An artist with a crazy mixture of thoughts and feelings, surrounded by stimuli of every sort, can reproduce and express the jumble by various means – among them, disjunction, open-endedness, disorderly presentation, non-linear development, and so forth. These approaches tend to result in forms that recapitulate the *processes* of experiencing, thinking, and making. Pound's *Cantos* exemplify this process-oriented poetic.

A second move is to sort, arrange, and balance disorderly elements to form a logical pattern, thus expressing the outcome or *product* of thought in a form polished and rounded. By this strategy art becomes a kind of antidote to, or respite from, chaos. It serves not merely to amuse or divert and not necessarily to suppress contradiction and confusion but rather to manage and contain them by recourse to paradox, temporary balance, or closed poetic forms. The most sustained project of this kind may be the poetry of Wallace Stevens, who set himself the difficult task of contemplating "the poem of the mind in the act of finding / What will suffice . . ." ("Of Modern Poetry"). Robert Frost described poetry as "a momentary stay against confusion" ("The Figure a Poem Makes"). Indeed, many of Frost's poems center on the achievement of poise or the effects of choice between two things: the boy swinging from tree top to ground in "Birches," the farmer contemplating staying or going in "Stopping by Woods on a Snowy Evening," the walker who recalls "The Road Not Taken." Edna St. Vincent Millay makes the ordering of a threatening disorder her subject in the sonnet "I will put Chaos into fourteen lines." Here a female speaker personifies Chaos as an unruly male "held" by the sonnet form: "I have him. He is nothing more nor less / Than something simple not yet understood." Millay employs form and gender here in a telling way, sonnets having long been addressed to women but written by men. A later execution of this strategy is Elizabeth Bishop's "One Art," in which the strict order of the villanelle form is made to contain – just barely – emotion at the loss of increasingly significant objects.

To the first strategy of a difficult disorder and the second of a delicate balance of order and disorder, we may add a third: radical simplicity. Pound's "A Few Don'ts by An Imagist" (1913) insists upon "direct treatment of the thing" without ornamentation or the imposition of artificial structures. Imagism as a movement (quickly abandoned by Pound but continued by H.D., Amy Lowell, and others) employed an approach characterized by spareness. This aesthetic applies as well to other poems not allied with a movement. William Carlos Williams's well-known "The Red Wheelbarrow" singles out the chickens, the rain, the wheelbarrow as things upon which "so much depends." A note of apology for eating the plums in the icebox becomes elegant when carefully arranged into lines ("This is Just to Say"). Similarly, Marianne Moore's meticulous description of animals such as the jerboa, the plumet basilisk, and the pangolin makes careful observation and precise selection of vocabulary into acts that suggest a template for moral action: humility, attention, care, concentration. Gertrude Stein's *Tender Buttons* evinces a similar fascination with the objects of everyday life. To comprehend the "thingness" of things close-up requires tactics and attitudes quite different from the panoramic sweep of poems that present, as do Pound's *Cantos*, Eliot's *The Waste Land*, or Hart Crane's *The Bridge*, the "variety and complexity" of civilization.

In the stories modernist artists tell about themselves, the confrontation with chaos is a major thread of the narrative. A remarkable aspect of literature written between 1900 and 1930 particularly is the frequency with which writers explain what they are doing and why it is important. Whether in manifestos, memoirs, letters, reviews, or collections of essays, they created a substantial body of work akin to a set of "how-to" manuals for the reader. Pound was especially prolific in this genre with books such as *Guide to Kulchur* and *ABC of Reading*, but the more reticent Wallace Stevens also wrote explanatory essays (*The Necessary Angel*) and Marianne Moore, too, explained her aesthetic commitments in essays on the poetic virtues of humility, concentration, and gusto. This didactic phenomenon suggests, first, that by the twentieth century advertising oneself was increasingly understood as a necessity and, second, that as much as the often "difficult" writing of modernism might appear purposely rebarbative, its authors still wanted to be read. This is not to say that writers routinely sought large audiences, but rather that this period saw a high degree of self-consciousness and seriousness about the absolute value of what writers were doing. For American writers, this seriousness was a product not only of a general move toward professionalization in all occupations, but also of a yearning to raise the status of literary pursuits in the national consciousness, to be understood as doing real work. "The difficulties of modernism," to use Richard Poirier's double-edged term, may be read as art's struggle to get itself noticed.[3]

Among the many motives for and techniques of experimentation in modernist art, one will help to organize the following discussion: perception. As a set of ideas about the relations of subject and object, the reliability of what is seen or experienced, the stability or instability of selves, and even the nature of artistic materials, the category of perception, in one way or another, accounts for much of what happened in the arts just before World War I and until World War II. The shifts in the understanding of these topics, it must be noted, did not begin or end with the wars: they had been evolving for at least the previous half-century, and they continue to develop now.

"At the turn of the century," explains Sanford Schwartz in *The Matrix of Modernism*, "the human sciences were undergoing a global shift from the developmental (or 'before and after') paradigms of the nineteenth century to the structural (or 'surface and depth') paradigms of the twentieth."[4] "Before and after" paradigms have a teleology: patterns of thought that emphasize succession and development (whether from Bronze Age to Iron Age, or primitive to complex) coordinate well with notions of progress and perfectibility, such that the most recent manifestation of a society is seen as superior to what went before. This mode tends therefore to privilege the present and to arouse expectations for a still better future. "Surface and depth" paradigms, by contrast, suggest that what meets the eye is not all there is to know. Here, the Freudian conception of the unconscious is a classic example. "In seemingly independent developments," Schwartz writes, "the study of the psyche, the sign, and society were reorganized around the opposition between the world of ordinary awareness and the hidden structures that condition it" (p. 5). If there is more to the mind than meets the eye, perhaps there are effects over which one has no control; responses to that lack of transparency might range from suspicion to fear of one's own motives and methods of self-control, but it might also signify sources of energy and renewal still to be tapped. In psychology, anthropology, linguistics, and philosophy, Schwartz argues, this paradigm shift enabled new ways of thinking, including new ways of thinking about thinking.

Consider, for example, this statement in William James's *Principles of Psychology*, published in 1890 while James was a professor at Harvard University:

> No doubt it is often *convenient* to formulate the mental facts in an atomistic sort of way, and to treat the higher states of consciousness as if they were all built out of unchanging simple ideas. . . . But . . . we must never forget that we are talking symbolically, and that there is nothing in nature to answer to our words. *A permanently existing "idea" . . . is as mythological an entity as the Jack of Spades.* (emphasis in original)[5]

To take this statement as seriously as James intends it is to substitute flux for stability, contingency for certainty, instrumental formulations for permanently existing ideas. Flux is another way of naming the "stream of consciousness," James's metaphor for the movement of thought as fluid rather than "chopped up into bits" ("Stream of Consciousness," 1892). In the hands of Dos Passos, Faulkner, and other modernist writers (in Britain, Woolf and Joyce), attempts to record this stream became characteristic of experimental fiction.

Here is the opening of the second section of *The Sound and the Fury* (1929). It is dated "June Second 1910."

> When the shadow of the sash appeared on the curtains it was between seven and eight oclock and then I was in time again, hearing the watch. It was Grandfather's and when Father gave it to me he said, Quentin, I

give you the mausoleum of all hope and desire; it's rather excruciating-
ly apt that you will use it to gain the reducto absurdum of all human
experience which can fit your individual needs no better than it fitted
his or his father's. I give it to you not that you may remember time, but
that you might forget it now and then for a moment and not spend all
you breath trying to conquer it. Because no battle is ever won he said.
They are not even fought. The field only reveals to man his own folly
and despair, and victory is an illusion of philosophers and fools.

Passages like this one generate questions: In what time frame is this
occurring? Despite all the references to time – the date, the shadows,
the hour, the watch – much of the passage appears to be not "in time,"
as the speaker says he is, at least not in the sense of contemporaneous
action. He is out of time; the speech of Father is recalled from the
past. Where are the conventional signals of quoted speech? Why is
thought presented in this way, the ticking clock and shadow calling
up a phrase about "the mausoleum of all hope and desire"? How, if
at all, does time as a subject cohere with the legacy of the watch and
the references to "battle" and "victory"? Are Father's words the reason the central consciousness of the passage is aware of the hour? An
educated reader in 1929 would recognize a passage of *memento mori*
and would easily see how a ticking sound might arouse thought
about the passing of minutes and generations. What is new about this
passage (actually one of the clearer ones in the section) is the authorial
refusal to employ conventional explanatory and expository devices, the
attachment to *not* explaining. Devising explanations is left to the reader.
   The paradigm shift of which James was only one spokesman has
profound consequences in addition to the demands placed on readers
by this form of narration. Acceptance of contingency restores stature
to the specificities of experience and questions the value of abstract
ideals. If theories are instruments and not, in James's words,
"answers to enigmas," the search for truth, that is to say, provisional
truths, becomes an unending process of vision and revision. This
constant state of becoming, in turn, raises questions about the nature
of selfhood. If this process is ongoing, is it possible to conceive of a
unitary self? Lastly, the emphasis on epistemological *means* rather than
ends promotes attention to the media of thought and creativity, whether
language, image, sound, or movement. For example, a significant revision of perception for painters changed the uses of light, color, shape,
perspective, and subject matter and in part accounts for the move from
representation to impressionism, expressionism, and abstraction.

What, then, is real? And what can be known about what appears to be real? If those questions cannot be answered conclusively, what are the implications for observing and managing physical processes (as in science) or understanding and communicating with another human being? How does one reconcile one's own point of view – itself subject to change – with that of another? For people who think about such things – and many of the modernists did – this line of questioning can foster quite opposite emotional reactions. On the one hand, it is disorienting and alienating to find that one cannot depend on previously held views nor entirely rely upon one's perceptions. On the other hand, it is thrilling and liberating to know that what seems to obtain now may be subject to reinvention and revision in the next minute. We might think about these complementary responses as we would about the making and breaking of habits, a subject that, not incidentally, greatly interested William James. Habits simplify life: not having to think consciously about certain repetitive procedures frees one from trivial business and, in addition, provides comforting, familiar rhythms to one's day. But habits also stifle new ideas, obstruct new perceptions, and settle into deadening routines. On the whole and speaking very generally, experimental art of the twentieth century was primarily interested in disrupting habit.

Shock tactics are the most obvious way to shake a populace out of its habits, to *épater les bourgeois*, defamiliarize the familiar, and disturb the complacent. The design for the first issue of the magazine *BLAST* – hot pink paper and a large, bold, black font, for example – combines attention-seeking and nose-thumbing. But among Americans sledgehammer tactics were less frequently practiced than other forms of defamiliarization. Make it strange, make it different, make it surprising, make it mysterious, make it elliptical, make it discontinuous, make it kaleidoscopic – these were all ways to "make it new," as Pound exhorted his peers. Examination of three techniques – *multiple perspectives, juxtaposition,* and *allusion* – will introduce the much larger range of invention that characterizes many modernist texts. As will become clear, the three techniques are often interdependent.

Multiple perspectives

The stream-of-consciousness passage from *The Sound and the Fury* quoted above illustrates a mind's ability to be (or to feel as if it is) in several places at once. Although the reading eye moves in one direction at a time and the reading "ear" hears one word at a time, a writer may nevertheless disrupt the *sensations* of linearity and sequence. Even the most straightforward sort of tale can "flash back" to an earlier scene to supply background or motivation. An extension of this kind of multiplicity is Faulkner's use of multiple focalizations in the novel. Each of the novel's four sections offers the perspective of a different character: Benjy, Quentin, Jason, and Dilsey. In the first three, a Compson brother narrates, each in a highly distinctive voice and about highly personal obsessions; in the last section, the narration is omniscient but the center of consciousness is the Compson family's servant, Dilsey. Faulkner's next novel, *As I Lay Dying*, is also structured on the principle of multiple points of view but with considerably shorter episodes and more frequent shifts. Faulkner extends the narrative scope within this relatively brief novel by allowing the story to be told by each of the Bundren family members, their neighbors, and even townspeople they happen to pass on their journey to Jefferson.

In *The Waste Land*, this sort of time- and space-travel is also presented through multiple speakers, though often glimpsed so briefly that we cannot consider them "characters." Arguably, the reader too is writing the poem as he or she pieces together the meanings of this highly fragmentary and allusive work. Thus memory and desire (or past and future) are mixed not only within a given individual mind but, for lack of a better phrase, within the mind of a civilization. The sudden shifts from contemporary to ancient settings and from one voice to another make the events of the poem seem to be happening simultaneously. In the last thirty-three lines of section III ("The Fire Sermon"), the reader moves from Queen Elizabeth I and the earl of Leicester to the Rhine Maidens of Richard Wagner's *Götterdämmerung* to Dante's *Purgatorio* to what Eliot's footnote explains is a "collocation of . . . two representatives of eastern and western asceticism," Buddha's Fire Sermon and St. Augustine's *Confessions*. Throughout the poem, this effect of simultaneity is sustained by similar juxtapositions, by the polyphony of the poem's "voices" (both those of dramatized speakers and those of literary allusions), and by the use of languages other than English (Latin, Greek, German, French, Sanskrit). Ezra Pound's editing of Eliot's manuscript, which can be studied in a widely available facsimile of the original, eliminated, with Eliot's consent, many connectives and transitions so that the poem became more radically fragmentary. This eschewal of syntactic coherence was to become a major stylistic technique of Pound's *Cantos*, first begun in 1915 and continued almost until his death in 1972. Not particular to Pound, the breaking of syntax was also a feature of the *transition* manifesto quoted earlier and indeed was a key modernist tool for investigating the nature of language.

Whether designed to move between one "eye" or "voice" and another or between one historical moment and another, techniques of discontinuity require a reader to move mentally as well. Whereas a traditional narrative usually offers a single protagonist or an omniscient narrator to give the story coherence, these methods intentionally court incoherence so as to expose the constructed nature of all stories, an acknowledgment that any story changes with a change of teller and that every point of view is limited. Further, multiple points of view *within* a character, the rendering of self-consciousness, and the adoption of multiple roles and masks dramatize the alienation and psychic fragmentation characteristic of modernism. As the examples of Faulkner, Eliot, and Pound suggest, the presentation of multiple perspectives often depends upon the second technique we will consider: juxtaposition.

Juxtaposition

Placing two or more things side by side can create an effect or tell a story. Thus, for example, the juxtaposition of images in a film (usually called *montage*) is a method of narration. Indeed, the placing of any two things next to one another invites the spectator to compare or imagine connections between them. An example of juxtaposition at work in prose narration has already been considered at some length in chapter 2. John Dos Passos's *USA* trilogy combines pieces of biography, stream-of-consciousness writing, "newsreels" of headlines, advertisements, and song lyrics, and narratives about several different characters whose lives intersect. His methods are in the service of an ambitious project to represent change and continuity, success and failure, and a nation divided by class and ethnic tensions at a particular moment in American history.

Though the methods are less elaborate, the effects of Jean Toomer's *Cane* (1923) and Hemingway's *In Our Time* (1925) can also be attributed in large part to juxtaposition. *Cane* is a loosely connected set of stories interspersed with poems. About half the stories are set in the South and half in the North. There is one recurring character, but he does not appear in every story and thus cannot sustain continuity as a conventional protagonist would do. Several kinds of juxtaposition operate in the text and require the reader's attention to and questioning of effects: those of *genre* (how the poem as a form comments on the story as a form, and how the work's last piece, "Kabnis," which uses theatrical conventions, comments on the previous genres); *theme or imagery* (the praise of Georgia's natural smells and sights, like its pine tree forests, inflecting the praise of black women's bodies); *setting* (how the collection's rural settings resonate with the urban ones); and those of *style* (how a surrealist story like "Rhobert" affects a reading of a realist one like "Bona and Paul").

Hemingway's collection invites similar attention, with its alternating stories and vignettes and the occasional reappearance of characters, notably Nick Adams. Since war is a clear text and subtext in the collection, violence is a predictable theme of the collection as a whole. The arrangement of stories and vignettes or interchapters (designated with numbers) encourages the reader to treat the collection like a novel, to read straight through from beginning to end. For those readers who do, a web of connections emerges to imply that war is only one of many forms of violence: barely suppressed divisions between men and women ("The Doctor and the Doctor's Wife," "The End of Something," "Soldier's Home"); competition and destructive behavior in sport ("The Battler," "Out of Season"); uncontrolled outbreaks of panic or cowardice manifest in humiliating bodily evacuations (vignettes IX and XV), devastating moral failures ("My Old Man"). The original cover of the collection in 1925 was a collage of headlines, itself, of course, a form of juxtaposition.

Juxtaposition as a literary technique is like and unlike putting together a puzzle, assembling a whole from parts. Fragments are themselves suggestive, especially when not yet fitted into a whole object. The possibility that a puzzle fragment might go any number of places is amusing. But only for a time: the ultimate aim is to discover its place in a larger picture, in short to complete the puzzle. Nor is this sort of mental exercise limited to jigsaws. Consider the extent to which a shard of pottery or a scrap of papyrus might suggest a civilization to a trained eye. Readers of texts that employ juxtaposition in the dense ways we've observed experience a similar pleasure when they can see how one piece (a line, an image, a word) connects to another. However, unlike a puzzle piece or chunk of pottery, a literary fragment can have numerous possibilities of "fit": multiple meanings, scores of connotations, and its own history. Consider the heft of a single phrase from the Bible or Shakespeare or, for that matter, a phrase from *The Waste Land* that alludes to the Bible *and* Shakespeare: "Co co rico co co rico." A gloss of this line in a popular anthology offers English folklore, *Hamlet,* and the book of Matthew in the New Testament as sources. Since the meaning of each element in a juxtaposition is polyvalent, and since meaning is dependent upon such variables as linguistic and social contexts, levels of education, and point of view, it is rare that a juxtaposition of two elements can serve as a formula for a single meaning. Not surprisingly then, modernist works that make heavy use of this method may close ambiguously or not at all. The *Cantos*, for example, simply stop; they do not end.

Allusion

"Co co rico" demonstrates the polyvalent nature of allusion. As a literary device, it operates as a kind of shorthand that paradoxically enlarges rather than reduces. Thus the cockcrow permits simultaneous reference to ghosts, sons and fathers, revenge, cowardice, and betrayals, among other effects. At the same time, it functions as a palimpsest. A palimpsest is a writing surface on which one text has been written over another. On a piece of parchment, for example, an original text might be erased or effaced so that a second text can be written over it, and this "recycling" can continue into multiple layers of writing. The superimposition of one layer upon another, like geological strata, records history. Similarly, a single word, a pair of lines, or juxtaposed images can evoke materials ranging broadly in time and space. The palimpsest is analogous to Schwartz's "surface and depth" paradigm. One of the things Eliot most admired about *Ulysses* was Joyce's "manipulating a continuous parallel between contemporaneity and antiquity" ("Ulysses, Order, and Myth"). He employed the method in *The Waste Land* as well.

Allusion to another text may also be employed as a tactic of revision. Both H. D. and Louise Bogan revisited mythology as a means of challenging the representation of women in Western culture. H. D. wrote poems on the subjects of Leda and Helen of Troy, Bogan on Medusa and Cassandra. Later in the century, Sylvia Plath continued this tradition in "Lady Lazarus." Similarly a writer might refer to another literary tradition in the very form of his or her writing. The section of *The Waste Land* detailing the relations of the "typist" and the "young man carbuncular," for example, mimics the rhyming couplets of *The Rape of the Lock*, thus deepening the satire by contrasting the matter-of-fact coupling of the contemporary pair with the mock-heroic qualities of Pope's poem. In adopting and adapting blues and jazz forms in his poetry, Langston Hughes offers homage to the unidentified authors of a still evolving folk tradition. His use of these forms invokes the history of African Americans, even as it employs a contemporary and highly popular form. Thus he speaks simultaneously in the voice of past and present, of written and oral cultures.

Finally, in the more self-reflexive writers, allusion operates as a cross-referencing system. Because much of Faulkner's work is set in his fictional world of Yoknapatawpha County, place names, family lines, and even events from previous fiction recur. The critic Hugh Kenner suggests that Pound's sprawling *Cantos* derive coherence from rhythms of recurrence and "subject rhymes"; this is another way of saying that the *Cantos* often refer not only to events in history, to people, to texts, and so forth, but also to themselves.[6] Thus each iteration of a favored image, such as "light" (instances of which occur over 140 times), will, in the course of the poem's development, recall previous instances, thus building layer upon layer of meaning. These iterations become guideposts in the thicket of allusion.

Remembering Schwartz's description of the paradigm shift – from "before and after" to "surface and depth" – we can see that multiple perspective, juxtaposition, and allusion are tools for bridging the two paradigms. Schwartz refers to these and other methods of modernism as "relational structures." Multiple-perspective techniques acknowledge the constructedness of what we perceive, thus linking mind and eye or one's own view with someone else's; juxtaposition assists us in seeing the relationship between two otherwise disparate elements and may suggest an additional meaning arising from their connection; allusion can connect past with present and text with text. Literary relational structures, seen from this perspective, become modes of making order out of disorder and vice versa: learning to read these structures provides, in the critic Kenneth Burke's phrase, "equipment for living" in the modern world.[7]

The long shadow of modernism

Why do women writers, compared to figures such as Eliot or Faulkner, appear less frequently in the standard histories of modernism? Feminist scholarship since about 1970 has altered the contours of the literary terrain by writing a counter-history to the "men-of-1914" narrative, that is, an alternative to a largely Eurocentric or expatriate story of male writers. Recovering previously ignored work, building a more complete picture of the history of modernism's genesis and development, devising theories about the relationship between gender and modernity, and re-evaluating works with criteria not provided by the modernists themselves, this scholarship has made it necessary to rethink what modernism was. First it has enabled a more inclusive awareness of art (by both men and women) that did not conform to the disjunctive, defamiliarizing aesthetic normally thought of as modernist and, second, it has provided evidence that the very pressures giving rise to modernist experiment may also have contributed to the critical dismissal of writing by women.

Read in the twenty-first century, some twentieth-century commentary written about female poets is genuinely shocking. These comments have been much rehearsed. Theodore Roethke's litany of weaknesses in poetry by women is one of many examples, worth quoting as a summary of the usual complaints: "lack of range – in subject matter and emotional tone – and a lack of sense of humor . . . the embroidering of trivial themes; a concern with the mere surfaces of life . . . lyric or religious posturing . . . lamenting the lot of the woman; caterwauling; writing the same poem about fifty times, and so on."[8] Earnestness, decoration, domesticity as the realm of the shallow and precious, cheap sentimentality rather than real emotion, too much "I": these complaints evoke the modernist list of "shalt nots," for they had the odor of gentility and Victorian parlors about them. In America, the drive toward professionalism in all the occupations, along with respect for enterprise and hard work, meant that, to be taken seriously, male artists felt they must dissociate themselves from any taint of amateurism or femininity. Harold Stearns, editor of *Civilization in the United States* (cited above) complained that "our cultural interests and activities have been turned over to the almost exclusive custody of women."

The misogynist remarks of some male modernists seem overwrought, as if the writer feels threatened or defensive about work produced by women; comments by both artists and literary critics indicate that powerful beliefs about female biology (and its consequences for the ability of women to think and work) held sway over any evidence to the contrary. Both kinds of comment are a tacit acknowledgment that women were not as they had been, that the relationships between men and women were not likely to be exempt from the forces of modernization.

Ever since Nathaniel Hawthorne lashed out at that "damn'd mob of scribbling women" in the nineteenth century, women had established a foothold as fiction writers and, while they rarely won accolades, that tradition of female prose writing continued. In the 1920s, for example, there was Edna Ferber's *So Big* (1924) and *Showboat* (1926), Ellen Glasgow's *Barren Ground* (1925), and Willa Cather's *Death Comes for the Archbishop* (1927). Pearl Buck's *The Good Earth* (1931) and Margaret Mitchell's *Gone With the Wind* (1936) were bestsellers in the following decade, though such popularity would have won them only negative attention from the prominent American culture critics. Women poets, rather than fiction writers, seem to have suffered most under the regime of high modernism. Male-authored reviews of work by writers like Elinor Wylie, Sara Teasdale, and Edna St. Vincent Millay were often scathing. Some poets, like Louise Bogan, were nearly paralyzed with self-doubt as they attempted to find a voice sufficiently impersonal and precise to suit the times. In critical writing such as *Achievement in American Poetry*, her self-presentation is more confident. Babette Deutsch and Laura Riding, too, were respected more for their criticism than their poetry. H. D. made a difficult transition from writing the kinds of Imagist poems Pound said she should write to the longer forms that captured her interest. Marianne Moore, though sometimes treated with respect, did not immediately attain the status she would gain in later decades.

The women contemporary to the major male modernists were not the only ones to be dominated by the likes of Pound and Eliot. As we have noted already, writers like William Carlos Williams and Hart Crane, too, felt that the moves made by Eliot and company necessitated counter-moves from them. In the course of the 1930s Eliot became an icon of modernism's mandarin tendencies, and modernism's stylistic innovations and demands seemed to some writers to have diverted energy from writing that was more fully engaged with issues of social justice. The catastrophic economic situation of 1930s America contributed, of course, to this shift in opinion. To increasing numbers of critics and writers, innovations of technique appeared to deflect attention from content and to make modernist writing an activity done by the select for the select. The continuing attempt of poets and critics of the 1940s and 1950s to free themselves of the "heavy father" that was experimental modernism will be a subject of the next chapter.

Making It New II: The Other Arts

For students of literature, the experiments of modernism are highly significant, shaping taste, literary criticism, and syllabi. The modernist model influenced subsequent generations of writers, some of whom were inclined to smash the idol. For most Americans, however, the proclaiming of literary manifestos and the raucous vying for attention of one "ism" after another would scarcely have registered. The poor and disenfranchised had attention focused on needs more basic than artistic experimentation. And although F. Scott Fitzgerald's *Flappers and Philosophers* (1920) and *Tales of the Jazz Age* (1922) present the 1920s as an endless gin-soaked party, plenty of Americans were displeased with, fearful of, or disgusted by modern art, modern thinking, and modern fashions of any sort.

While most indicators pointed the way toward an increasingly pluralist society, receptive to change and open to experiment, the years following World War I saw a backlash of racism, isolationism, nativism, and puritanism. The Ku Klux Klan was revived, and by 1923 had attracted a membership in the millions. Race riots erupted in Chicago in 1919. The US Senate, despite President Wilson's urging, refused to ratify the nation's entrance into the League of Nations. The "Red Scare," a national hysteria about immigrants and anarchists, was in full cry. Immigration quotas were imposed in 1924: no more than 3 percent of any nationality was to be admitted, and even this admission was limited to nationalities already represented in the United States. Congress passed the Prohibition Act in 1919 in a quixotic attempt to eradicate the drinking of alcohol. The famous "Scopes Monkey Trial" of 1925, in which a Tennessee high school biology teacher was convicted of teaching the theory of evolution, proved that acceptance of "foreign" ideas was by no means widespread. For many citizens, the wholesome Norman Rockwell families on the covers of the *Saturday Evening Post* represented the true America.

Nevertheless, the sense of the new made itself felt in daily life between the wars. Increasing numbers of labor-saving devices, with streamlined design that embodied the beauties of efficiency, were introduced into American homes. There were movies to go to, radio programs to tune into, jazz bands to dance to, Victrola record-players on which to play their tunes at home. By the end of the 1920s, some 700 radio stations and 8,000 movie theaters served a population of about 123 million. Automobiles were affordable, and miles of good roads were being laid to drive them on; the Ford Motor Company made its fifteen-millionth car in 1927. In Yankee Stadium, Babe Ruth was hitting home runs. You could work a crossword or peruse the "funny papers," read a Book of the Month Club selection, take photos with your personal Kodak camera, or go to one of the recently opened art museums. Between 1920 and 1930 there was a 56 percent increase in the number of art museums across the country: the Museum of Modern Art opened in 1929; the Whitney Museum of American Art in 1931. With a little cash to spare and a bit of leisure time, an American could choose among novelties galore, all along the spectrum of "high" and "low" culture, to edify and amuse. This jubilant atmosphere would, of course, vanish with the onset of the Depression and the slow economic recovery of the 1930s, followed shortly after by America's participation in World War II. During the hardest times, the federal government took over the role of patron and, through agencies such as the Works Progress Administration, supported artists, particularly in projects that heightened a consciousness of national identity or "Americanness." Following the war, historical events would again allow sufficient leisure and money for artistic expression, but the 1920s remain an extraordinary decade in American history for energy and innovation in the arts.

Artists in every medium wrestled with many of the same issues and strategies that occupied writers: speed, multiplicity, complexity, the jumble of simultaneous stimuli in urban settings, the opening up of permissible subject matter, new thinking about the potentialities of one's medium, and, in some instances, competition with new media and other forms of mechanized entertainment. The remaining pages of this chapter will offer a brief survey of developments in the visual arts, architecture and design, movies, and music. Two major ideas govern this review. First, despite the many differences among these disciplines, it is possible to see certain continuities that we may call "modern" and even "modernist." Many of the features associated with literary modernism and discussed in the previous section appear, albeit in modified form, in these works as well: cross-fertilization among the arts is characteristic of this period, one innovation suggesting another. Second, the tension between tradition and innovation, Europe and America, is once again made manifest. Introduction of the new often came in stages. American artists received training in Europe; they participated in introducing European imports to Americans, thus serving an educational function; and they found ways to incorporate the old with the new as their careers developed, including finding ways to express the Americanness of American culture.

Visual arts

Collage and assemblage in painting bear comparison with the treatment of fragments in literature. Their effects of simultaneity and disjunction in *The Waste Land* or *Cane* appear also in the skewed perspectives of Marsden Hartley's *Portrait of a German Officer* (1914) or the shard-like components of Max Weber's *Chinese Restaurant* (1915). In both, the reader/observer confronts multiple perspectives and must do the work of assembling the parts into a whole. A painter like Edward Hopper, on the other hand, employing more conventional techniques of representation, handled his subjects and landscapes in ways that revise notions of beauty and extend subject matter: a woman in an automat (*Automat*, 1927), a lighthouse (*Light at Two Lights*, 1927). Continuing into the 1940s, Hopper's project captured the scenes of everyday life in America: filling stations for cars, an office, a late-night diner (*Gas*, *Office*, and the much–reproduced *Nighthawks*). Similarly, the Precisionist painter and photographer Charles Sheeler induced viewers to rethink the aesthetic value of factories and smoke stacks, in, for example, his paintings of elevated railways and factories (*Church St. El*, 1920; *American Landscape*, 1930) and photographs of the Ford Motor Company plant in Dearborn, Michigan (1927). This attention to recognizably American settings is consonant with the objectives of William Carlos Williams and other writers who consciously employed native materials to make an identifiably American art. And, in this regard, painters like Hopper and Sheeler continue the tradition of the Ash Can school discussed in chapter 1, for whom unromanticized urban streets were worthy subjects. Sheeler's work also employs what might be called the "clean" aesthetic that shaped some modernist poetry: exactitude, sharp lines, simplicity, clarity. With the opening up of new topics for art, visual artists became major contributors to the depiction of what it was and what it had been to be black in the USA. Aaron Douglas's mural *Aspects of Negro Life* (1934) and Jacob Lawrence's sixty-panel series *The Migration of the Negro* (1940–1) are clearly influenced by the geometries and flat planes of other modernists, such as Picasso, who were themselves influenced by African art. These painters were also motivated by a desire to record the stories and iconography of a race's challenges and achievements.

The introduction of modernist painting and sculpture to America followed a trajectory common to most of the arts. A period of education and introduction – and resistance – was followed by a coming of age.

FIGURE 7   *Fugue*, 1940 (tempera and graphite on gessoed Masonite) by
Charles Sheeler (1883–1965)
© Museum of Fine Arts, Boston, Massachusetts, USA / Arthur Mason
Knapp Fund / The Bridgeman Art Library
Sheeler's precision revises the definition of the beauty of American
landscape.

The 1913 Armory Show has become the symbol of the introduction
of modernist art to the American public, as we've seen. But this was
invasion by invitation. The Association of American Painters and Sculp-
tors, whose members included Arthur B. Davies, Maurice Prendergast,
Robert Henri, John Sloan, George Luks, and William Glackens, sponsored the show. Inspired by what they had seen in travels abroad and
in the more avant-garde galleries of New York, they introduced new
methods in the visual arts, in part as an educational project and in
part as a means of creating audiences for new work. They expected
the art to be controversial and actively sought publicity. They treated
journalists to a beefsteak dinner before the show's opening. They also

expected that once the hurricane of controversy had subsided, the interest that had been aroused would remain, at least for some.

Earlier, Alfred Stieglitz's 291 Gallery in New York functioned similarly as an educational enterprise, both for artists and for the viewing public. Stieglitz opened the space in 1905. In the beginning, exhibitions centered on European art: Auguste Rodin, Henri Toulouse-Lautrec, Paul Cézanne, Pablo Picasso, Francis Picabia, Constantin Brancusi, Vassily Kandinsky. There were also shows of Japanese woodcut and African sculpture. "It was from all this fresh influx," the painter Marsden Hartley recalled, "that I personally was to receive new ideas and new education. . . . There was life in all these new things, there was excitement, there were healthy revolt, investigation, discovery, and an utterly new world opened out of it all."[9] The journal *Camera Work*, a quarterly edited and published by Stieglitz between 1903 and 1917, also spread the modernist message, including American elements of its vocabulary, notably in the stunning photographs by Paul Strand. 291 was followed by Intimate Gallery (1925–9) and, finally, by An American Place, which presented work by Ansel Adams, Arthur Dove, Charles Demuth, Marsden Hartley, John Marin, and Georgia O'Keefe. What had begun as a showcase of European modernism became one for American modernism.

New materials and new ways of imagining the distribution of space affected architectural and interior design as well. Frank Lloyd Wright, America's most famous architect, had been a student of Louis Sullivan, the pioneer of skyscrapers at the end of the nineteenth century. A long-lived man (1867–1959), he completed 532 works, not only private homes but also public buildings such as churches, schools, libraries, and museums, including the Guggenheim Museum in New York. His styles were eclectic; his philosophy, that a building should harmonize with its setting. Among his attempts to create an American vernacular is the "Prairie-style" home. The best example of this style is the 1909 Robie House in Illinois. Low and horizontal with an open-plan interior, the Prairie-style home was literally close to the earth. Wright also used modernist geometries in his house designs, as in the astonishing graduated cantilevers of Fallingwater in Pennsylvania (1936), and decorated interiors with details that have clear antecedents in the Arts and Crafts movement and in Japanese design. Other architectural innovators were European émigrés to America – among them Le Corbusier, Walter Gropius, Mies van der Rohe, Josef and Annie Albers, and Marcel Breuer. They brought the aesthetic commitments of modernism to American design: function, precision, clean lines, and eschewal of historical reference, all features of the German Bauhaus movement. The so-called "International Style" in architecture, an extension of that design philosophy, became especially influential in the 1930s when important members of the Bauhaus school emigrated from Germany to the US. The style dominated urban architecture after World War II.

On a smaller scale, one more accessible to acquisition by the middle classes, were articles of everyday use, from furniture to cutlery to glasses. The 1934 Machine Art exhibition at the Museum of Modern Art indicates a growing awareness of the potential complementarity of business and art. The catalogue for the show opens, rather defensively, with quotations from Plato and St. Thomas Aquinas on the nature of beauty. The foreword, written by Alfred H. Barr, then director of MOMA, explains the machine's potentiality for creating beauty: geometry, rhythm, the sensual surfaces of aluminum, brass, and steel. A brief essay on the history of machine art was contributed by Philip Johnson, later to become an architect in the International Style (a phrase he coined with the historian Henry Russell Hitchcock). The catalogue includes industrial units (machine parts, propeller blades), household and office equipment, kitchenware, scientific instruments, and laboratory glass and porcelain. The expected Breuer and Le Corbusier chairs are represented, but so are drinking glasses, spoons, perfume bottles, clocks, ashtrays, and cigarette lighters. Perhaps most modern and most American of all, given the national investment in technology, were the inventive ways that architects and designers found to use rather than to resist materials like synthetic resins, steel, concrete, aluminum, and glass, and methods such as the prefabrication of parts and the assembly line.

Music in the concert hall

Whether employing unusual kinds of sound or adapting folk forms to concert-hall pieces, composers experimented with their medium and its history in many of the same ways writers tested the limits of language and the history of literary forms. They also absorbed European musical training and sought to integrate tradition with their individual talents and national heritage. Premiered at Carnegie Hall in 1927, George Antheil's *Ballet mécanique* employed, among other instruments, a siren borrowed from a fire department, airplane propellers, a player piano, and a wind machine (which proved too gusty for the audience).

FIGURE 8   Roycroft tabouret
Photograph L. & J. G. Stickley, Inc.

FIGURE 9   Eileen Gray end table
Photograph European Furniture Warehouse
The shift from handicraft to machine art as expressed in domestic furnishings.

It was not a success. But the episode is a useful illustration of modernist experimentation in music, comparable to contemporary literary innovations. Antheil was influenced by European modernism, especially Dada; he was rethinking his medium, wedding high and low, conventional and unconventional, and employing machine art in the making of music. Ezra Pound was a fan.

Most experiments with the new presuppose some familiarity with what went before. Antheil's methods are analogous to the bright pink cover and large, bold typefaces of Wyndham Lewis and Ezra Pound's *BLAST*. Composer Samuel Barber's attitude toward the requirements of making twentieth-century music might be better compared to T. S. Eliot's emphasis on tradition, on "the mind of Europe." Schooled in such modernist methods as dissonance, Barber employed them judiciously, but his work does not break dramatically with the music of the past. Instead, it bears comparison to the music of late nineteenth-century composers like Richard Strauss, whose work continued the Romantic tradition. Barber employed European forms such as the opera, the concerto, and the art song, and his aim was to create comparable works for the American concert hall. In short, he did not feel compelled to employ specifically American musical traditions. His much-performed *Adagio for Strings* began life as the second movement of a 1936 string quartet. Played at the funerals of both President Franklin Roosevelt and President John F. Kennedy, the adagio has become an American tradition at moments of public grief.

Although modernism is often thought of as an elitist enterprise, the adaptation of American folk or popular forms was a fundamental mode of expression in compositions by musicians as diverse as Aaron Copland, Charles Ives, and Virgil Thomson. As Carol Oja remarks of Aaron Copland, "Some of his compositions – *Fanfare for the Common Man, Lincoln Portrait, Appalachian Spring* – have become virtual signifiers of American culture."[10] Copland's career evolved in native and international contexts: study in Paris with Nadia Boulanger, broad knowledge of the work of contemporaries at home and abroad as reviewer for the journal *Modern Music*, and increasing interest among American concert-hall composers in the possibilities of American forms and subjects. In *Music for the Theatre* (1925) and *Piano Concerto* (1926), he employs jazz idiom. In *Appalachian Spring* (1944), he builds his melodies around the Shaker hymn "Simple Gifts." *Appalachian Spring* was commissioned as a dance piece by the choreographer Martha Graham, herself a pioneer in modern dance. Other Copland dance works that allude to American popular forms are *Billy the Kid* (1938) and *Rodeo* (1942). Like Copland,

FIGURE 10   Isamu Noguchi's set for the ballet *Appalachian Spring*
Photograph: Library of Congress
A confluence of modern arts: Martha Graham's choreography,
Aaron Copland's music, and Noguchi's set design.

Charles Ives mixed old and new. Ives, who like Wallace Stevens worked full-time in the insurance business, was influenced by nineteenth-century Transcendentalism but employed twentieth-century tonal and polytonal music and popular song forms, from hymns to ragtime.

Virgil Thomson's eclectic resources ranged from the Baroque to Baptist hymns. In music written for the Pare Lorentz films *The Plow that Broke the Plains* (1936) and *The River* (1937) he alludes to spirituals, cowboy songs, and banjo music, while in *Acadian Songs and Dances*, his inspiration is Cajun music (1948). Among other modernist credentials are his collaborations with Gertrude Stein, the operas *Four Saints in Three Acts* and *The Mother of Us All* (the latter a work about suffragist Susan B. Anthony). Stein's text for *Four Saints* is based on the lives of Teresa of Avila and Ignatius Loyola, among other sixteenth-century Spanish saints. Thomson's music is not conventionally operatic, but a collage of Protestant hymns, bits of popular songs, dance music, and other forms. First performed in 1934, the production's cast was entirely African American and the sets made of such modern materials as cellophane. As this summary suggests, the piece mixes tradition and innovation in extraordinary ways.

Perhaps the most famous "cross-over" from popular form to the concert hall was the 1924 debut of George Gershwin's *Rhapsody in Blue*, one act in jazz bandleader Paul Whiteman's evening called "An Experiment in Modern Music." Gershwin is an exemplary musician of his period. He wrote scores of popular songs and was thought of as the leader of "Tin Pan Alley," so called because of the sound of tinkling pianos on 28th Street in New York, where composers had their studios. With his brother Ira as lyricist, he composed songs for many Broadway musicals. With *Rhapsody in Blue*, he added jazz and a piano concerto to his repertoire. For an American musician with broad interests and an ear for the contemporary, jazz had to be a part of one's musical life. It is indisputably an American form.

Jazz

In its beginnings jazz was not just music, it was metaphor; depending on one's point of view, a metaphor either for everything that was right with America or for everything that was wrong with America. Champions of the form cited its youthful spirit, joy, energy, speed, urbanity, and sensuality, while the naysayers deplored its vulgarity, its association with illegal alcohol and lascivious dancing, and – the point is unavoidable – its having been created by African Americans. If modernity meant going to hell in a hand-basket, there was sure to be a jazz accompaniment. The roots of jazz are mixed: it is an amalgam of blues and ragtime, with lineages in spirituals and African harmonies as well. Ragtime, a form for piano, began in the brothels of Storyville, a neighborhood in New Orleans, Louisiana, and that shady reputation was never quite erased; nevertheless, ragtime became a craze, causing a major increase in piano sales and launching various dances like the Turkey Trot. As ragtime became popular as dance music, "syncopated" orchestras formed, creating work for musicians, black and white. The northern migration of African Americans after World War I assisted the diffusion of the music called jazz, from the Deep South to Chicago, New York and, later, Kansas City. It also had its expatriate moment, taken more seriously in Paris than in America, and admired by classical composers such as Darius Milhaud and Igor Stravinsky. This stamp of approval would, as we have seen, have repercussions in compositions for every concert hall in America.

A significant moment in American theater and music history is *Shuffle Along* (1921), the first musical produced, directed, written, and performed by African Americans. The work of Eubie Blake and Noble Sissle, the musical made the reputations of two major twentieth-century artists, Josephine Baker and Paul Robeson. Baker was introduced to Paris in "Le Revue Nègre" in 1926, where her numbers included an erotic *danse sauvage*. Whether dancing in a revealing costume that appeared to be made from bananas or walking her pet leopard, Baker became the rage of Paris, cannily profiting from the vogue for all things African and exotic. Paul Robeson played major roles in Broadway musicals, including *Porgy and Bess* and *Showboat*, acted Shakespeare's *Othello* many times, and (in a less visible venue) shared billing with the poet H. D. in an experimental film called *Borderline*.

The roll call of great Jazz Age musicians includes Louis Armstrong, Sidney Bechet, Bix Beiderbecke, Duke Ellington, Coleman Hawkins, Fletcher Henderson, Bessie Smith, and Fats Waller. This list includes, significantly, both black and white musicians. One oddity of this period is the position of black musicians vis-à-vis their white audiences: at the Cotton Club in Harlem, black musicians entertained an exclusively white audience and played to the demands for a safe primitivism. Duke Ellington renamed his band the Jungle Orchestra. Jed Rasula points out the irony: "The entire public furor over jazz, along with any sense that jazz and modernism were overlapping phenomena, evaporated just as Duke Ellington's career was getting started."[11] Recordings and radio, increasingly accessible technologies, worked to spread the sound of jazz across America. Bessie Smith's "Downhearted Blues" sold 780,000 copies in 1923.[12] And, unsurprisingly, the more the music spread and the more middle-class white people heard it, the more commercialized and domesticated it became. It found a place in concert halls, living rooms, and dance halls, and lost the aura of the forbidden. Jazz's outsider label would return with bebop and the cult of "cool" in the 1940s and with rock-and-roll in the 1950s.

The movies

Historians of modernist practices in the arts have observed a similarity of method between the juxtapositions of image in poetry, collage in painting, and montage in film. The "Odessa Steps" sequence of Sergei Eisenstein's film *Battleship Potemkin* is the classic example, but the principle can be illustrated by two frames of a Charlie Chaplin, Buster Keaton, or Lillian Gish movie, too, since storytelling in movies is nearly unthinkable without this method. Around 1919, the Russian Lev Kuleshov performed experiments to see what meaning would be generated by juxtaposition of images. One of the images remained unchanged – an archive clip of the actor Ivan Mozhukhin, a close-up of a face showing no particular emotion. The sequence "frame 1: man's face," followed by "frame 2: bowl of soup" caused viewers to construe the meaning as "the man is hungry"; the same face followed by a picture of a child's coffin was read as "the man is sad." It is this sort of syntactic experiment that is at work in the juxtaposition of fragments in a poem. Film, like other media of modernism, has an international genealogy, with contributions from Russia, France, Germany, and other nations. Immigration from Europe to America, and Jewish immigration in particular, was decisive in the success of the American film industry: among prominent leaders in the studios were Samuel Goldwyn and Louis B. Mayer (who became partners in Metro-Goldwyn Mayer), Harry Cohn (Columbia Pictures) and Jack, Harry, Albert, and Sam Warner (Warner Brothers). In addition to actors, stories, and techniques, what America brought to film was talent for the big business of movie-making. "Hollywood," shorthand for this industry, became the nexus for scriptwriters, actors, producers, directors, technicians, designers, scientists who specialized in image and sound, and advertising executives – a mix that made for a sometimes uneasy alliance of art, science, and business. Much of what the world knows about America, for good or ill, is courtesy of this collaborative industry.

Conclusion: the example of Showboat

The arts usually thought of as typically American – jazz, movies – are collaborative. Another candidate for the title of "most American" is similarly a team effort, the Broadway musical. The historian Raymond Knapp suggests, in *The American Musical and the Formation of National Identity*, that all three of these arts share faults and strengths – or, more precisely, faults that are also strengths – that mark them as distinctively American. The musical's collaborative form, for example, may raise the standard of excellence through the pooling of talent, but cooperation may degenerate into discord, and dispersal of energy may damage the coherence of the final product. A financial backer may insist on a shorter running time to save on paying the pit musicians.

A "star" may demand a turn that doesn't harmonize with the show's objectives. Audience tastes, labor costs, available theaters, and other such variables dictate almost every feature of the project: casting, length, the book, the musical vocabulary, the look of the show. Despite these contingencies, and despite frequent rumors of the form's demise (Broadway has long been known as "The Fabulous Invalid"), the musical was extremely hardy for most of the twentieth century. "Over the course of the twentieth century," Knapp writes, "jazz, film, and the musical have achieved and maintained greater relevance to greater proportions of the population than any other performance-based arts, notwithstanding the erosive effects on that relevance . . . by television and rock-and-roll beginning in the 1950s."[13]

Knapp's argument has an antecedent in the work of Gilbert Seldes, one of the first champions of popular culture forms as quintessentially American. In *The Seven Lively Arts* (1924), he delights in the slapstick of Mack Sennett's Keystone film comedies; the songs of Irving Berlin, George Gershwin, Jerome Kern, and Cole Porter; the "smeared" notes of jazz trombone; Ring Lardner's demotic humor in *You Know Me, Al*; burlesque shows, circus acrobats, and the *Krazy Kat* comic strip. For Seldes, the lively arts are "entertaining, interesting, and important," not at odds with a Picasso painting and also not inferior to it. His view is that there is room for both kinds of art and that America clearly has something to contribute in its "lively" arts. "There must be ephemera. Let us see to it that they are good."[14]

In the 1927–8 season, of the 280 new productions in eighty theaters on Broadway, the most significant was *Showboat*, a musical based on Edna Ferber's successful novel of the previous year. Immediately, the commercial requirements of theater are evident: people had already heard of the book. The composer, Jerome Kern, was already famous. Along with several of his contemporaries, notably Irving Berlin and George Gershwin, Kern had developed the melodic conventions of European operetta into a distinctive American musical idiom. The lyricist, Oscar Hammerstein II, would soon join with Richard Rodgers in the creation of some of the American musical theater's most memorable works: *Oklahoma!*, *Carousel*, and *The Sound of Music*. The producer was one of Broadway's most flamboyant figures, Florenz Ziegfield, the man responsible for the perennially popular *Ziegfield Follies*. *Showboat* was a milestone in the development of American musical theater because it converted the two prevailing musical theater traditions, the operetta and the vaudeville revue, into an essentially new form. Instead of the fairy-tale characters of operetta and the unrelated songs, skits, and dancing girls of the *Follies*, the creators unified lyrics, music, and plot into a continuous story.

The subject matter of *Showboat* was also unusual: miscegenation and racial conflict are its major topics, but it also dramatizes alcoholism, gambling addiction, and marital discord. The plot centers on the love-affairs of two women: one, a performer in the *Cotton Blossom*'s show, Julie La Verne, a black woman sufficiently light-skinned to "pass" for white, and the other, Magnolia Hawks, the white daughter of the boat's Captain Andy. Both are unlucky in love. Julie is married to a white performer and, in singing "Can't Help Lovin' Dat Man," reveals to the black members of the show her racial background. The tune, actually composed for the show, is presented as a "heritage" song that only black people would know. Julie lives with the fear of exposure and the irrational jealousy of her husband. Magnolia's husband is an unfaithful gambler, whom she idealizes and indeed idolizes.

Perhaps the most famous of the show's songs is "Ole Man River," written for Paul Robeson (eventually performed by him in 1928, and again in the film version of 1936). It appears to be based on the spiritual "Deep River"; as in many songs of that tradition, the river acts as symbol for both religious salvation and the escape from slavery, encoded, for example, in references to crossing over the River Jordan. As is clear from the song's title, the creators of *Showboat* employed dialect in the songs. This is one of the many mixed modes in the musical. It is an artful blend of waltzes, blues, spirituals, ragtime, Tin Pan Alley, and, in the Little Egypt scene on the Midway, faux Middle Eastern. The dances are similarly varied: waltz, polka, foxtrot, and black dance styles like tap. Musical leitmotifs signal themes and character in the show (Julie's motif is "Can't Help Loving Dat Man"; Magnolia's, "Make Believe") and when the white musical forms blend with black, the music often acts as commentary on the action.

The critical reception of *Showboat* has changed over time, with concerns emerging over its depiction of African Americans and its use of language that has become deeply offensive, but one point critics seem to have agreed on: the second act is weaker than the first. The musical raises questions it cannot answer and sets in motion action it cannot resolve. The early scenes of the first act allow the audience to imagine a country in which the racial mix of America can be a source of creativity and strength. The final scenes deflate that possibility.

Like Mark Twain's *Huckleberry Finn*, also set on the Mississippi River, *Showboat* looks back to an earlier period. Twain's 1885 novel recalls the era before the Civil War; Ferber's 1926 work takes place in the 1890s, well after the conflict. Both works may be accused of nostalgia – glancing back to a more innocent time. Neither novel, however, ignores the terrible cost of America's persistent racial tensions. In the musical version of *Showboat*, the first act takes place on the boat, called the *Cotton Blossom*, and the second is on the Midway of the Columbian Exposition of 1893. Past and present, black and white, intersect: the boat's name alludes to the Southern crop most strongly linked to slavery; the Exposition boasted of American progress and symbolized its ideals with the so-called White City. It was on the Midway where the exotic and "primitive" cultures of the world were represented. Technological progress was demonstrable; progress in human relations was not.

Both *Huckleberry Finn* and *Showboat* can be said, in theatrical parlance, to have "second-act" problems. Many readers have found the final sections of Twain's novel unsatisfactory: how can Huck allow Tom to make a game of Jim's escape? When composers of *Showboat* wrote the finale, they composed nothing new; instead they resurrected "After the Ball," a sentimental and melodic piece of 1892. Composed by Charles K. Harris, it was the first American song to sell sheet music in the millions of copies. This choice not only increases the air of nostalgia but shifts the emphasis away from the musical's troubling subjects onto the more readily accepted notion of a broken heart. As extraordinary as Twain's novel remains, as groundbreaking as the musical *Showboat* was, both works revert to the familiarity of old times. Imagining a different future, both works are dogged by the past.

CHAPTER 4

Free

FIGURE 11   Fort Dix 1918, human Statue of Liberty
Photograph: National Archives (NWDNS-165-WW-521B(1)

This nation has placed its destiny in the hands and heads and hearts of its millions of free men and women. . . . Freedom means the supremacy of human rights everywhere. Our support goes to those who struggle to gain those rights or keep them. Our strength is our unity of purpose.
Franklin Delano Roosevelt's address to Congress, January 6, 1941

Great concepts like "due process of law," "liberty," "property" were purposely left to gather meaning from experience. For they relate to the whole domain of social and economic fact, and the statesmen who founded this Nation knew too well that only a stagnant society remains unchanged.
Felix Frankfurter, Supreme Court Justice, dissenting opinion in the case National Mutual Insurance Co. v. Tidewater Transfer Co., 1949

We conclude that in the field of public education the doctrine of "separate but equal" has no place. Separate educational facilities are inherently unequal.
Earl Warren, Chief Justice of the Supreme Court, Brown v. Topeka Board of Education, 1954

Everything free in America!
For a small fee in America.
"America," West Side Story,
lyric by Stephen Sondheim, 1957

There never was a war that was
not inward; I must
fight till I have conquered in myself what
causes war, but I would not believe it.
I inwardly did nothing.
O Iscariot-like crime!
Marianne Moore, "In Distrust of Merits," 1944

In mid-nineteenth-century America, saloon-keepers customarily posted the sign "Free Lunch" in a conspicuous spot as an inducement for passers-by. Attracted by the promise of something for nothing, the visitor would pay for the drinks and sample the free food. For hungry people, the price of a drink seemed preferable to the price of a meal. In addition, the congenial atmosphere would as often as not lead to another drink. The phrase "There's no such thing as a free lunch" has an unclear provenance, but its meaning is transparent. One way or another, we pay for what we get. Despite the tautology "free gift," beloved of marketers, it is rare to receive a commodity with no strings attached. "Freedom" and "liberty," as abstract nouns, also suggest an unencumbered state – no strings. Theoretically, one is free because one is born free, by virtue of being a human being. Thus, Thomas Jefferson describes the premises of the Declaration of Independence as "self-evident": "We hold these truths to be self-evident, that all men are created equal, that they are endowed by their Creator with certain unalienable Rights, that among these are Life, Liberty and the pursuit of Happiness." However, as Justice Felix Frankfurter argued in the 1949 Supreme Court case cited above, a tenet that is self-evident at one point in a society's development may be considered arguable at another stage. In short, the meaning of "freedom" is not unassailable and ahistorical. It is a condition most discernible in its absence. We know when we don't have it but may not notice when we do.

The philosopher and critic George Santayana was among those unconvinced by America's boasts about freedom: "Although it has always thought itself in an eminent sense the land of freedom, even when it was covered with slaves," he writes in *Character and Opinion in the United States* (1920), "there is no country in which people live under more overpowering compulsions."[1] In the course of this book, some of the compulsions Santayana observed will have become clear: the Puritan insistence on employing time and materials to glorify God; the expectation that immigrants adopt American speech and customs; the boss's demand that workers obey specified and (sometimes) unspecified rules of behavior; the "other-directed" suburbanite's need to be accepted as normal. Complaints about America's provincialism and conformity were a refrain among American intellectuals and artists in the 1920s, as we have seen. Pressures to "fit in" have historically been just as powerful as the mythology of the self-reliant non-conformist. Were the population not so scattered geographically and not so various in ethnicity, national background, level of education, religious beliefs, and degree of affluence, then the persistent problem of how best to balance the elements of the one with the many might not be so intractable. The Great Seal of the United States carries the motto *e pluribus unum* ("out of many, one" or "from many, one"). Certain moments in the nation's life demanded a showing of solidarity, an emphasis on the *unum.*

In his speech to Congress in January 1941 appealing for permission to offer material support to the Allies, President Roosevelt cited unity of purpose as the source of the nation's strength. His emphasis on shared beliefs simultaneously acknowledges the differences that otherwise characterize so diverse a population. In particular, he was aware that US neutrality regarding contemporary European conflicts had great appeal for Americans. In this speech, often referred to as the "Four Freedoms," he outlines a national commitment to freedoms *of* and *from* – of speech and expression, of religious worship, and from want and fear. As he spoke to Congress, US citizens were only emerging from the Great Depression that, for many, had provided direct and memorable experience of want. And FDR's reference to fear was also topical, given the rise of Nazism and fascism. That he should choose "Freedom" as his theme is telling – and not only because of current events. More immediately, he required a word that encapsulated compelling values that would mean something, if not precisely the *same* something, to the many constituencies that made up the America people. He sought to articulate what his wife Eleanor had described in her book as *The Moral Basis of Freedom* (1940), that is, a universally or at least widely accepted view of the dignity of the individual. "Since the beginning of our American history," he asserted, "we have been engaged in change – in a perpetual peaceful revolution – a revolution which goes on steadily, quietly adjusting itself to changing conditions." His phrase "perpetual peaceful revolution" acknowledges, as does Frankfurter's judicial opinion, the paradoxical nature of freedom as it is experienced, as it evolves; it must at once be an ideology (a self-evident truth) and a practice (subject to re-creation, redefinition, experience, and social construction). In time of war, American leaders have emphasized ideology and consensus about foundational values. In time of peace, however, the specific rights and privileges of freedom are negotiated in every branch of government and in every city block.

About the meaning of the word "free," then, as about that of other adjectives providing chapter titles in this text, there are multiple plausible opinions, its significance inflected, as is any abstraction, by the interpreter's perspective. Consider an example from the American theater: Leonard Bernstein's musical *West Side Story* is loosely based on Shakespeare's *Romeo and Juliet* but relocated to 1950s New York, where the rivalry is not between families but gangs, one group of "white" boys and one group of Puerto Rican immigrants. In the process of retelling this well-known tragedy, Bernstein and his lyricist Stephen Sondheim insert a wry and humorously rhymed debate about the relative merits of America and Puerto Rico. Anita defends "the isle of Manhattan," while her two homesick friends praise the island of Puerto Rico. What has America to offer? Automobiles, televisions, washing machines. Anita's friends say they will take these marvels back to Puerto Rico. In the following section, the first voice is that of the girls missing Puerto Rico; the second, Anita's deflating response:

I'll drive a Buick through San Juan.
　If there's a road you can drive on.
I'll bring a T.V. to San Juan.
　If there's a current to turn on!
I'll give them new washing machine.
　What have they got there to keep clean? . . .
When I will go back to San Juan
　When you will shut up and get gone?
Everyone there will give big cheer!
　Everyone there will have moved here.

Conducted in Latin dance rhythms the women have imported from their homeland, the witty, irony-laden debate encapsulates the division between the individual dream and the national dream, between gains in comfort and losses of native culture. Characters with nearly identical backgrounds have opposite views of their adopted country. Freedom for Anita is comfort: "knobs on the doors"; "wall-to-wall floors." As we will see, this comfort became increasingly identified with the meaning of "freedom" following World War II.

Santayana's image of a land "covered with slaves" points to an egregious blot on the country's record of guaranteeing freedom, a betrayal of founding principles the legacy of which continues to the present. This too is a reality that is obscured but not erased by the rhetorics of freedom. The landmark Supreme Court case Brown v. Topeka Board of Education was one of several measures taken during the latter half of the twentieth century to end legal justification for so-called "Jim Crow"[2] treatment, a set of practices given the legal imprimatur of the Supreme Court in the case of Plessy v. Ferguson in 1896. Under Jim Crow laws, separate schools, separate toilets and water fountains, separate railroad cars, even separate blood banks were countenanced, on the grounds that, so long as "separate but equal" public facilities were made available to African Americans, forced segregation did not violate constitutional protection of the law for African Americans under the 14th Amendment. Such customs persisted long after the Civil War, despite the Emancipation Proclamation, the Harlem Renaissance, and the strides made by the "New Negro." Brown v. Topeka Board of Education declared that "separate educational facilities were inherently unequal."

While Booker T. Washington's Atlanta Compromise address in 1895 had served as justification for a separate (fingers) but equal (hand), approach to rights for African Americans, his proposal was made at a time when temperate rhetoric seemed to Washington the most pragmatic route to progress. Increasingly over the course of the twentieth century, however, the gradualism and conciliation of that speech became insupportable to African Americans. Following each of the world wars, they demanded privileges and rights commensurate with the responsibilities they had accepted as defenders of freedom abroad and supporters of the wartime economy at home. And, spurred by the Civil Rights movement as it evolved after World War II, other ethnic minorities and women also demanded rights and freedoms they felt had been denied them.

This chapter investigates some of the meanings of "freedom" for Americans in the twentieth century, examining changes in the idea of "liberty" in the course of the century; literature addressing the United States at war; cultures of opposition and the "inward" war; and the Civil Rights movement.

The Multiple Meanings of Freedom

In *Spheres of Liberty: Changing Perceptions of Liberty in American Culture* (1986), Michael Kammen argues that, in the course of US history, the concept of liberty changed partners from era to era. "Liberty and property," crucial to the country's founding and early development, gave way by the middle third of the nineteenth century to "liberty and order" as the population grew and cities became more complex. Later, in a change he dates as occurring in the 1930s, the emphasis shifted again – this time to "liberty and justice." His assertions are carefully documented in surveys of public discourse, newspapers, speeches from the political platform, sermons from the pulpit. Why did "order" edge out "property" as the central concern of the nineteenth century, and why did the primacy of "order" as a value persist through the first three decades of the century? The work of Progressives at the turn of the century would seem to have focused far more on issues of social justice than on order. And indeed Kammen suggests that, while nineteenth-century thinkers considered order a "precondition of liberty," the Progressives in the last decades of the nineteenth century "were moving toward an intellectual inversion – the belief that liberty provides a precondition for order, and a necessary context for order to be both acceptable and meaningful."[3] In other words, activists like Jacob Riis and Jane Addams saw want and fear as the ordinary lot of immigrants and concluded that such needs do not conduce to an orderly population. Until want and fear were addressed, they believed, order would be a subordinate concern to the populations they sought to aid.

But this opinion was not widely shared outside Progressive circles. In the main, Americans associated immigrants with anarchism and socialism, hence the numerous expressions of nativist suspicion about anyone not "100 percent American," prejudice against Roman Catholics, and the denigration of ethnicities by a special vocabulary of insult: Yids, Polacks, Chinks, Micks, Wops (derogatory terms for Jews, Poles, Chinese, Irish, and Italians). Cities, the arrival point for many newcomers, were viewed as unsavory stews – full of disease, crime, danger, and temptations to sin. For those Americans already well settled in the nation, fear led to demands for order. And these demands furnished impetus and justification for government actions that indisputably trampled civil rights. The decade after World War I saw a powerful resurgence of suspicion regarding "other" Americans: a rash of lynchings of African Americans, the anti-communist Palmer raids of 1920, the notorious trial of Sacco and Vanzetti in 1927, and appalling exploitation of recent immigrants by business-owners. However, Kammen argues that, by the 1930s, "the idealism that accompanied [America's] participation in World War I as well as the critical pessimism stimulated by the Great Depression" brought a concern for "justice" to the fore. This is not to say that protection of property and support for law and order were ignored; indeed, concerns about both continue to spur debates between conservative and liberal interpreters of the nation's laws. Jurists who insist on strict construction of the Constitution are said to subordinate human values to property and personal wealth, while judges favoring broader constructions are accused of making rather than interpreting the law, of using "legal activism" to fulfill a social agenda. This agon between individual rights and the public good remains at the heart of American politics.

Despite this unresolved conflict, life under the New Deal initiatives of the 1930s accustomed Americans to more caretaking and regulation by the federal government. "Free enterprise" philosophy, the belief that capitalism and individual action should be restrained as little as possible, gave way for a time to a philosophy that governmental regulation of individuals and their business enterprises could be justified in the name of "justice for all." As Maury Maverick, a congressman from Texas, put it in 1939: "You cannot fill the baby's bottle with liberty." This view of the priority of basic and immediate human needs gained ascendancy over a more abstract, but nevertheless fundamental, American value, the desirability of a non-interfering federal government. Instead, public discourse in the 1930s focused on interdependent interests and the connection of all enterprises to the nation's common good. Tensions and conflicts between the individual and the larger community have marked American writing in every era and, while this theme is hardly exclusive to America, it is certainly one of the hardiest in the nation's literature. Thus literature, too, has provided a venue for the conduct of this ongoing debate.

As part of the general economic recovery overseen by Roosevelt's administration, the federal government enlisted the arts as never before in projects to define the commonweal in America. What was America apart from or in addition to a congeries of individual interests? Writers in the Federal Writers Project, together with photographers, graphic designers, and other artists, were employed on projects that emphasized America's heritage and its progress: research in federal, state, and local archives that led to town histories and state guidebooks; filmed and photographic documentation of American lives; collection and recording of folk music; panoramic murals on American themes in public buildings; striking posters advertising undertakings like the Rural Electrification Project. The cumulative effect of this work was to create a sense of the nation as a common enterprise in counterpoise to the excesses of entrepreneurial energy and sheer greed evident in the boom economy of the 1920s. Similarly, educational organizations and governmental offices promoted the view that the common values and beliefs unifying Americans were far stronger than the differences that divided them. In 1937, the Progressive Education Association established the Commission on Intercultural Education. By 1938, the program was called "Education for Democracy." The US Office of Education devised a series of radio programs broadcast in 1938–9 on the topic "Americans All . . . Immigrants All." A theme of the New York World's Fair of 1939 was "unity without uniformity." Organizations outside government also contributed to the project of defining shared values and community. In 1937, for example, *Life* magazine published Margaret Bourke White's memorable photo-essay on Muncie, Indiana, the "real 'Middletown.'" Thus, by the end of the 1930s the country was primed to begin what Daniel T. Rodgers calls its "intense fling with the word freedom";[4] the word became a portmanteau for these commonly held values. An affair in full swing during World War II, the partnership continued into the years of the Cold War.

War and the Affirmation of American Values

During and following World War II, the majority view of American citizens was that the "G.I.s" (soldiers) sent to Europe and the Pacific were emissaries of liberty, engaged in noble work. Making the world "safe for democracy," as Woodrow Wilson had described the task in the previous war, gained credibility as a worthy aim between the end of the first war and the beginning of the next. This chapter will focus on the later period, World War II and the Cold War; however, in order to trace the changing perceptions of America's relationship to the rest of the world in the course of the twentieth century, we must briefly consider how radically public opinion altered between Woodrow Wilson's declaration in 1917 and Franklin Roosevelt's in 1941.

The United States entered World War I reluctantly and belatedly in 1917, three years after the fighting in Europe had begun. Indeed Wilson had been nominated for a second term as president in 1916 on the strength of the slogan "He kept us out of war." The initial feeling among the great majority of Americans was that it was in the country's better interest to remain neutral. A notable exception to this disinclination was the attitude of some young American men, often college graduates, who enthusiastically signed up for the French foreign legion or the ambulance corps. Among the participants were poet e. e. cummings, novelists John Dos Passos, Dashiell Hammett, and Ernest Hemingway, and critics Malcolm Cowley and Edmund Wilson. Memorable American writing following the war derives from their experiences. Most Americans, however, were less concerned about Europe and more concerned that the war would interfere with national progress, both material and social. Those of an anti-Old World bent, seeing Europe as decadent, interpreted the conflict as a squabble among countries "over there," a dispute that was none of America's business. But a series of events built up pressure for the nation to enter the war as an "associate" of the Allies: Germany's declaring British waters a war zone, thus inhibiting US trade with the Allies; the sinking of the *Lusitania*; revelation of a potential alliance between Germany and Mexico; and repeated German U-boat attacks. Once the United States had committed troops to the conflict, the federal government, anticipating popular resistance, launched an ambitious program of propaganda – in print and film. "Four-minute" men, presenters of brief rallying speeches, addressed gatherings at theaters, exhorting the audience to support the war. Congress passed an

Espionage Act (1917) and a Sedition Act (1918) as stays against opposition to the war. Anti-German sentiment rose to such an extent that certain books and music, along with the teaching of the German language in schools, were banned in towns throughout the country. Public support for the war went from hesitant to wholehearted, and soldiers were celebrated for coming to the aid of the Old World. In Irving Berlin's song "Over There," the lyrics suggested that America was on a rescue mission.

> O-ver there, o-ver there, send the word, send the
> word, o-ver there,
> That the Yanks are com-ing, the Yanks are com-ing,
> The drums rum-tum-ming ev'ry where
> So pre-pare, say a prayer, send the word, send the
> word to be-ware
> We'll be o-ver, we're com-ing o-ver,
> And we won't come back 'til it's o-ver O-ver There!

But the enthusiasm was short-lived. After the Armistice was signed in November 1917, many concluded that the war had been futile. Many also felt Wilson had been outwitted by David Lloyd George (England) and Georges Clemenceau (France) in the Treaty of Versailles. And Wilson's idealistic aim of creating a League of Nations failed to capture the public imagination. Increasingly, Americans, including many who had served as combatants, felt as Ezra Pound did about the "war to end all wars":

> There died a myriad,
> And of the best, among them,
> For an old bitch gone in the teeth,
> For a botched civilization,
>
> Charm, smiling at the good mouth,
> Quick eyes gone under earth's lid,
>
> For two gross of broken statues
> For a few thousand battered books.
> (*Hugh Selwyn Mauberley*,
> section V, 1920)

The sense of waste and futility similarly shaped Dos Passos's *Three Soldiers*, Hemingway's *A Farewell to Arms* and *In Our Time*, e. e. cummings's *The Enormous Room*, and Faulkner's *Soldier's Pay*, all of which demythologize the glories of war and heroism in battle. "I was always embarrassed by the words sacred, glorious, and sacrifice and the expression, in vain," says Hemingway's protagonist Frederic Henry. Disillusionment was the order of the day. To what ends had this war been fought and these thousands of lives lost? And what had become of the dream of continual progress toward a great society? Of course deflation of hope for the future was felt even more deeply in countries where the battles had been fought and the losses far heavier than they had been for the United States. World-weariness and suspicion of high-flown rhetoric and sentimentality became a keynote in many canonical literary texts of Anglo-American modernism: T. S. Eliot's *The Waste Land*, Virginia Woolf's *Mrs. Dalloway*, Ford Madox Ford's *The Good Soldier*. The lives and work of the "Lost Generation" were frequently marked by defeat and exhaustion.

In the United States "debunking" became a favorite activity of intellectuals, and American heroes were dethroned.[5] Works like Stearns's collection *Civilization in the United States*, discussed in the previous chapter, insisted that there was more wrong than right with America: it was provincial, dull, prudish, anti-intellectual. Historian Charles A. Beard's *Rise of American Civilization* (1923) emphasized not the schoolhouse narrative of the Founding Fathers' wisdom and virtue but the less lofty realities of economics. This willingness to look skeptically at America's foundational myths partially explains the expatriation of American writers and artists in the 1920s. On the other hand, the majority of Americans were less critical. The country emerged from the war more prosperous than ever, and the Jazz Age ethos of exuberant spending and enthusiastic testing of social boundaries ensued. For many young Americans particularly, this was a blissful time; leading cultural observers like Santayana or the more caustic culture critic and journalist H. L. Mencken, however, offered stinging criticism of America's shallower pleasures and rampant materialism. Nevertheless, the jazz band played on until the party was abruptly closed down by the stock market crash and the decade-long effort to recover from its effects.

In the 1930s domestic issues absorbed most Americans' full attention. And the economic crisis was made still more intolerable for the rural poor when windstorms took control of their livelihoods out of their hands. Effects of drought and soil erosion in the so-called Dust Bowl created hardship across the southern Great Plains for most of the 1930s. Meanwhile, England and France felt increasingly threatened by the regimes of Adolf Hitler, Benito Mussolini, and Francisco Franco and the aggressions of Japan in Asia. The title of Sinclair Lewis's novel *It Can't Happen Here* (1935) sums up the isolationist mood of the

American majority – though the novel was intended as an indictment of just that attitude. Lewis imagines a homegrown Hitler named Senator Berzelius (Buzz) Wildrip, who replaces FDR as the Democratic nominee in the 1936 election. Backed by an organization called The League of Forgotten Men, led by a radio-priest named Bishop Prang, Wildrip pretends to be the folksy champion of ordinary people, but is in fact planning a dictatorship. His power base comprises an underclass susceptible to the idea of an international Jewish and communist conspiracy. As he had done in *Elmer Gantry* (1927), Lewis reveals the power of appeals to Americans' basest instincts and stresses their attraction to charismatic leaders. As before, too, characters in the novel have contemporary models: Huey Long's populist reign in Louisiana, Henry Ford's public anti-Semitism, Father Charles Coughlin's "Shrine of the Little Flower" radio station, the white underclass's resentment as expressed in organizations like the Ku Klux Klan. Wildrip moves toward militarism and terrorist tactics with implausible rapidity, but his tyranny is countered by liberal journalist Doremus Jessup, who organizes an underground resistance. The novel concludes inconclusively but with the suggestion that the resistance forces will fight on. No critic counts this work as Lewis's masterpiece. R. P. Blackmur's review stressed that the novel was propaganda, not art, an instance of the category war fought throughout the 1930s in the pages of *Partisan Review* and elsewhere.[6] Critics more kindly disposed to the work usually conceded that the ideas, not the artistry of the prose, merited attention. Whether the novel was art or propaganda (and whether the categories can be separated at all), it sold well and toured in a dramatic adaptation sponsored by the Federal Theatre Project, thus spreading its influence. Spain also drew the attention of American writers: the civil war between the republican loyalists and General Franco's fascists (1936–9) occasioned a flood of pamphlets, fiction, poetry, and plays, among them Hemingway's *For Whom the Bell Tolls*. This novel, too, sought to depict America's interests as inseparable from those of the rest of world. Hemingway's title alludes to John Donne's "Meditation XVII": "never send to know for whom the bell tolls; It tolls for thee." Neither a man nor a country could be an island "entire of itself." Given the conditions of Dust Bowl America, however, it was hard for folks scrabbling for a living to attend to this proposition.

The "Four Freedoms" speech discussed above came just days before FDR's request for Congress to pass the Lend-Lease Act, which permitted the US to lend material aid to the Allies (much of it in the form of armaments the President referred to as the "arsenal of democracy"); by

August 1941, FDR had signed the Atlantic Charter with England's Prime Minister Winston Churchill, outlining the "common principles" that contained their "hopes for a better world." On December 7, 1941 the Japanese bombed the US naval station in a surprise attack at Pearl Harbor in Hawaii, killing over two thousand Americans, including civilians. On December 8 Congress, by unanimous vote, declared war on Japan. Terms of the Tripartite Pact of 1940 made inevitable Germany's and Italy's declaration of war against the United States on December 11. For the next four years, America's main business was the business of war.

And the rallying cry was "Freedom." Stubborn divisions of political philosophy, class, race, ethnicity, gender; skepticism about America's moral health; critiques of the country's intellectual poverty; the pitting of one political or economic interest against another – all were muted (though not entirely silenced) by cries for solidarity against Hitler and what he represented. Indeed the poet Archibald MacLeish, in *The Irresponsibles* (1940), accused his fellow writers of the 1920s of having shirked their cultural responsibility to America: "Instead of studying American life, literature denounced it. Instead of working to understand American life, literature repudiated it." He was roundly criticized by the literati for this point of view; Dwight Macdonald, an editor of *Partisan Review*, declared MacLeish's accusation "totalitarian."[7] Such disputes aside, however, this was a war and a cause that most Americans could support with fervor. To simplify: if the 1920s and early 1930s had exposed the rough seams barely holding the country together, the late 1930s and 1940s ignored the pieces in favor of the whole cloth.

In 1938, when the US position was "aid to Britain short of war" and the attack on Pearl Harbor had not yet ignited widespread belligerence, Henry R. Luce published an influential editorial entitled "The American Century." His was a recognizable and authoritative voice: having created *Time* magazine in 1923, *Fortune* magazine in 1930, and *Life* magazine in 1936, he was also behind the highly popular *March of Time* radio series first aired in 1931. Luce's essay, broadly disseminated in newspapers and published as a book in 1941, articulated reasons for America to assert itself in global politics. In doing so, however, Luce laid out a controversial agenda that would continue to affect American politics for the remainder of the century – and beyond.

In the field of national policy, the fundamental trouble with Americans has been, and is, that whereas their nation became in the twentieth-century the most powerful and the most vital nation in the world, nevertheless Americans were unable to accommodate themselves spiritually and practically to that fact. Hence they have failed to play their part as a world power – a failure which has had disastrous consequences for themselves and for all mankind. And the cure is this: to accept wholeheartedly our duty and our opportunity as the most powerful and vital nation in the world and in consequence to exert upon the world the full impact of our influence, for such purposes as we see fit, and by such means as we see fit.[8]

This passage will strike many readers as staggeringly arrogant and good cause for other nations and peoples to resent American hegemony. Luce seems to declare that America's "vitality" and wealth justify America's right to exert global power. In the remainder of his essay, he spells out the purposes and means by which "American internationalism" will justify itself because of the good America can do. Luce calls for the vision of an American century to be realized in four areas: enabling "free economic enterprise"; sharing "technical and artistic skills"; feeding all the destitute and hungry people of the world; and spreading "great American ideals," specifically freedom, equality of opportunity, self-reliance and independence, cooperation, and the principles of Western civilization – "above all Justice, the love of Truth, the ideal of Charity." This is American exceptionalism on an operatic scale. It recalls and unquestionably builds upon the Puritan vision of a "city on a hill," moral leader of all nations; it recognizes globalism as a feature of modernity, but without a suggestion that global interchange will come not only *from* America but will happen *to* America; it elucidates basic assumptions underpinning the politics of the Cold War, in which "freedom" American style came to mean the sole alternative to communism and fascism.

Entry into World War II spurred new levels of patriotism and talk of shared values, but public discussion of such topics was not a sudden turn in American intellectual life. In the course of the 1930s substantial energy was expended on defining what America was. This national self-assessment appeared in the attempts of social scientists to define the American character and American values, in the efforts of literary historians to identify the characteristics that made American literature "American," and in the work of historians who evaluated the country's past to discern the patterns and values critical to national strength. Work of this bent had begun in the 1920s but increased markedly in the 1930s, thus reinforcing the New Deal agenda of highlighting America's common values. The war made this agenda more urgent still. The motivation to study American character, culture, and literature was not, however, only political. "Culture" as a concept had entered public discourse because of developments in the social sciences that provided a new vocabulary and a new set of questions about the elements that cause societies to cohere.

Of works that contributed to what is now routinely referred to as "American Studies," a remarkable number appeared in the late 1930s and early 1940s. Among these publications are titles that still have interest for students of American culture:

Charles A. and Mary Beard, *The American Spirit: A Study of the Idea of Civilization in the United States* (1942)
Van Wyck Brooks, *The Flowering of New England, 1815–1865* (1936)
Merle Curti, *The Growth of American Thought* (1943)
John Dollard, *Caste and Class in a Southern Town* (1937)
Edward Franklin Frazier, *The Negro Family in the United States* (1939)
Louis M. Hacker, *The Triumph of American Capitalism* (1940)
William T. Hutchinson, ed., *Democracy and National Unity* (1942)
Alfred Kazin, *On Native Grounds: An Interpretation of Modern American Prose* (1942)
Robert S. and Helen Merrell Lynd, *Middletown in Transition* (1937)
F. O. Matthiessen, *American Renaissance: Art and Expression in the Age of Emerson and Whitman* (1941)
Perry Miller, *The New England Mind: The Seventeenth Century* (1939)
Samuel Morison and Henry Steele Commager, *The Growth of the American Republic* (1930)
Ralph Barton Perry, *Shall Not Perish from the Earth* (1940)
Arthur Schlesinger and D. R. Fox, eds., *A History of American Life*, 13 vols. (1927–48)

Plans for a *Literary History of the United States* were first mooted in a 1939 meeting of the American Literature Group of the Modern Language Association (still the premier organization for teachers of English and other modern languages). Not surprisingly, given the sweep and ambition of the project, professional and political factors complicated discussion: negotiations about editorial control, competing definitions of literary history, whether the discipline of American literature was sufficiently "mature" to warrant a history, and who should write what. World War II also retarded the project, but when the history was finally published in 1946, the editors declared that the war had been a spur to the completion of the book: "The disruptions of the war and postwar eras, far from presenting handicaps, have stimulated interest by emphasizing the need for cultural redefinition." The history came at an appropriate moment in the development of the American university curriculum. The Servicemen's Readjustment Act of 1944, commonly known as the G.I. Bill of Rights, provided grants and loans to veterans of the war seeking education and additional support to educational institutions for their tuition, books, and fees. In 1947, veterans comprised 49 percent of all college students. The institutionalization of American literature, including twentieth-century literature, within universities can in large part be explained by this influx of students newly alert to the position of the United States as a world power.

Writing War

W. H. Auden's poem "The Shield of Achilles" (1955) juxtaposes the heroic with the banal. In an episode described in detail in book VIII of Virgil's *Aeneid*, Achilles' mother Thetis observes the making of his shield. As Auden's Thetis looks over the armorer's shoulder as he works, the speaker presents, in four shorter-line stanzas, what she expects to see and, in five longer-line stanzas, what she sees instead. In place of olive trees and grape vines, marble cities, "ritual pieties" of "libation" and "sacrifice," and beautiful human bodies dancing, she sees a bare plain, an "unintelligible multitude" represented by "a million boots in a line," hears a disembodied voice cite statistics about a just cause, sees barbed wire enclosures, "bored officials," a "ragged urchin" stoning a bird, rapes, and a murder. Epic deflated, the hero dwarfed, men of action become men of bored acquiescence, the *polis* as dump. Auden became a US citizen in 1946 but he wrote from a broader perspective. The poem emphasizes what the political philosopher Hannah Arendt called the "banality of evil," evident not only in time of war but in the ordinary cruelties of humankind.

Depictions of heroic action in a just cause are far more likely to be found in Hollywood movies than in the fiction or poetry emerging from World War II. Films made to boost morale and support the Allied cause would, of course, portray the American soldier at his best: brave, resourceful, kind to civilians, a little too naive or a little too tough but always good at heart. In movies such as *Sahara, Flying Tigers, Bataan*, and *Back to Bataan*, major Hollywood stars like John Wayne, Robert Taylor, Humphrey Bogart, and Spencer Tracy reinforced appreciation for the armed forces and promoted the view that the war was worth fighting. For Americans at home in wartime, Hollywood provided a sense of the justness of this war. Long after the victory had been declared, the World War II movie continued to be popular: *From Here to Eternity* (based on James Jones's bestselling novel of 1951), *Run Silent, Run Deep, Stalag 17*, and the films of Audie Murphy, the most decorated soldier of the war now turned actor, in particular *To Hell and Back*.

Valiant soldiers also appear in popular fiction after World War II, but the novels that received the most critical attention and that, arguably, most influenced other writers do not sound the heroic note. Irony, as in Auden's poem, was the prevailing tone, anti-heroism the organizing principle. Two examples, one published just after the war and one issued over a decade later, share a view of war's absurdities, though to different effect. *The Naked and the Dead* (1948) was one of the most powerful novels to come out of World War II, and it was certainly the making of Norman Mailer's reputation. Joseph Heller's *Catch-22* (1961) echoes many of the themes of *The Naked and the Dead* but presses them to outrageous and often hilarious extremes.

Mailer follows the maneuvers of a reconnaissance platoon on the fictional island of Anopopei in the South Pacific. The techniques of the novel are comparable to those of John Dos Passos's *USA*: well-developed characters who are also "types," dense detail, action interrupted by short biographies, occasional stream-of-consciousness writing. In his fiftieth-anniversary preface to the novel, Mailer recalls that he began writing it at age 23 and published it at 24 and that, during the fifteen months of its composition, he read Tolstoy daily. His own novel

> reflect[s] what [I] learned about compassion from . . . the old man – Tolstoy teaches us that compassion is of value and enriches our life only when we can perceive everything that is good and bad about a character but are still able to feel that the sum of us as human beings is probably a little more good than awful. In any case, good or bad, it reminds us that life is like a gladiators' arena for the soul and so we can feel strengthened by those who endure, and feel awe and pity for those who do not.

Mailer's metaphor of the Roman Colosseum is apt. The gladiator's life or death was in his own hands and protected by his own ability – up to a point. But the odds were against survival, and ultimately the Roman rulers, not the gladiators, decided who would live and who die. Thus Mailer evokes in this simile, as in his novel, the paradox of the man of action under the command of a distant bureaucracy whose decisions he cannot alter or influence. An Emersonian self-reliance is both required and irrelevant. The characterizations and the plot lines of the novel depend upon this maddening paradox.

As in naturalist writing generally, Mailer creates characters whose will is subject to larger forces, whether in their home lives or as soldiers on battlegrounds. Each of the biographical vignettes is built upon the disjunction between aspiration and actuality. The variety of characters makes the military unit a microcosm of the larger society: ethnicities represented by the names and nicknames (Martinez, Polack, Goldstein); varying levels of education (the platoon sergeant, Croft, is uneducated; Hearn, the lieutenant sent to lead Croft's platoon went to Harvard); brief mentions of religion (Catholic, Protestant, and Jew are all present). Some of the men are choleric, some sensitive, some gifted at survival, some hopeless. In a series of "Time Machine" sections, so labeled, Mailer familiarizes the reader with the backgrounds of the major figures: Martinez has grown up in San Antonio and knows the ways in which his Mexican ethnicity and poverty have limited his choices: "Tired? Restless? Knock up a dame? Join the Army." And yet his choices remain limited in the army; his background, it is clear, will slow or prevent his rising in the ranks. Still, in his last appearance, he muses that he will probably re-enlist: "Army no goddam good, but Army okay. Nice pay."

Mailer calls attention to his own methodology and to the limits of any explanatory model even as he presents such details. In his biography of Sergeant Croft, he introduces him in an italicized headnote to the section as a man who "hated weakness and . . . loved practically nothing." The biography then addresses the question that readers routinely ask about a fictional character's behavior: "But why *is* Croft that way?" The narrator responds with a series of answers that, while perhaps plausible, are unsatisfactory:

> Oh, there are answers. He is that way because of the corruption-of-the-society. He is that way because the devil has claimed him for one of his own. It is because he is a Texan; it is because he has renounced God. He is that kind of man because the only woman he ever loved cheated on him, or he was born that way, or he was having problems of adjustment.

The tone makes clear, as does the arch hyphenation of society's "corruption," that the usual explanatory paradigms (sin and evil, betrayal in love, nature, and nurture) are insufficient. And yet the biography offered is made up precisely of those kinds of explanations. Croft's father thinks he was born "mean"; he spends his childhood tracking deer; he has been shaped by his work as a ranch hand, "busting" or taming horses; as a National Guardsman, he killed a man while breaking a strike; his sexual life has been violent and so has his marriage. Increasingly, he is defined by the things he destroys.

The events of the novel are similarly structured. General Cummings has his men build a bivouac to his very particular and perfectionist dictates. When it is finished, a storm lays waste to the camp. Lieutenant Hearn must negotiate Cummings's passive-aggressive demands upon him. Infuriated by the General's nagging, Hearn grinds a cigarette into Cummings's spotless tent floor, but must then humiliate himself by picking up the butt at the General's command or risk insubordination. Roth, a sensitive and intelligent soldier in Sergeant Croft's platoon, finds an injured bird that does more to lift his fellows' morale than any single event in the novel, but Croft crushes it in his hand. When Wilson, who has been presented as a sexual adventurer, is wounded in the stomach, four of the platoon members must carry him back to the beach, knowing that he will soon be dead from venereal disease, if not from his wound. And, most futile of all, Croft demands that the men climb Mount Anaka at the center of the island, believing this to be the best way to ascertain Japanese presence on the island but also compelled by the existence of the mountain itself. It is finally not the Japanese who defeat his purposes, but a nest of hornets. In any event, unknown to Croft and his men, the battle has meantime been won through a series of bumbling decisions made by Major Dalleson, whose primary job to that date has been office and supply management. Encountering a pilot on their return, they learn the campaign is over. The pilot remarks:

> "Jesus, I forgot you men were out on patrol for six days."
> Polack swore. "The whole thing's over, huh?"
> "Just about."
> "And we broke our ass for nothin.'"
> The pilot grinned, "Higher strategy."

When the remaining members of Croft's platoon learn what has happened in their absence, they respond with laughter. Mailer depicts this moment of release in terms of sexual humiliation, which has been a subtext in every encounter between enlisted men and officers. As the men imagine what their next assignment may be, the self-mocking jokes tumble out and grow increasingly sexist:

"We're gonna be Red Cross girls."
"They're puttin' the division on permanent KP" [kitchen patrol].
"Aaah, get the hell out, you're a bunch of goddam women."

Their laughter is "hysterical" and "close to tears." The mirth concludes with a bawdy song:

> Roll me over
> In the clover
> Roll me over,
> Lay me down
> And do it again.

The "higher strategy" directing military operations functions in the novel metonymically: like many aspects of the men's lives – parentage, upbringing, education, occupation – plans have been determined for them by a distant and indifferent power. Readers are invited to judge their behavior, whether heroic or craven, with compassion because we see how it has been motivated. General Cummings is driven by a Nietzschean will-to-power based in his conviction that the only "morality of the future" will be based upon the command of "superior" men over inferior. The events of the novel, however, do not bear out Cummings's view. If the men have risked their lives pointlessly in climbing Mount Anaka, the General's plans too have been thwarted. Because of happenstance, not he but the unimaginative bureaucrat Major Dalleson will receive credit for the breaking of the Japanese line. A further irony helps to structure *The Naked and the Dead*: the pervasive anti-Semitism of the soldiers. Hitler's view of mankind, his conviction that all men were *not* created equal, the Nazi conception of an Aryan "master" race – all these were crucial elements in the argument that World War II was a "just" war. But the soldiers of Mailer's army, except those who are themselves Jewish, express disdain and contempt for Jews throughout the novel. Similarly, the Japanese they fight are presented as having little regard for human life, but the American soldiers who kill them are also trained to set aside pity and respect. Encountering a faceless and nearly naked corpse, Red Valsen realizes "with surprise and shock, as if he were looking at a corpse for the first time, that a man was really a fragile thing." He thinks of battle as "the way a bunch of ants would kill each other." But by the time the whiskey he's drunk has turned into a headache, he mutters, "There damn sure ain't anything special about a man if he can smell as bad as he does when he's dead."

Praise for the novel centered on its realistic depiction of men at war – the book was "brutal" and "stark." It may be surprising then to see that Mailer considers compassion to be the book's major virtue. Mailer's fiction, in the course of a long career, has consistently threaded a narrow path between brutality and compassion. On the one hand, man's (*not* woman's) competitive, survivalist, dominating urges are unapologetically presented in his fiction and nonfiction as natural and necessary components of a functioning masculinity. Such a position put him at odds with twentieth-century feminists, sometimes in very public (and publicity-seeking) ways. He is dedicated to describing the powerful forces of modernity in America that distort men, making them unnatural, criminal, and murderous. Speaking broadly, all his novels are war novels: the embattled male seeks dignity even as he concedes he has little control over "higher strategy."

If Mailer's soldier serves in a repetitious and humiliating Hell, Heller's serves in a madhouse. Mailer's characters are distinguished one from another by class, education, and ethnicity, in keeping with the naturalist premises of the novel, but Heller's men and their commanders are distinguished primarily by their individual expressions of insanity – hypochondria, narcissism, manic depression, masochism, sadism, the full menu of twentieth-century disorders. The bombardiers are subject to "higher strategy" emanating in this case from a colonel whose ambition inspires him to increase the number of required missions each time the fliers reach the previously mandated number of required missions. To choose to opt out of this Sisyphean task, as the character Yossarian spends the novel attempting to do, is to confront "Catch-22." The regulation is explained, fittingly enough, by a doctor: Yossarian asks, "Is Orr [a fellow soldier] crazy?"

> "He sure is," Doc Daneeka said.
> "Can you ground him?"
> "I sure can. But first he has to ask me to. That's part of the rule" . . .
> "That's all he has to do to be grounded?"
> "That's all. Let him ask me."
> "And then you can ground him?" Yossarian asked.
> "No. Then I can't ground him."
> "You mean there's a catch?"
> "Sure there's a catch," Doc Daneeka replied. "Catch-22. Anyone who wants to get out of combat duty isn't really crazy."

Such nonsense can be seen in American vaudeville and film comedy – this is Laurel and Hardy, Abbott and Costello, and Groucho and

Chico Marx exchanging puns and other forms of double-talk. Also relevant and chronologically closer to the novel are the vaudeville-style conversations of Vladimir (Didi) and Estragon (Gogo) in Samuel Beckett's *Waiting for Godot* or the non sequiturs of Eugene Ionesco's *The Bald Soprano*. Language play in the "Theater of the Absurd," as it was named by critic Martin Esslin, had by the time of Heller's novel given artistic form to the premises of French existentialism. The chop-logic of these plays dramatizes the premise that a full explanation of life's purpose (whether in religious, philosophical, or scientific terms) was not merely deferred until some point of future revelation or discovery but was flatly non-existent. It is on the meaning of meaninglessness that Groucho and Chico, Didi and Gogo converge. "Nonsensical" sense has always implied the limits of rational meaning and the inadequacy of logic as an instrument for explaining human behavior.

Heller's methods of doubling and doubling back in *Catch-22* include not only the circularity of the titular military regulation, but scores of formal devices that reinforce the sense of a disorientation so complete as to be normal. Alliteration abounds (Colonel Cathcart, Doc Daneeka, Major Major, Dori Duz, Milo Minderbender), as do oppositions (Captain Black/Chief White Halfboat; General Dreedle and General Peckem, the novel's Tweedledee and Tweedledum). Even the double letters within names seem significant: Yossarian, Dreedle, Orr, Daneeka, Duckett, Dobbs, and Aardvaark. So do the puns on halves: Clevinger ("cleave"), Havermeyer. And the mirror-image pseudonym adopted for censoring letters is alternately Washington Irving or Irving Washington. Puns and capital letters explode the pomposity of military slogans: the Great Loyalty Oath Crusade, the Great Big Battle of Bologna ("Bologna," known in America primarily as a kind of meat, is pronounced "baloney" and is slang for meaninglessness). Heller for the most part eschews chronology in favor of replaying, with variations, a few major situations – the bombing of Bologna; Yossarian's repeated hospitalizations for a non-existent liver complaint; two passes over Ferrara; two missions to Bologna. the death of Snowden. The latter hellish incident, in which the young soldier is shot almost in two, becomes the occasion of painful wordplay. "Ou sont les Neigedens d'antan?" echoes the sadness of François Villon's question, "Where are the snows [*neiges*] of yesteryear?" When Milo Minderbender's capitalist deals come to a climax as he sells private planes to the Germans and directs from a control tower the bombing of his own outfit, the novel seems to have reached the apex of absurdity. But, in the final turn, he is forgiven because he has made a profit.

On the evidence of Mailer's and Heller's novels of World War II, the ideals of making the world "safe for democracy" and defending fundamental human rights seem naive, even ludicrous. Theirs was not the majority view. Today, the marking of special anniversaries of the war such as D-Day continues to honor the soldiers not only for the risks they took but for the principles their presence in the war symbolized. Nevertheless, even as the USA was praised for its role in war, critics asked how the country could assert itself globally on such issues when democratic principles and human rights were flouted within its own institutions? How could the nation justify the internment after 1941 of nearly 120,000 Japanese and Japanese Americans, two-thirds of whom were *nisei*, American citizens born in the USA.? Reception of the "Freedom Train" dramatically exposes the faultlines implicit in these questions. Between 1947 and 1949 a kind of mobile museum called the Freedom Train toured the United States. One car contained core documents of America's history: Jefferson's first draft of the Declaration of Independence, the Constitution as it had been annotated by George Washington, Lincoln's Gettysburg Address. A second car carried documents of Germany's and Japan's surrenders. The train drew thousands of Americans, and contemporary reports suggest that the slowly moving and quiet lines of citizens having come to reflect on these artifacts was a moving spectacle. And yet the city officials of Birmingham, Alabama, and Memphis, Tennessee, demanded that Jim Crow lines and separate visiting hours be established for African Americans. The organizers of the Freedom Train refused this request, but that the question should have been raised at all proves that "liberty and justice for all" was a pledge still unmet.

Upstream Against the Mainstream

The received wisdom about post-World War II America is that the 1950s were, in Robert Lowell's oft-quoted description, "tranquilized" ("Memories of West Street and Lepke"). This vision of American life would seem to contradict FDR's notion of "perpetual peaceful revolution." Stepping back from the events of the twentieth century, as one might step back from a pointillist painting to allow the dots to merge into an image, we can see that Lowell's conception of a decade of quietism seems largely accurate. Of the periods associated with radical rethinking of American laws and *mores*, one thinks of the Progressive Era (roughly the years 1890–1914), the 1930s, and – an era that falls outside the scope of this book – the 1960s. This perspective suggests a roughly thirty-year interval between major efforts at change; further, it suggests that American art and culture might have been substantially altered had the eras of change not been interrupted by two major wars. Certainly, male artists associated with literary modernism often spoke of their efforts having been arrested by the 1914 war. But Lowell's metaphor of the tranquilizer (also for him a regimen throughout much of his adult life) suggests that the complacency, normalcy, and domestic contentment portrayed in narratives of the 1950s conceal a psychological upheaval as potent as the social upheavals of more radical decades, a need for psychopharmaceutical tranquility when genuine tranquility is elusive.

In the sanitized version of the 1950s, mothers happily putter in their clean and conveniently outfitted kitchens; their husbands smoke pipes, carry briefcases, and announce, "Honey, I'm home" at the end of a day's unspecified work at an unspecified office; children are mischievous but also polite and basically well-behaved; houses are suburban and comfortable; schools are orderly if uninspiring; daily life is comfortingly predictable. This image of American life is largely a product of the mass media and advertising industry, though it is not without a basis in fact. This was the era in which the imagery of the American Dream and the American Way of Life became fixtures of America's self-presentation. When World War II concluded, a wave of strikes, releasing resentments held back during wartime, made it look as though economic recovery would be problematic. However, measures like the G.I. Bill eased the transition to a peacetime economy. The Bill effectively managed the number of re-entering workers by channeling them into training or education and also, via grants for home ownership, solidified commitment to the health of the economy and provided displaced female workers with a physical and psychological place to come home to. Home ownership surpassed renting; by 1960, one-quarter of the houses in which Americans lived had been built in the past decade. Television entered these homes and stayed there: in 1946, only 6,000 televisions were manufactured; by 1953, 7 million. Increasingly, Henry Luce's conception of life in the American Century was altered: his call for global dominance became for the majority of citizens a matter of domestic affluence, the American Way of Life defined as material well-being.

Alternative narratives to what we might call, after the popular television series, the "Father-Knows-Best" version of the 1950s, however, expressed barely repressed anxiety and potent forms of rebellion and resistance. It is in these stories that we will likely find the traces of "perpetual . . . revolution" running counter to the status quo, setting in motion the more dramatic eruptions of protest that characterized the 1960s. The most obvious manifestation of postwar anxiety is the Cold War itself. This tense rivalry and animus between the USA and the USSR comprised, on the American side, policies of "containment" regarding communist regimes; constant vigilance via international spy and counter-spy rings; "races" to stay ahead in science and technology, particularly in the build-up of nuclear armaments; "proxy" wars like the Korean "conflict" (never an officially declared war) of 1950–2; and directives from the US Office of Civil Defense about how to build a fallout shelter so as to survive nuclear war. Elementary school children were drilled to "duck and cover" under their desks in case of bombing. Many families kept supplies of canned food and bottled water – just in case. In the midst of prosperity and comfort, a family affluent enough to build a shelter could keep in its backyard a constant reminder of nuclear holocaust. Attacks on the "Un-American" were further evidence of fear: the House Un-American Activities Committee hearings and the wave of McCarthyism (discussed in chapter 1) were fueled by fear of communism; the CIO, one of two major labor organizations, conducted an anti-communist drive in 1949, leading to the expulsion of eleven unions. The civil defense instructions and drills responded to the prospect of invasion; the hunt for communists, to the possibility that the invasion had already occurred and dissidents moved among "us." Movies like *Invasion of the Body Snatchers* (1956) offered a barely disguised metaphor for alien takeover; a bit later, *The Manchurian Candidate* (a 1962 film based on a Richard Condon novel of 1959) dispensed with the metaphor entirely, depicting a US presidential candidate programmed by Chinese communists and managed by high-level American political insiders.

It would, however, be misleading to suggest that Americans were living in constant terror. On the contrary, critics of contented suburbanites complained that "the good life" engendered passivity and mindless acquiescence. John Kenneth Galbraith predicted, in *The Affluent Society* (1958), that public spaces, what is now often referred to as infrastructure, seemed to belong to nobody and therefore to be nobody's problem. Americans, he argued, drove their cars past billboards, litter, and polluted streams on roads that remained unpaved. This absence of a civic impulse was a frequent refrain of cultural commentary in the 1950s and 1960s. In contrast to calls for a sense of responsibility to the body politic were defenses of those forms of self-expression asserting the importance of individual eccentricity. At bottom, critiques of 1950s culture, whether emphasizing the common good or the exceptional individual, shared a similar motivating perception: surely there had to be something more to the American Dream than a brand-new car. The rebellious teenager, the "beat" aesthetic, the shift from the impersonal to the personal in American poetry, and the paintings of Abstract Expressionism chronicle that discomfort with comfort.

Delinquents and beats

In the Jazz Age, the bobbed hair, short skirts, and rouged lips of the flapper symbolized liberation to the young and degeneration to the old. In an Age of Anxiety, the young man in tight blue jeans and a black leather jacket was the image of youth gone wrong. In the same period that saw efforts to purge the nation of "Reds" and fellow travelers, America also turned anxious eyes toward its youth – particularly toward the group labeled "juvenile delinquents." In general, the juvenile delinquent (at least in the public mind) was a small-time law-breaker in a city, usually from a working-class family. Sociologists and psychologists implied that if delinquency were not curbed or treated and its breeding ground (the dysfunctional family, the city) not cleaned up, it would spread like a communicable disease. The work of the psychotherapist Dr. Fredric Wertham on the relationship between mass media and violence, in particular comic books, is a case in point. At a period in which the comic book was selling over 60 million copies a month, largely to a youth market, Wertham argued that images of violence and identification with superheroes were contributing to criminality among boys and young men. Publishing his theories in widely circulated magazines, *Saturday Review, Reader's Digest,* and the *Ladies Home Journal,* beginning in 1948, and in his book *Seduction of the Innocent* (1953), Wertham contributed to rising panic about dangerous tendencies in the young. Delinquency, like communism, got the attention of state and federal government. The New York State Joint Committee to Study the Publication of Comics conferred from 1949 to 1952. The US Senate Subcommittee to Investigate Juvenile Delinquency, established in 1953, began televised hearings in 1954 and issued the *Comic Books and Juvenile Delinquency Report* in 1955.

Comic books were only one cause of concern. Two other aspects of popular culture – rock-and-roll and movies – also seemed to many parents capable of tainting developing minds and undermining the values of the American Way of Life. Rock-and-roll, with its insistent percussion, made the sexual subtext of social dancing explicit, and the swiveling hips of Elvis ("the Pelvis") Presley epitomized sexual abandon and lawlessness. When the 21-year-old Elvis first appeared on the highly visible Ed Sullivan show in 1956, his hip movements so outraged the viewing public that by the time of his third appearance in the next year, he was filmed only from the waist up. Presley became (and remains for many) an icon of youthful sexual energy. But sex was not the only message. Buddy Holly, Bill Haley and his Comets, the Platters, Ritchie Valens, radio "disc jockeys," the television show *American Bandstand* – all gave to the American young a sense of themselves as a subculture, a mode of identity separate from the more regimented aspects of adult life in the 1950s. Being a teenager became an occupation and an affiliation.

It also became a market sector to be exploited. The film industry was quick to cater to this audience, using rock-music soundtracks and teenage settings (the high school, the malt shop, the drive-in) and devising plots for young, angry, but somehow sensitive anti-heroes. In *Blackboard Jungle* (1955), Glenn Ford, a World War II veteran and new teacher, must find a way to break through the disrespect and anger of his inner-city students. Music for the opening credits of the film was Bill Haley and his Comets' "Rock Around the Clock." More popular still were films that took the point of view of the outsider or misfit. Here the classic examples are Marlon Brando in *The Wild One* (1954) and James Dean in *Rebel Without a Cause* (1955). Though very different physical types, both actors were trained in the Method style of acting, which aimed for an effect of authentic feeling – one not playing to the audience or the camera. The combination of rough good looks and underplaying suggested a new kind of cool – one that chose not to fit in. The motorcycle gang leader played by Brando is introduced by a long shot of the open road; as the cycles draw nearer and come into focus, the inevitable effect is menace. What the gang brings to a small town is not so much crime as misrule: drinking, dancing, and dangerous competitions with their cycles. To Kathie, Johnny's (Brando's) love interest in the film, the life he represents is both tantalizing and frightening. When he tells her that he and his gang "have a ball" on the weekends, she asks, "And what do you do? I mean, do you just ride around? Or do you go on some sort of a picnic or something?" Johnny replies:

"A picnic? Man you are *too* square . . . Now, listen, you don't *go* any one special place. That's cornball style. You just go. [He snaps his fingers.] A

FIGURE 12   *The Wild One*, 1953
Photograph Columbia Pictures / Album / akg-images
Marlon Brando in "bad-boy" mode. When asked what he is against,
the character replies, "What've you got?"

bunch get together after all week it builds up, you just . . . the idea is to
have a ball. Now if you gonna stay cool, you got to wail. You got to put
somethin' down. You got to make some jive. Don't you know what I'm
talkin' about?"

She doesn't but she'd like to. His leather jacket and tight denims, his speech littered with hipster vocabulary borrowed from black jazz musicians and their followers, and his insouciance all represent an exotic and free-wheeling world of which she has had no experience. As the young men and women dance in Kathie's father's bar, someone shouts: "Hey, Johnny. What are you rebelling against?" He replies, "What've you got?"

In *Rebel Without a Cause*, the source of the character's angst is similarly amorphous. Jim Stark (Dean) is introduced to the viewer as a drunk in a gutter. We learn that he is new to the town, that he has been in trouble before, that he has a difficult relationship with his parents, that he is profoundly lonely. But the background is not deep and his problems not sufficiently defined to be solvable. The two teenagers with whom Jim bonds form a surrogate family, with Jim as father-figure to the childlike Plato and Judy as the mother; all three teenagers feel alienated from their families because of inadequate love and attention. Here are young people from the middle class capable of the delinquency previously tied to poverty and urban life, and yet they are also sensitive and sympathetic with one another. Jim is no tough guy but cries openly. Despite the more contained and sanitized environment in which these characters live, they feel empty and can imagine no better future for themselves. James Dean's death in a car crash at the age of 24 helped to glamorize the notion of a young person too "good" for the world, one who saw through the fakeries of materialism and the repression of feeling seemingly required by American normalcy. To live fast and die young seemed an appealing alternative to the deadness of habit and compliance on offer in the American suburbs. Neither Brando's Johnny nor Dean's Jim has an identifiable "cause" for rebellion; nor does their younger literary brother Holden Caulfield of J. D. Salinger's *The Catcher in the Rye*. The cause, we are given to understand, is so pervasive as to be American culture itself.

In literature the cognate form of youthful rebellion was the beat movement, though its chief figures were hardly teenagers. Allen Ginsberg was 30 years old when he wrote *Howl* (1955), the long poem that is the touchstone for the movement; Jack Kerouac was 35 when he published *On The Road* in 1957. To be beat, as Kerouac and Ginsberg glossed the term, was to declare both a condition of mind and a remedy. "Beat" meant exhausted and beaten down, at odds with the system, an unapologetic declaration of unfitness for the workaday world, and defiance of authority. "Beat," for Ginsberg particularly, also implied "beatitude," a perspective inspired by revelations, drugs, sexual ecstasy, and a madness saner than sanity, seeking to be one of the "angel-headed hipsters" of *Howl* "burning for the ancient heavenly connection." Inspiration, taken literally, means being breathed into by the spirit and made capable of prophecy. The beat aesthetic prized spontaneity, orality, protest, improvisation, freedom of movement, an ecstatic present. Johnny's speech to Kathie in *The Wild One* is a reasonable summary of the values: "You just go." The movement began in New York but prospered and became famous in San Francisco, particularly after *Howl* was judged obscene and copies confiscated by San Francisco police. Other writers associated with the movement include Kenneth Rexroth, Gary Snyder, Lawrence Ferlinghetti, Diane di Prima, William Everson, and Gregory Corso. Far from being thoughtless or merely contrary, the beat movement was a conscious return to an opposition as old as that between Dionysus and Apollo. More immediately, the roots were Romantic. Ginsberg claimed to have had a vision of William Blake, and his stance against Moloch (materialism, repression, mechanization) in *Howl* has much in common with Blake's "mind-forg'd manacles" and "charter'd streets" in his poem "London." The beats' strongest American precursor is Walt Whitman, whose *Leaves of Grass* extolled a vision of liberty in mind and body – and in the body politic – and whose commitment was to erase divisions of class, race, and property in favor of universal brotherhood. A less obvious American model is Emily Dickinson. Her form, of course, has little in common with the long lines of Ginsberg's poetry and the rhythms of Kerouac's prose, but her attachment to eccentricity, her conviction that "Much madness is divinest sense / To a discerning eye" is a touchstone for the beats' sense of reality. Indeed, the equation of madness with sense, central to *Catch-22*, would serve as a common premise in work by Ken Kesey (*One Flew Over the Cuckoo's Nest*, 1962) and other writers of the 1960s who shared the "beat" point of view.

The beat writers, for all the drama and eccentricity of their lives, had counterparts in popular culture. Indeed, part of the irony of the beat, as of the "hippie" culture of the 1960s, was the rapidity with which a set of ideas was translated into consumables. The word "Beatnik" was a coinage of the popular press. If to *be* beat meant a radical change in one's way of life, to *appear* beat meant to wear black turtlenecks, sunglasses, a goatee (for men) or heavy eyeliner (for women) – essentially a matter of shopping – and to frequent coffee houses, jazz clubs, and poetry readings – essentially a matter of selecting forms of entertainment. By 1959 the Beatnik had been domesticated in the bumbling Maynard G. Krebs of the television comedy *The Many Loves of Dobie Gillis*; a year earlier, the hipster had transmogrified into the hair-combing, finger-snapping parking-lot attendant and amateur private investigator Kookie in *77 Sunset Strip*. Commercialization of the anti-commercial is a reliable pattern of capitalism.

Poetry and the New Criticism

The beats' embrace of the irrational and its return to Romantic principles may be understood not only as a response to Moloch, but also as a strategic defense against the institutionalization of modern poetry. The exemplary poem of modernism's avant-garde was, from 1922, T. S. Eliot's *The Waste Land*. But just as the anti-commercial has a way of becoming a sales item, so does the avant-garde become the mainstream. By 1949, Delmore Schwartz was complaining in *Partisan Review* about "The Literary Dictatorship of T. S. Eliot." How this dictatorship came about is a complex history about which opinions are divided and conclusions still unclear. But a number of markers offer solid evidence that Schwartz assessed the situation correctly. By the end of World War II there was no longer any question about modern poetry's acceptance in the university curriculum. In fact, enrollments in modern literature courses increased remarkably, and universities routinely appointed poets to academic posts. As Cynthia Ozick recalled in a 1989 memoir of those days, T. S. Eliot was "absolute art, high art, when art was at its most serious and élitist."[9] In part, Eliot's stature was a result of his influential critical essays and books and his editing of the journal *Criterion*, which had in turn given impetus to the method of literary study known as the New Criticism. The New Critics, among them Allen Tate, John Crowe Ransom, William Wimsatt, Cleanth Brooks, and Robert Penn Warren, espoused a set of practices involving microscopically close reading of the text, which, while aiming to attend to the tensions, paradoxes, and ambiguities of the poem, also sought to demonstrate the cooperation of those forces in creating a unified object.[10] Although well versed in history themselves, their methods paid little attention to historical context, the poet's biography, or other matters tangential to the words on the page. The textbook *Understanding Poetry* (a 1938 anthology devised by Brooks and Warren) forbade notice of such matters. The titles of Cleanth Brooks's *The Well-Wrought Urn* and William Wimsatt's *Verbal Icon* suggest the New Critical premise of the autotelic, self-contained poem. Many of these highly influential methods were derived from an Eliotic principle, first articulated in *The Sacred Wood* in 1920, that poetry was to be treated as poetry, and not some other thing: not a sermon, not a thinly disguised biography, not a *cri de coeur*, not merely a vehicle for pleasure. In short, the poem was to be understood as an object worthy of concentrated intellectual attention on its own terms, freed of the demand for usability. New Critical practice put a premium on discernible and unified complexity, and these criteria, in turn, meant that university curricula and criticism favored some kinds of poetry over others. The professionalization of criticism, both inside the universities and in scholarly and journalistic venues, meant that between (roughly) 1930 and 1960, some kinds of poetry received attention and plaudits, while other sorts – less suited to analysis by New Critical methods – were given brief or dismissive notice.

A simplified version of the break from academically approved poetry is Robert Lowell's exposure to the San Francisco scene, which occasioned his turn from the densely allusive, intellectually challenging, and "closed" poetic forms that characterized his early work (*Lord Weary's Castle* in 1946; *The Mills of the Kavanaughs* in 1951) to the more personal and painful topics and open forms of *Life Studies* (1959). Lowell characterized the difference as the "cooked" versus the "raw." The Lowell conversion often serves in literary histories as a synecdoche of the larger shift in American poetic practice during the 1950s and 1960s. It is, like many convenient stories, not entirely true, for it overlooks poetry not fitting the "confessional" category with which Lowell became associated. It neglects the poems being written by so-called New York poets, especially the highly personal poetry of Frank O'Hara, for example. It ignores Black Mountain, the experimental college in North Carolina where Charles Olson was working out the concept of Projective Verse and the work of Robert Creeley, editing the *Black Mountain Review* from Mallorca and basing his poetic line on breath and chance. It does not account easily for the Objectivists (among them, Louis Zukofsky, Lorine Niedecker, and George Oppen), nor for the deep image poets (Robert Bly, Louis Simpson, William Stafford, and James Wright). In short, while the official version of modern American poetry dominated the schools and publishers, vigorous revision and change were already in place, and these revisions extended beyond the "rawness" of confessional poetry. Donald Allen's 1960 anthology *The New American Poetry* brought these other poetries into public view.

The rebellion against New Critical dicta and poetic orthodoxy took many forms, from the length of the line to the lack of closure to the conception of how ideas come to a poet and how fully in control the poet can or should be. Another important principle, espoused by Eliot at times, and by New Critics nearly always, was that the poem should be impersonal. Ginsberg's oeuvre takes the opposite stance: the poem *must be* personal, must be a representation of intense feeling and opinion; further, whatever critique of society the poem undertakes must be understood to have personal consequences. These working assumptions are clearly tied to a Romantic ethos of sincerity and authenticity. Poetry normally designated as "confessional," that is, work by John Berryman, Anne Sexton, Sylvia Plath, W. D. Snodgrass, and Robert Lowell, takes sincerity to excoriating extremes. Steeped in the language of psychoanalysis, colored by dream imagery and recollections of trauma, and revelatory of feelings and subject matter that can shock readers, these poems differ one from another in nearly every way but this one basic commitment to a kind of fierce truth-telling. While the poems are rarely overtly political in subject matter, they carry political force of another sort, depending as they do on the articulation of intimacies rarely speakable in public – suicide, self-loathing, sexual function and dysfunction, menstruation, murderous hatred and anger.

Abstract Expressionism

Anglo-American literary modernism had begun with iconoclastic energies – breaking free of "gentility," sloughing off sentimentality, blasting complacencies, revising form. But, as the previous brief history of postwar American poetry suggests, modernism, as established in universities and journals, along with the critical practices that modernism (or, at least, Eliot) had dictated, became for many writers the icon to be smashed. The causes for this turn range from "the anxiety of influence" to boredom with another generation's vocabularies and strategies, from a need to make a mark of one's own to temperaments that chafed against any sort of officialdom.

These attitudes had consequences in painting, too. While allowing for the manifest differences between painting and writing, we can observe throughout the twentieth century notable partnerships and cross-fertilizations. William Carlos William and Charles DeMuth; Frank O'Hara and Larry Rivers. Robert Creeley and R. B. Kitaj. There are parallels in critical practice as well. Clement Greenberg's installation of the Abstract Expressionists as the true representatives of American art employs rhetoric strikingly comparable to that of the early Eliot, which was echoed throughout the years of high modernism. Here again is Eliot explaining why poetry must be difficult:

[I]t appears likely that poets in our civilisation, as it exists at present, must be *difficult*. Our civilisation comprehends great variety and complexity, and this variety and complexity, playing upon a refined sensibility, must produce various and complex results. The poet must become more and more comprehensive, more allusive, more indirect, in order to force, to dislocate if necessary, language into his meaning. ("The Metaphysical Poets," first published *Times Literary Supplement*, 1921)

And here is Greenberg on why painting must change:

the closed-form canon – the canon of the profiled, circumscribed shape – as established by Matisse, Picasso, Mondrian, and Miró – seems less and less able to incorporate contemporary feeling. ("Art," *The Nation*, 1948)

These statements by influential taste-makers share a number of assumptions: that the times in which their readers live require a new kind of art, that this new art must be clearly different from what went before if it is to reflect contemporary reality, and that the discerning audience being addressed (implicitly because of the publishing venues selected) will assist the project of taking taste in its proper direction.

These pronouncements are at least in part self-serving: Eliot was remarkably successful in creating readers for his poems, and Greenberg had already declared his allegiance to "high art" over "kitsch" in "Avant-Garde and Kitsch" (*Partisan Review*, 1939). For Greenberg, American art could renew itself only by a strong move away from figurative representation and the populist, social-realist values of the 1930s. A strong art was necessary for the world's strongest nation. In language invoking Henry Luce's "American Century," Greenberg declared that "the main premises of Western art have at last migrated to the United States" ("The Decline of Cubism," *Partisan Review*, 1948). As supporter-in-chief of the painters who came by 1950 to be labeled "Abstract Expressionists," Greenberg exerted influence on criticism, gallery shows, and the art market that made his power comparable to Eliot's "literary dictatorship."

But just as the "difficult" privileges only one of the aesthetic standards followed in the early years of modernist writing, "abstract" is a term that obscures the specific qualities of paintings and painters, including the Abstract Expressionists themselves. In the galleries of the Museum of Modern Art where the paintings of Jackson Pollock, Clyfford Still, Barnett Newman, Mark Rothko, Willem de Kooning, and Robert Motherwell may be observed *seriatim*, the range of styles

in the paintings resists the effort to define what Abstract Expressionism was. Pollock's famous "drip" paintings have an utterly different
effect from Rothko's mesmerizing squares of color; Willem de Kooning's
color palette is nothing like the black ovoids of Motherwell's (for
example in *Elegy to the Spanish Republic, 54*). What the paintings share
most is what they eschew, that is, they do not represent the human
figure (and de Kooning's *Woman* series gives the lie even to this
distinction); they do not, except in their titles, suggest narrative content; they do not seek to hide their painterliness in tricks of the eye.
The canvases are usually large (significantly, much too large for most
domestic settings) and the painted surface often flat (apart from the
texture of the Pollock drips). The paintings are, though in different
ways, assertive and arresting.

The size and assertiveness of Abstract Expressionist painting may
well have contributed to the sense that America now had an art fit
to be at the center of the world stage. The painters were presented by
the art press as evidence that America had not just "caught up" with
Europe but surpassed its achievements. A show entitled "The New
American Painting" toured Europe in 1958–9, spreading this message.
Jackson Pollock, filmed and photographed as he stood above the
canvas he had laid on the floor, moved over its surface with athletic
grace and exemplified the "action" in action painting. As Erika Doss
explains, Pollock became a symbol of the virility and seriousness
of American painting, mythologized as "a freedom-seeking postwar
individual, a tormented hero/artist outcast, the alienated figure of
Kierkegaard, Camus, and Sartre's existential philosophy.... such
imagery cast the American Expressionists as serious artistic tough
guys, and the movement itself as an all-male club."[11] And indeed many
of the painters lived in New York, competed with one another, and
met to drink and argue at "clubs" like the Cedar Tavern. The women
artists whose work is comparable – Lee Krasner, Helen Frankenthaler,
Grace Hartigan, and Elaine de Kooning – received, in comparison,
little attention. The work of African American painters Romare Bearden
and Norman Lewis was similarly slighted. In this exclusivity, too, the
retailing of Abstract Expressionism is strikingly similar to the high-
modernist literary narrative.

To read essays and interviews with the painters under consideration here, however, is to learn how little the artists saw themselves
as ambassadors for America. In the *Museum of Modern Art Bulletin*
1956–7, Pollock discounted the notion of a specifically American
painting:

The idea of an isolated American painting, so popular in this country during the thirties, seems absurd to me, just as the idea of creating a purely American mathematics or physics would seem absurd. . . . An American is an American and his painting would naturally be qualified by that fact. But the basic problems of contemporary painting are independent of any country.

Similarly, Robert Motherwell's 1951 comments about the motives of painting resemble those of the beats, not what would be congenial to the State Department:

abstract art represents the particular acceptances and rejections of men living under the conditions of modern times. If I were asked to generalize about this condition as it has been manifest in poets, painters, and composers during the last century and a half, I should say that it is a fundamentally romantic response to modern life – rebellious, unconventional, sensitive, irritable . . . (*MOMA Bulletin*, 1951)

Both artists show a consciousness of their place in a larger art-historical context, not easily reducible to either an assertion of nationality or a manifesto for a specific school of painting. Further, if the paintings seem to direct us to the surface of the canvas, comments from the painters direct us to psychological depths, Jungian analysis, the search for a personally meaningful mode of expression, the use of movement or action or other routes to spontaneity to unleash emotion and allow the painting a life. Pollock spoke of being *in* his painting: "I have no fears about making changes, destroying the image, etc., because the painting has a life of its own. I try to let it come through."

An important critique of the kind of formalist approach associated with Clement Greenberg appeared in 1972, and thus is outside the scope of this text. But it is worth quoting from Leo Steinberg's "Other Criteria" because its expression of the limits of formal analysis is relevant both to current revisions within art history and to the ways in which poets developed alternatives to the New Critical poem. Steinberg writes that he finds himself "constantly in opposition to what is called formalism," not because he distrusts formal analysis or its serious practitioners, but "because I mistrust their certainties, their apparatus of quantification, their self-righteous indifference to that part of artistic utterance which their tools do not measure. I dislike above all their interdictory stance – the attitude that tells an artist what he ought not to do, and the spectator what he ought not to see."[12]

Steinberg's comment is applicable also to the interdictory stances that New Criticism sometimes took, its list of what we are not to wonder about when we read a poem, its inability to provide positive criteria for the long poem, or indeed for any poem that fell outside its idea of complexity.

The perturbations considered here – teenage angst, rock-and-roll, beat poetry, confessional poetry, and an expressionism that is more vital, personal, and various than its critical promotion suggested – are vivid against the bland background of normalcy, national power, and material well-being. But, borrowing Erika Doss's term, why did the "tough guys" need to be – or at least appear to be – tough? Why the enchantment with motorcycle riders, jailhouse rockers, rebels? In the years of high modernism, 1900–1930 or so, there was a similarly masculinist and rebellious rhetoric, though without the overtly criminal overtones or glamour. It seemed important to writers like Joyce, Eliot, Pound, and others to assert masculine rights to the arts and to avoid the taint of softness or sentimentality. As a result of feminist scholarship, these rhetorics have been identified and analyzed for some thirty years now. When we survey postwar writing or peruse the tables of contents of anthologies, we note that the number of women included in the literary histories is small, though it is clear that women were writing and publishing with considerable success. The history of Black Mountain College is largely about its men (with little to say about M. C. Richards or Francine duPlessix Gray); Denise Levertov, considered part of the "school," was never in fact present at the college. Occasionally, women are mentioned in histories of the beat movement, Diane di Prima for example, but no revision of the history will cause Ginsberg or Kerouac to yield up their roles as central figures. For the mid-century poets who might be thought of as "second-generation" modernists – John Berryman, Theodore Roethke, Randall Jarrell, and so forth – only Elizabeth Bishop rates as much attention. Adrienne Rich, a bit later, was lauded by male critics and fellow poets for her craft when she wrote poetry of the expected sort, but her reception would change as she began to explore life outside the domestic sphere. Only with the confessional poets, those most overtly personal, did women begin to receive as much attention as that accorded men.

When we think broadly about the cultural scene in the postwar period (1945–60), it once again seems to be a man's world. The shift of the workforce back to a male majority, the renewed emphasis on full-time mothering and housewifery, and the war itself may all have

assisted in valorizing masculine physical traits and reinstating a patri-
archal order. The Hollywood vogue for "tough broads" and "irreverent
dames" in the 1930s and 1940s had ended. All signs point to forces
that sent women back home. Attention turned to men – their re-
entry into civilian life, their need to earn a living, their traumas, their
pain. The plight of the returning veteran was insistently tied to the
reaffirmation of men's virility in the domestic sphere, as breadwin-
ners and as husbands and fathers. William Wyler's *The Best Years of
Our Lives*, a film of 1946, portrays the physical adaptation of an amputee
to an altered sexuality, the reassertion of respect for the father's lead-
ership of the family, the right of a man to marry a decent girl who will
give him children and stability. The consolations of home and family
were, understandably, high on the list of desires, and thus a modernized Victorian angel of the hearth reappears, keeping house without
servants but with the aid of electronic appliances, and dressed in the
wasp-waisted, stereotypically feminine clothing inspired by Christian
Dior's "New Look."

The privileging of the nuclear, father-centered home could not,
however, please all or please long. "Outsider" status, promoted primarily but not exclusively by the younger generation, gave breathing
room to modes of life not validated by the stamp of normalcy. Ginsberg
and O'Hara articulated homosexual eroticism and friendship; Plath,
Sexton, and Rich, the entrapments of being a "good girl"; Kerouac
and the motorcyclists, the freedom of the road to nowhere in particular. The paintings of Abstract Expressionism, like John Berryman's
Dream Songs, portrayed the unconscious, the irrational, the depths
below the surface; rock-and-roll celebrated unregulated, exuberant
sexuality. Added to these artistic means of imagining and acting upon
alternatives to the mainstream was a critical literature, some of it
from émigrés with direct experience of totalitarianism, arguing that
the line between voluntary consensus and state-mandated agreement
was easily crossed. Thus, commentators like Wilhelm Reich and Herbert
Marcuse kept alive the minority opinion that repression, whether as a
result of capitalism, conformist practices in business and social life, or
the privileging of some sexualities over others, did not exist only in
overtly tyrannical regimes. Resistance to the "normal" in all these
arenas was conducted largely on behalf of the personal, of the inter-
nal emotional, sexual, and psychological depths and eccentricities of
the individual. Once the outer "hot" war was concluded and peace
restored, these writers and artists explored the insight expressed by
Marianne Moore quoted in the headnote to this chapter: "There never

was a war that was / not inward; I must / fight till I have conquered in myself what / causes war."

"An Inescapable Network of Mutuality"

The title of this section is taken from Martin Luther King, Jr.'s "Letter from Birmingham Jail": "Injustice anywhere is a threat to justice everywhere. We are caught in an inescapable network of mutuality, tied in a single garment of destiny." In 1963, imprisoned for a "direct action" demonstration against segregation, King composed the letter in response to a newspaper-published letter from eight Alabama clergyman criticizing his actions. What, they asked, was King doing in Alabama? His own flock was in Georgia. Why not give the newly elected mayor of Birmingham time to act before instigating demonstrations? Why, as a churchman, did he condone lawbreaking? Ostensibly a direct response to these questions, the "Letter from Birmingham Jail" is far more: a document reiterating Gandhi's principles of nonviolent resistance and a restatement of justification for civil disobedience comparable both to the Declaration of Independence and Henry David Thoreau's "Resistance to Civil Government" (or "Civil Disobedience") in 1849. "Unjust laws exist," Thoreau wrote,

> shall we be content to obey them, or shall we endeavor to amend them, and obey them until we have succeeded, or shall we transgress them at once? Men, generally, under such a government as this, think that they ought to wait until they have persuaded the majority to alter them. They think that, if they should resist, the remedy would be worse than the evil. But it is the fault of the government itself that the remedy is worse than the evil. . . . Why does it not cherish its wise minority?

America had historically cherished *no* minority, as King reminded his readers. In particular, African Americans had "waited for more than 340 years for our constitutional and God-given rights." And, while individuals might become enlightened, "it is a historical fact that privileged groups rarely give up their privileges voluntarily." The clergymen, he gently remonstrates, have asked the wrong question; they should worry not about the demonstrations but about the conditions that had occasioned them. King extends the notion of America's "destiny" to include full rights for all its citizens. Pointedly employing not only the language of the Constitution but the metaphor of the nation as a whole cloth (a "garment"), he turns the rhetorical bases of freedom into evidence of their inapplicability to millions of American citizens.

The same reminder of unkept promises finds another, equally American, metaphor – money – in his famous speech ("I Have a Dream") at the march on Washington in the same year:

> In a sense we've come to our nation's capital to cash a check. When the architects of our republic wrote the magnificent words of the Constitution and the Declaration of Independence, they were signing a promissory note to which every American was to fall heir. . . . It is obvious today that America has defaulted on this promissory note, insofar as her citizens of color are concerned. . . .
>
> But we refuse to believe that the bank of justice is bankrupt. We refuse to believe that there are insufficient funds in the great vaults of opportunity of this nation. And so, we've come to cash this check, a check that will give us upon demand the riches of freedom and the security of justice.

The themes of unkept promises, of the God-given dignity of every person, of the unequally shared wealth of a large and powerful nation with more than adequate resources – America's critics have repeatedly measured the realities of their lives against these ideals as a means of calling America to account. In the era before the Civil War, abolitionists built their argument on these premises; in 1848 at Seneca Falls women based their declaration of rights on the Declaration of Independence; Progressives at the turn of the century pressed for social policies to ameliorate the inequities faced by immigrants and the urban poor; in the 1920s, the writers and artists of the Harlem Renaissance called for racial equity and racial pride; in the 1930s, the communist and socialist systems seemed to a significant number of careful, idealistic thinkers to offer a social vision more cognizant of human needs and rights than did that of their native country; after World War II, these same idealists faced the disappointment of those expectations and, further, disappointment in their fellow citizens for the ease with which they settled for less than universal equality. The language of freedom, especially as espoused in the nation's founding, has proved a durable means by which to assert America's failings and urge change.

The Civil Rights movement is normally dated from about 1954 to 1965, from the Supreme Court ruling Brown v. Topeka Board of Education to the Voting Rights Act that prohibited the use of literacy tests and poll taxes to prevent African Americans from voting. These dates are coincident with the development of so-called "counter-cultures" discussed in the previous sections. Notably, the apotheosis of the misfit and the premium placed on personal expression observable in those trends is primarily a phenomenon of the white middle classes. While white rebels opposed conformity and thus the idea of "belong-ing," the Civil Rights movement advocated collective action. Here was group identification in the service of a different form of liberatory action that could not be effective without a politically and racially defined agenda.

In 1955, two African American men were murdered for trying to register African American voters. The case created little interest. In the same year, a 14-year-old Mississippi boy, acting on a dare from his friends, spoke in flirtatious tones to a white woman as she left a local store. The boy, Emmett Till, was murdered. He was found in the Tallahatchie River, one eye gouged out and his neck wound round with barbed wire. Despite eyewitness testimony against them, the brother and husband of the woman Emmett had spoken to were found not guilty by a jury composed entirely of white males. This case, perhaps because it focused on the death of a child, got national attention. In the same year, a 43-year-old African American seam-stress in Montgomery, Alabama, Rosa Parks, refused to give up her seat on a bus to a white man. She was arrested. Fifty leaders of the African American community met at a church the following night to consider what to do, among them Martin Luther King, Jr. The outcome was the Montgomery bus boycott. The bus company lost revenues; King was fined $500. Within the year, the Supreme Court had ruled that bus segregation, like school segregation, was unconstitutional.

Although the case against the school board of Topeka, Kansas, had been decided three years earlier (in Brown v. Topeka Board of Education), the schools of Little Rock, Arkansas, did not begin deseg-regation until 1957. On the first day the new policy was to operate, nine African American students were blocked from entering the school by National Guardsmen – acting on the orders of the state's governor. When an injunction prevented the governor from continuing that practice, the students returned to the school – to find their entrance obstructed by a mob of townspeople. Before the students could begin their school year, President Dwight D. Eisenhower ordered 1,000 para-troopers and 10,000 National Guardsmen to assure their safe entry. This was the last of the major episodes in the 1950s. In 1960, an

African American student in Greensboro, North Carolina, was refused service at a lunch counter at a downtown Woolworth's. The next day, he returned with three friends. And then, still not served, they returned day after day. *The New York Times* newspaper ran a story. More local students, including white students, joined them. And their example was followed by students in other cities over the next two months. Senator John F. Kennedy, a presidential candidate, sent a message of support to the students in Atlanta, Georgia. They had shown, he suggested, a way to stand up for rights – by sitting down. King and other leaders would employ this tactic of passive resistance for the next several years as the movement gathered momentum.

For the next five years, until the passage of the Voting Rights Act, Civil Rights activism received unprecedented notice, in part because television had become available in most American homes. Televised dissent was a strategy employed throughout the decade, and the meanings of television as a form of mass culture generated lively debate. For the Canadian Marshall McLuhan (*Understanding Media*, 1964), for example, a mass medium like television was a powerful tool of reform, capable of creating a "global village"; on the other hand, the equation of mass media with totalitarianism, passive spectatorship, and the routinization of violence – the equation of mass culture with debased intellectual and moral values, in short – called into question the true usability of the medium for the public good. While this is not a debate that has closed, nor perhaps one that is even capable of conclusion, the Civil Rights movement was *seen* by Americans in a way uncommon in the history of US dissent to that date.

Whether because of public awareness or because of other conditions long in the making, some of which have been explored in this book, the idea of "rights" as a primary meaning of "freedom" took hold in postwar American culture. The cry "Freedom now," the rhetoric of liberation from slavery, the employment of the biblical story of Exodus, the refusal to be ignored, the methods of passive resistance – the African American precedent provided models and inspiration for other movements in the following decades: for women, for those gay or lesbian, for the disabled, for oppressed ethnic and racial minorities, Native Americans, Hispanic Americans, Asian Americans, and others. These and like movements have combined collective action with rhetorical emphasis on the individual. Each *individual* has rights to equal treatment and equal access, whether to protection under the law in such matters as pay and education, or control of the body in such matters as reproduction and sexual expression. Simultaneously, however, group identification, affiliation according to ethnicity, color, sexual orientation, gender, or other markers of likeness, has provided a sense of common cause. And beyond these two modes of self-understanding there lies another: King's "inescapable network of mutuality" that defines the interdependence of a nation's citizens and a sense of global responsibility.

In *The Souls of Black Folk* (1903), W. E. B. Du Bois described the burden of double-consciousness:

> the Negro is a sort of seventh son, born with a veil, and gifted with second-sight in this American world, – a world which yields him no true self-consciousness, but only lets him see himself through the revelation of the other world. It is a peculiar sensation, this double-consciousness, this sense of always looking at one's self through the eyes of others, of measuring one's soul by the tape of a world that looks on in amused contempt and pity. One ever feels his two-ness, – an American, a Negro; two souls, two thoughts, two unreconciled strivings; two warring ideals in one dark body, whose dogged strength alone keeps it from being torn asunder. (p. 243)

Du Bois's concern is for the members of his race. Their history is unique because of the "peculiar" institution of slavery and the racism that kept it strong and then outlasted it. Without then discounting that specificity and its historical importance, we may also consider his formulation as relevant to the life of any person who expresses dissent because of personally experienced injustice and who nevertheless assents to and feels loyalty for the principles of American freedom, those inalienable rights that have been honored and dishonored in American history. To be an "American" (itself a contested label) and to be simultaneously oneself with the permutations and allegiances that shape identity – this, too, is a perpetual revolution furnishing endless motives for, and variations of, judgment, negotiation, inclusion, exclusion, acceptance, refusal, and commitment.

In 1960 Robert Lowell, invited to participate in the Boston Arts Festival, read "For the Union Dead," a poem commissioned by the festival organizers. Originally titled "Colonel Shaw and the Massachusetts 54th," the poem presents a central figure both historical and monumental: Shaw, a white man, led a regiment composed solely of black soldiers; the figure or memorial of him and his men, a bronze bas-relief designed by Augustus St. Gaudens, stands directly opposite the Boston State House. Shaw and his regiment were killed in the

Civil War battle at Fort Wagner and were buried together in a mass grave. Though the Confederate soldiers intended disrespect in this ditch-burial, they in fact complied with Shaw's expressed desire not to exercise his right as an officer to be returned home for burial. He wished instead to be buried with the men he led.

The monument is literally central to the work; it is described in stanzas 6 through 13 of a seventeen-stanza poem. The first five stanzas focus on a childhood memory of a visit to the now abandoned South Boston Aquarium and a more recent memory ("One morning last March") of watching steam shovels digging out space for a parking garage. In both, the speaker describes himself as pressed against a barrier, first the glass of the aquarium ("my nose crawled like a snail on the glass") and then the "barbed and galvanized / fence on the Boston Common." The image of a boy with a nose like a snail merges into one of "cowed and compliant" fish with "noses," which gives way to that of "yellow dinosaur steam shovels" – attributing animal traits to humans, human traits to animals, and animal traits to machines, and then describing machines as digging a large ditch for more machines. Mixed, permeable categories are established from line 2, where the aquarium "stands / in a Sahara of snow." Yet many of the oppositions in the poem lead the reader to expect clear boundaries: the past versus the present; the monument versus the parking garage; the war monument versus the Mosler Safe that withstood a nuclear blast; "sparse sincere rebellion" versus "savage servility"; the "bell-cheeked Negro infantry" of the monument (stanza 7) more vital than the "drained faces of Negro children" on the speaker's television (stanza 15); the fish of childhood memory (stanza 2) debased as the "giant finned cars" of the final stanza.

In the opposing images, the present appears consistently inferior to the past, but this effect is suggestively blurred by other elements in the poem. In stanza 2 we read, "my hand tingled / to burst the bubbles"; in stanza 5, the transition to description of the monument, "A girdle of orange, Puritan-pumpkin-colored girders / braces the tingling Statehouse, shaking." The remainder of the sentence is incomplete until the end of the next stanza: "over the excavations, as it faces Colonel Shaw / and his bell-cheeked Negro infantry / on St. Gaudens' shaking Civil War relief, / propped by a plank splint against the garage's earthquake." Two instances of tingling, two of shaking, and then an earthquake. The tremors of the poem lead to but never quite eventuate in breakdown. The tingling hand "draws back," the buildings are girdled, braced, and propped. The bubble never bursts, though Colonel Shaw "riding on his bubble" "waits for the blessed break." The faces of the Negro school children are drained and yet they "rise like balloons," pointedly analogous to the unburst bubble, as the speaker "crouches" before his television, once again on the wrong side of the glass.

Formal elements of the poem also tremble between stability and instability. The stanzas are all quatrains but the line-lengths are irregular. Lowell employs no end-rhyme but a highly dense pattern of alliteration and assonance: in stanza 4, for example, "grunting," "mush," "grass," "gouge," "garage." Lines in other stanzas repeat the pattern: "lots luxuriate like civic sandpiles"; "propped by a plank splint against"; stanza 17, "giant finned cars nose forward like fish / a savage servility / slides by on grease." The tone and meaning of the final stanza are a clear indictment of present values. Other meanings are not so stable. An established image like the ditch appears in an unexpected sentence: "The ditch is nearer." To whom? Nearer in space or in time? Then, "Space is nearer." Which space? The parking garage, outer space? What is near is uncertain.

Stanza 10 provides a paradox that may suggest a position that bridges the oppositions and braces the poem:

> He is out of bounds. He rejoices in man's lovely,
> peculiar power to choose life and die –
> when he leads his black soldiers to death,
> he cannot bend his back.

Lowell was no longer practicing Catholicism at this stage, though he had been an avid convert. In any case, he need not have studied religion to know the fundamental paradox of spiritual rebirth, to "choose death" (of one sort of self) and "live" (as another, presumably better, self). But here the phrase is a chiasmus of that expression: "to choose life and die." And the speaker resorts to diction unlike that of the rest of the poem: "rejoices," "lovely," and "peculiar power." Because the speaker has implicated himself in the destructive forces of the poem (he was the boy whose hand tingled to burst the bubbles, but drew back; he is the man who crouches passively as he watches the balloons rise), the disgust he expresses for "savage servility" is disgust with himself as man and citizen of the "Grand Army of the Republic." But the poem suggests a position beyond despairing self-flagellation and frayed flags. The juxtaposition of two historical moments, the Civil War and the Civil Rights movement, could, of course, be read as indicative of continued racism and oppression, as proof there had been little progress in a century. The erosion of all the monuments bespeaks disregard for what was once accomplished. Nevertheless, the speaker has offered an alternative to historical amnesia for he sees in the monument a world he cannot revive but also cannot dismiss.

"For the Union Dead" concludes this book because the poem traverses the historical era it represents. Lowell's name itself conjures up Boston, New England, and the Puritans. Shaw's monument recalls the bloodiest war fought on American soil. The horrors of that war led, as wars often do, to new technologies and ways of thinking, and these shaped the twentieth century. The division between North and South over the question of slavery and "states' rights" was not concluded when hostilities ceased, and Lowell conveys the legacies of slavery in the image of the televised schoolchildren. The Edenic innocence that was the myth of the New World appears in the childhood memories of the fish, and the fragility of that myth is evoked by the bubbles about to burst and the finned cars that replace the fish. Technology, in the form of steam shovels, Mosler safes, and atom bombs, has created instruments for building and for destroying what was built. In the poem's movement from innocence to experience, from the Grand Army of the Republic to "savage servility," from the poet as orator to the poet as guilty confessor, from the present to the past and back again, "For the Union Dead" movingly comprehends the divisions of America.

Notes

Introduction

1 Stephen Greenblatt, "Culture," in Frank Lentricchia and Thomas McLaughlin, eds., Critical Terms for Literary Study (Chicago: University of Chicago Press, 1990), p. 225.

Chapter 1 Big

1 R. W. B. Lewis, *The American Adam: Innocence, Tragedy, and Tradition in the Nineteenth Century* (Chicago: University of Chicago Press, 1955), p. 5.
2 D. W. Meinig, "The Beholding Eye," in D. W. Meinig, J. W. Jackson, et al., eds., *The Interpretation of Ordinary Landscapes: Geographical Essays* (New York: Oxford University Press, 1979).
3 Patricia Nelson Limerick, *The Legacy of Conquest: The Unbroken Past of the American West* (New York: Norton, 1987), introduction.
4 For an accessible treatment of this subject, see Louis Menand, *The Metaphysical Club* (New York: Farrar, Straus & Giroux, 2001).
5 T. J. Jackson Lears, *No Place of Grace: Antimodernism and the Transformation of American Culture 1880–1920* (New York: Pantheon Books, 1981).
6 An influential book on the subject of neurasthenia among Americans is Tom Lutz's *American Nervousness, 1903: An Anecdotal History* (Ithaca, NY: Cornell University Press, 1991).
7 The text of the speech may be found online at bartleby.com.
8 Houston Baker, "Harlem On Our Minds," in David A. Bailey et al., eds., *Rhapsodies in Black: Art of the Harlem Renaissance* (London: Hayward Gallery, Institute of International Visual Arts; Berkeley: University of California Press, 1997), p. 162.
9 For an articulation of "hybridity," see, for example, Homi Bhabha's books *The Location of Culture* (1994) and *Nation and Narration* (1990).

10 Quoted in Frank Lentricchia, *Modernist Quartet* (Cambridge: Cambridge University Press, 1994), p. 132.

11 See on this subject Lea Jacobs, *The Wages of Sin: Censorship and the Fallen Woman Film, 1928–1942* (Madison: University of Wisconsin Press, 1991).

12 Kenneth T. Jackson, *Crabgrass Frontier: The Suburbanization of America* (New York: Oxford University Press, 1985).

13 Bonnie Costello, *Marianne Moore, Imaginary Possessions* (Cambridge, MA: Harvard University Press, 1981), p. 18.

14 Sacvan Bercovitch, *The American Jeremiad* (Madison: University of Wisconsin Press, 1978), p. 25.

15 The view against which Bercovitch is arguing is that of Perry Miller in *Errand into the Wilderness* (Cambridge, MA: Belknap Press of Harvard University Press, 1956).

16 Flannery O'Connor, "The Regional Writer," in *Collected Works* (New York: Library of America, 1988), p. 847.

17 "Agrarianism in Literature," in Charles Reagan Wilson and William Ferris, eds., *Encyclopedia of Southern Culture* (Chapel Hill: University of North Carolina Press, 1989).

18 Eudora Welty, "Place in Fiction," in *The Eye of the Story: Selected Essays and Reviews* (New York: Random House, 1978), p. 127.

19 The comment was in his speech accepting the Republican Party nomination for the US Senate.

Chapter 2 Rich

1 "Muckraking" denotes a type of investigative journalism that exposes corruption. The man with the muckrake in *Pilgrim's Progress* is so focused on his work that he cannot look up. Thus, the word can be applied disapprovingly to someone too focused on the bad to see what is good. Theodore Roosevelt popularized the term.

2 Thorstein Veblen, *The Theory of the Leisure Class* (1899; repr. New Brunswick, NJ: Transactions Publishers, 1992).

3 Daniel T. Rodgers, *The Work Ethic in Industrial America, 1850–1920* (Chicago: University of Chicago Press, 1978), p. 126. Further citations are to this edition.

4 John Dewey, *Individualism Old and New* (1930; repr. New York: Capricorn, 1962), p. 36.

5 David Riesman, *The Lonely Crowd: A Study in the Changing American Character* (New Haven: Yale University Press, 1950), p. 21.

6 Implications of the social ethic are presented throughout the text. William Whyte, *The Organization Man* (New York: Simon & Schuster, 1956).

7 Nina Baym, "Melodramas of Beset Manhood: How Theories of American Fiction Exclude Women Authors," in Lucy Maddox, ed., *Locating*

American Studies: The Evolution of a Discipline (Baltimore: Johns Hopkins University Press, 1999), pp. 215–34.

8   Charlotte Perkins Gilman, *Women and Economics: A Study of the Economic Relations Between Men and Women as a Factor in Social Evolution* (London: G. P. Putnam's Sons, 1906), p. 86. Further citations are to this edition.

9   Another helpful resource is the website sponsored by the Illinois Labor History Society, which offers a curriculum of US labor history for teachers. See http://www.kentlaw.edu/ilhs/curricul.htm/

10 Cornell University's Kheel Center has an exemplary website describing the Triangle factory fire: see http://www.ilr.cornell.edu/trianglefire/

11 *On the Waterfront* is considered by some commentators to have been Elia Kazan's self-justification for "naming names" to the House Un-American Activities Committee in 1952 since it offers a defense of "ratting out" one's co-workers. Arthur Miller's plays *The Crucible* and *A View from the Bridge* may be understood, at least in part, as critiques of both HUAC and Kazan's decision to "out" eight members of the Communist Party.

12 This distinction is worked out in full in Warren Susman, *Culture as History: The Transformation of American Society in the Twentieth Century* (New York: Pantheon Books, 1984).

Chapter 3 New

1   C. Barry Chabot, *Writers for the Nation: American Literary Modernism* (Tuscaloosa: University of Alabama Press, 1997), p. 4.

2   Susan Hegeman, *Patterns for America: Modernism and the Concept of Culture* (Princeton, NJ: Princeton University Press, 1999), p. 21.

3   Richard Poirier, "Modernism and its Difficulties," in *The Renewal of Literature: Emersonian Reflections* (London: Faber & Faber, 1987), pp. 95–113.

4   Sanford Schwartz, *The Matrix of Modernism: Pound, Eliot, and Early Twentieth-Century Thought* (Princeton, NJ: Princeton University Press, 1985), pp. 4–5.

5   William James, "The Stream of Thought," in Frederick H. Burkhardt, Fredson Bowers, and Ignas Skrupskelis, eds., *The Principles of Psychology*, vol. 1 (Cambridge, MA: Harvard University Press, 1981), p. 236.

6   Hugh Kenner, *The Pound Era* (Berkeley: University of California Press, 1971), pp. 482–3.

7   Kenneth Burke, "Literature as Equipment for Living," in *The Philosophy of Literary Form: Studies in Symbolic Action* (Baton Rouge: Louisiana State University Press, 1941).

8   Quoted in Elaine Showalter, "Women Writers Between the Wars," in Emory Elliott, ed., *Columbia Literary History of the United States* (New York: Columbia University Press, 1987), pp. 826–7.

9   Waldo Frank, ed., *America and Alfred Stieglitz: A Collective Portrait* (New York: Octagon, 1975), p. 239.

10　Carol Oja, *Making Music Modern: New York in the 1920s* (New York: Oxford University Press, 2000), p. 237.

11　Jed Rasula, "Jazz and American Modernism," in Walter Kalaidjian, ed., *Cambridge Companion to American Modernism* (Cambridge: Cambridge University Press, 2005), p. 168.

12　Erika Doss, *Twentieth-Century American Art* (New York: Oxford University Press, 2002), p. 76.

13　James Knapp, *American Musicals and the Formation of National Identity* (Princeton, NJ: Princeton University Press, 2005), p. 4.

14　Gilbert Seldes, *The Seven Lively Arts* (New York and London: Harper & Brothers, 1924), p. 348.

Chapter 4　Free

1　George Santayana, *Character and Opinion in the United States* (New York: Scribner's, 1920), p. 209.

2　"Jim Crow" was a ludicrous black character of minstrel shows.

3　Michael Kammen, *Spheres of Liberty: Changing Perceptions of Liberty in American Culture* (Madison: University of Wisconsin Press, 1986), p. 111.

4　Daniel T. Rodgers, *Contested Truths: Keywords in American Politics Since Independence* (New York: Basic Books, 1987), p. 15.

5　"Bunk" is American slang for nonsense, as in Henry Ford's 1916 statement to the *Chicago Tribune*, "History is more or less bunk." This use of the word derives from the behavior of the senator from Buncombe, North Carolina, who began a windy speech just as everyone else was ready for a vote. For further details, see the *Oxford English Dictionary*. A popular novel in 1923 was William E. Woodward's *Bunk*. To debunk was to demythologize.

6　The distinction between art and propaganda was of special concern during the 1930s, when more writers and artists sought to depict social problems. The index to the *Partisan Review* would be an excellent place to begin study of this question. See Edith Kurzweil, ed., *Partisan Review: Cumulative Index*, vols. 1–66 (New York: AMS Press, 2000).

7　Dwight Macdonald, "Kulturbolschewismus Is Here," *Partisan Review* 8/6 (Nov.–Dec. 1941), p. 446.

8　Quoted in Warren Susman, *Culture and Commitment, 1929–1945* (New York: G. Braziller, 1973), p. 324.

9　Cynthia Ozick, "T. S. Eliot at 101," *New Yorker*, 20 Nov. 1989, pp. 119–54.

10　See also chapter 1 on the Fugitives.

11　Erika Doss, *Twentieth-Century American Art* (New York: Oxford University Press, 2002), p. 128.

12　Leo Steinberg, "Other Criteria," in *Other Criteria: Confrontations with Twentieth-Century Art* (New York: Oxford University Press, 1972).

Websites for Further Study of American Literature and Culture

American Studies Electronic Crossroads. Links to Syllabus Library, Essays on Pedagogy. American Studies Association and the Center for Electronic Projects in American Cultural Studies, Georgetown University
http://www.georgetown.edu/crossroads/

American Studies Research Portal. Developed by the Institute for the Study of the Americas of the University of London
http://www.asrp.info/

American Women's History Research Guide. Prepared by Ken Middleton, Middle Tennessee State University Library
http://frank.mtsu.edu/~kmiddlet/history/women.html/

British Association for American Studies
http://www.baas.ac.uk/

A Chronology of US Historical Documents, Pre-Colonial to the Present. University of Oklahoma College of Law
http://www.law.ou.edu/hist/

Electronic Archives for Teaching the American Literatures. Georgetown University
http://www.georgetown.edu/tamlit/tamlit-home.html/

Electronic Texts. Subjects of interest include Twentieth-Century American Poetry; Documenting the African American Experience. University of Virginia
http://etext.lib.virginia.edu/collections/subjects/

Humanities Text Intitiative (includes American Verse Project). University of Michigan
http://www.hti.umich.edu/index-all.html/

Library of Congress American Memory. Collections ranging from advertising to folk life to immigration
http://memory.loc.gov/ammem/

The Media History Project. Timelines, facsimiles, and other materials relevant to the study of print and other media. Hosted by the School of Journalism and Mass Commmunication, University of Minnesota
http://mediahistory.umn.edu/

Modern American Poetry: An Online Journal and Multimedia Companion to *Anthology of Modern American Poetry* (Oxford University Press, 2000). Edited by Cary Nelson
http://www.english.uiuc.edu/maps/

National Parks Service of the US Department of the Interior
http://www.nps.gov/

PAL: Perspectives in American Literature: A Research and Reference Guide. Project of Paul D. Reuben. California State University, Stanislaus
http://www.csustan.edu/english/reuben/pal/TABLE.HTML/

Twentieth Century American Literature. Prepared by the American Studies Program at Keele University
http://www.keele.ac.uk/depts/as/Literature/amlit-sallyanne.html/

Searchable archives of significant records of the US federal government
http://www.archives.gov/

Smithsonian Institution. Special exhibits and online resources for research in the arts, science, technology, and history. Links to Smithsonian Museums, including the National Museum of American Art
http://www.si.edu/

Bibliography

American Studies

Adamic, L. *My America* (New York: Harpers, 1938).

Baritz, L. *City on a Hill: A History of Ideas and Myths in America* (New York: Wiley, 1964).

Beard, C. A. and M. R. *The Rise of American Civilization* (New York: Macmillan, 1927).

Fisher, P., ed. *The New American Studies: Essays from "Representations"* (Berkeley: University of California Press, 1991).

Frank, W. *Our America* (New York: Boni & Liveright, 1919).

Gabriel, R. H. *The Course of American Democratic Thought*, 3rd edn. (New York: Greenwood Press, 1986).

Marx, L. *The Machine in the Garden: Technology and the Pastoral Ideal in America* (Oxford: Oxford University Press, 1964).

Mencken, H. L. *The American Language: An Inquiry into the Development of English in the United States* (New York: A. A. Knopf, 1923).

Miller, P. *Errand Into the Wilderness* (Cambridge, MA: Belknap Press of Harvard University Press, 1956).

Morison, S. E. and H. S. Commager. *Growth of the American Republic*, 2 vols. (New York: Oxford University Press, 1937).

Nettels, C. P. *Roots of American Civilization: A History of American Colonial Life* (New York: F. S. Crofts, 1938).

Parrington, V. L. *Main Currents in American Thought*, 3 vols. (New York: Harcourt, 1927–30).

Santayana, G. *Character and Opinion in the United States* (New York: Scribner's, 1920).

Schlesinger, A. M. and D. R. Fox. *History of American Life*, 13 vols. (New York: Macmillan, 1927–48).

Spiller, R. E. and E. Larrabee. *American Perspectives: The National Self-Image in the Twentieth Century* (Cambridge, MA: Harvard University Press, 1961).

Tuveson, E. *Redeemer Nation: The Idea of America's Millenial Role*. Chicago: University of Chicago Press, 1968).

American Literature and Literary Criticism

Allen, D., ed. *The New American Poetry, 1945–1960* (New York: Grove Press, 1960).

Baym, N. "Melodramas of Beset Manhood: How Theories of American Fiction Exclude Women Authors," in L. Maddox, ed., *Locating American Studies: The Evolution of a Discipline* (Baltimore, MD: Johns Hopkins University Press, 1999).

Blankenship, R. *American Literature as an Expression of the National Mind* (New York: Holt, 1931).

Brooks, C. *The Well-Wrought Urn: Studies in the Structure of Poetry* (New York: Harcourt, Brace, 1947).

Brooks, C. and R. P. Warren. *Understanding Poetry*, 3rd edn. (New York: Holt, Rinehart & Winston, 1960).

Chase, R. V. *The American Novel and its Tradition* (Garden City, NY: Doubleday, 1957).

Fiedler, L. *Love and Death in the American Novel* (New York: Criterion Books, 1960).

Foerster, N., ed. *The Reinterpretation of American Literature: Some Contributions Toward the Understanding of its Historical Development* (New York: Harcourt Brace, 1928).

Jones, H. M. *The Theory of American Literature* (1948; Ithaca, NY: Cornell University Press, 1965).

Lawrence, D. H. *Studies in Classic American Literature* (London: Penguin Books, 1971).

Lewis, R. W. B. *The American Adam: Innocence, Tragedy, and Tradition in the Nineteenth Century* (Chicago: University of Chicago Press, 1955).

Matthiessen, F. O. *American Renaissance: Art and Expression in the Age of Emerson and Whitman* (New York: Oxford University Press, 1941).

Pattee, F. L. *The New American Literature, 1890–1930* (New York: Century, 1930).

Poirier, R. *A World Elsewhere: The Place of Style in American Literature* (New York: Oxford University Press, 1966).

Shumway, D. R. *Creating American Civilization: A Genealogy of American Literature as an Academic Discipline* (Minneapolis: University of Minnesota Press, 1994).

Spengemann, W. C. *A Mirror for Americanists: Reflections on the Idea of American Literature* (Hanover, NH: University Press of New England, 1989).

Vanderbilt, K. *American Literature and the Academy: The Roots, Growth, and Maturity of a Profession* (Philadelphia: University of Pennsylvania Press, 1986).

Wagner-Martin, L. *The Mid-Century American Novel 1935–1965: A Critical History* (New York: Twayne, 1997).

Wagner-Martin, L. *The Modern American Novel, 1914–1945: A Critical History* (New York: Twayne, 1997).

Wimsatt, W. K. *The Verbal Icon: Studies in the Meaning of Poetry* (Lexington: University of Kentucky Press, 1954).

The Arts

Alexander, C. *Here the Country Lies: Nationalism and the Arts in Twentieth-Century America* (Bloomington: Indiana University Press, 1980).

Bailey, D. et al., eds. *Rhapsodies in Black: Art of the Harlem Renaissance* (London: Hayward Gallery, Institute of International Visual Arts; Berkeley: University of California Press, 1997).

Barr, A. *Cubism and Abstract Art*, introd. Robert Rosenblum (Cambridge, MA: Harvard University Press, 1986).

Corn, W. *The Great American Thing: Modern Art and National Identity, 1915–1945* (Berkeley: University of California Press, 1999).

Doss, E. *Twentieth-Century American Art* (New York: Oxford University Press, 2002).

Frank, W., ed. *America and Alfred Stieglitz: A Collective Portrait* (New York: Octagon, 1975).

Haskell, B. *The American Century: Art and Culture, 1900–1950* (Chapel Hill: University of North Carolina Press, 2000).

Knapp, J. *American Musicals and the Formation of National Identity* (Princeton: Princeton University Press, 2005).

Mickelson, J. C., ed. *Images of the American City in the Arts* (Dubuque, IA: Kendall/Hunt, 1978).

Oja, C. *Making Music Modern: New York in the 1920s* (New York: Oxford University Press, 2000).

Polcari, S. *Abstract Expressionism and the Modern Experience* (Cambridge: Cambridge University Press, 1991).

Seldes, G. *The Seven Lively Arts* (New York: Harper & Brothers, 1924).

Steinberg, L. *Other Criteria: Confrontations with Twentieth-Century Art* (New York: Oxford University Press, 1972).

Swain, J. P. *The Broadway Musical: A Critical and Musical Survey*, 2nd edn. (Lanham, MD: Scarecrow Press, 2002).

Cities, Towns, and Open Spaces

Boyer, P. *Urban Masses and Moral Order in America, 1880–1920* (Cambridge, MA: Harvard University Press, 1978).

Clarke, G., ed. *The American City: Literary and Cultural Perspectives* (New York: St. Martin's, 1988).

Conzen, M. *The Making of the American Landscape* (Boston: Unwin Hyman, 1990).

Cook, D. M. and C. G. Swauger. *The Small Town in American Literature* (New York: Harper, 1977).

Douglas, A. *Terrible Honesty: Mongrel Manhattan in the 1920s* (New York: Farrar, Straus & Giroux, 1995).

Hakutani, Y. and R. Butler, eds. *The City in African-American Literature* (Madison: Associated University Presses, 1995).

Gandal, K. *The Virtues of the Vicious: Jacob Riis, Stephen Crane, and the Spectacle of the Slum* (New York: Oxford University Press, 1997).

Hilfer, A. C. *The Revolt from the Village, 1915–1930* (Chapel Hill: University of North Carolina Press, 1969).

Jackson, K. T. *Crabgrass Frontier: The Suburbanization of America* (New York: Oxford University Press, 1985).

Kolodny, A. *The Lay of the Land: Metaphor as Experience and History in American Life and Letters* (Chapel Hill: University of North Carolina Press, 1975).

Kolodny, A. *The Land Before Her: Fantasy and Experience of the American Frontiers, 1630–1860* (Chapel Hill: University of North Carolina Press, 1984).

Limerick, P. N. *The Legacy of Conquest: The Unbroken Past of the American West* (New York: Norton, 1987).

Malone, M. P. and R. W. Etulain. *The American West: A Twentieth-Century History* (Lincoln: Nebraska University Press, 1989).

McCurdy, H. E. *Space and the American Imagination* (Washington, DC: Smithsonian Institution, 1997).

McShane, C. *Down the Asphalt Path: The Automobile and the American City* (New York: Columbia University Press, 1994).

Meinig, D. W., J. W. Jackson, et al., eds. *The Interpretation of Ordinary Landscapes: Geographical Essays* (New York: Oxford University Press, 1979).

Merck, F. *Manifest Destiny and Mission in American History: A Reinterpretation* (New York: Knopf, 1963).

Mumford, L. *The Culture of Cities* (New York: Harcourt, 1938).

Nash, R. *Wilderness and the American Mind* (New Haven: Yale University Press, 1967).

Smith, H. N. *Virgin Land: The American West as Symbol and Myth* (Cambridge, MA: Harvard University Press, 1950).

Stansell, C. *American Moderns: Bohemian New York and the Creation of a New Century* (New York: Metropolitan Books, 2000).

Stimpson, C. R., ed. *Women and the American City* (Chicago: University of Chicago Press, 1981).

Taylor, G. R., ed. *The Turner Thesis: Concerning the Role of the Frontier in American History* (Lexington, MA: D. C. Heath, 1972).

Turner, F. J. *The Frontier In American History* (Tucson: University of Arizona Press, 1986).

Class

Beach, C. *Class, Language, and American Film Comedy* (Cambridge: Cambridge University Press, 2002).

Denning, M. *Mechanic Accents: Dime Novels and Working-Class Culture in America* (New York: Verso, 1987).

Dollard, J. *Caste and Class in a Southern Town* (New Haven: Yale University Press, 1937).

Foley, B. *Radical Representations: Politics and Form in U.S. Proletarian Fiction, 1929–1941* (Durham, NC: Duke University Press, 1993).

Gilbert, D. L. and J. L. Kahl. *The American Class Structure: A New Synthesis*, 3rd edn. (Belmont, CA: Wadsworth, 1987).

Hapke, L. *Daughters of the Great Depression: Women, Work, and Fiction in the American 1930s* (Athens: University of Georgia Press, 1995).

Keister, L. A. *Wealth in America* (New York: Cambridge University Press, 2000).

Mills, C. W. *The Power Elite* (New York: Oxford University Press, 1956).

Mills, C. W. *White Collar: The American Middle Classes* (New York: Oxford University Press, 1951).

Peiss, K. *Cheap Amusements: Working Women and Leisure in Turn-of-the-Century New York* (Philadelphia: Temple University Press, 1986).

Reissman, L. *Class in American Society* (London: Routledge, 1960).

Riis, J. *How the Other Half Lives* (1st edn. 1901; New York: Penguin, 1997).

Rossides, D. W. *Social Stratification: The American Class System in Comparative Perspective* (Englewood Cliffs, NJ: Prentice Hall, 1990).

Sorokin, P. A. *Social Mobility* (New York: Harper, 1927).

Stadum, B. A. *Poor Women and their Families: Hard Working Charity Cases, 1900–1930* (Albany: State University of New York Press, 1991).

Streby, S. *American Sensations: Class, Empire, and the Production of Popular Culture* (Berkeley: University of California Press, 2002).

Warner, L. W., et al. *Social Class in America: A Manual for the Procedure of Measurement of Social Status* (Chicago: Science Research Associates, 1949).

Warner, L. W. and P. S. Lunt. *The Social Life of a Modern Community* (New Haven: Yale University Press, 1941).

Consumerism/Economics/Labor History

Banta, M. *Taylored Lives: Narrative Production in the Age of Taylor, Veblen, and Ford* (Chicago: Chicago University Press, 1993).

Beard, C. A. *Economic Origins of Jeffersonian Democracy* (New York: Macmillan, 1915).

Beard, C. A. An *Economic Interpretation of the Constitution of the United States* (1st edn. 1913; New York: Macmillan Brothers, 1925).

Bell, D. *Cultural Contradictions of Capitalism* (New York: Basic Books, 1976).

Bernstein, M. *The Great Depression: Delayed Recovery and Economic Change in America, 1929–39* (Cambridge: Cambridge University Press, 1988).

Boorstin, D. *The Image; or, What Happened to the American Dream* (New York: Atheneum, 1962).

Cohen, L. *Making a New Deal: Industrial Workers in Chicago, 1919–1939* (Cambridge: Cambridge University Press, 1990).

Cullen, J. *The American Dream: A Short History of an Idea That Shaped a Nation* (New York: Oxford University Press, 2003).

Galbraith, J. K. *The Affluent Society* (Boston: Houghton, 1958).

Gilman, C. P. *Women and Economics: A Study of the Economic Relations Between Men and Women as a Factor in Social Evolution* (1898; London: G. P. Putnam's Sons, 1906).

Glickman, L. B., ed. *Consumer Society in American History: A Reader* (Ithaca, NY: Cornell University Press, 1999).

Goodrum, C. and H. Dalrymple. *Advertising in America: The First Two Hundred Years* (New York: Abrams, 1990).

Gordon, I. *Comic Strips and Consumer Culture, 1890–1945* (Washington, DC: Smithsonian Institution Press, 1998).

Hacker, L. M. *The Triumph of American Capitalism: The Development of Forces in American History to the End of the Nineteenth Century* (New York: Simon & Schuster, 1940).

Harrington, M. *The Other America: Poverty in the United States* (Baltimore: Penguin, 1963).

Kurtz, S. *Wasteland: Building the American Dream* (New York: Praeger, 1973).

Lasch, C. *The Culture of Narcissism: American Life in an Age of Diminishing Expectations* (New York: Warner, 1979).

Leach, W. *Land of Desire: Merchants, Power, and the Rise of a New American Culture* (New York: Pantheon, 1993).

Lears, T. J. J. *Fables of Abundance: A Cultural History of Advertising in America* (New York: Basic Books, 1994).

Marchand, R. *Advertising the American Dream: Making Way for Modernity, 1920–1940* (Berkeley: University of California Press, 1985).

Marcuse, H. *One-Dimensional Man: Studies in the Ideology of Advanced Industrial Society* (Boston: Beacon Press, 1964).

Packard, V. O. *The Hidden Persuaders* (New York: D. McKay, 1957).

Potter, D. M. *People of Plenty: Economic Abundance and the American Character* (Chicago: Chicago University Press, 1954).

Rodgers, Daniel T., *The Work Ethic in Industrial America, 1850–1920* (Chicago: University of Chicago Press, 1978).

Szalay, M. *New Deal Modernism: American Literature and the Invention of the Welfare State* (Durham, NC: Duke University Press, 2000).

Tarbell, I. *The History of the Standard Oil Company* (New York: McClure, Philips, 1904).

Terkel, S. *Hard Times: An Oral History of the Great Depression* (New York: Pantheon, 1970).

Veblen, T. *The Theory of the Leisure Class* (New Brunswick, NJ: Transaction Publishers, 1992).

Watts, E. S. *The Businessman in American Literature* (Athens: University of Georgia Press, 1982).

Weber, M. *The Protestant Ethic and the Spirit of Capitalism*, trans. Stephen Kalberg (Chicago and London: Fitzroy Dearborn, 2001).

Whyte, W. H. *The Organization Man* (New York: Simon & Schuster, 1956).

Labor History

Bok, D. C. and J. T. Dunlop. *Labor and the American Community* (New York: Simon & Schuster, 1970).

Denning, M. *The Cultural Front: The Laboring of American Culture in the Twentieth Century* (New York: Verso, 1996).

Fink, L. *In Search of the Working Class: Essays in American Labor History and Political Culture* (Urbana and Chicago: University of Illinois Press, 1994).

Stephenson, C. and R. Aster, eds. *Life and Labor: Dimensions of American Working-Class History* (Albany: State University of New York Press, 1986).

Immigration, Nativism, Pluralism

Ferraro, T. *Ethnic Passages: Literary Immigrants in Twentieth-Century America* (Chicago: University of Chicago Press, 1993).

Fine, D. M. *The City, the Immigrant and American Fiction, 1880–1920* (Metuchen, NJ: Scarecrow, 1977).

Handlin, O. *Boston's Immigrants 1790–1880: A Study in Acculturation* (Cambridge, MA: Harvard University Press, 1959).

Higham, J. *Strangers in the Land: Patterns of American Nativism, 1860–1925* (1st edn. 1955; New Brunswick, NJ: Rutgers University Press, 1994).

Inglehart, B. F. and A. R. Mangione. *The Image of Pluralism in American Literature: The American Experience of European Ethnic Groups* (New York: Institute on Pluralism and Group Identity of the American Jewish Committee, 1974).

Klein, M. *Foreigners: The Making of American Literature, 1900–1940* (Chicago: University of Chicago Press, 1981).

Michaels, W. B. *Our America: Nativism, Modernism, and Pluralism* (Durham, NC: Duke University Press, 1995).

Ngai, M. N. *Impossible Subjects: Aliens and the Making of Modern America* (Princeton: Princeton University Press, 2005).

Stave, B. *From the Old Country: An Oral History of European Migration to America* (New York: Twayne, 1994).

Takaki, R., ed. *From Different Shores: Perspectives on Race and Ethnicity in America*, 2nd edn. (New York: Oxford University Press, 1994).

Modernism

Baker, H. *Modernism and the Harlem Renaissance* (Chicago: University of Chicago Press, 1987).

Beebe, M. "What Modernism Was," *Journal of Modern Literature*, 3 (1974),· pp. 1065–84.

Boone, J. A. *Libidinal Currents: Sexuality and the Shaping of Modernism* (Chicago: University of Chicago Press, 1998).

Bradbury, M. *The Modern American Novel* (New York: Viking, 1992).

Bradbury, M. "The Nonhomemade World: European and American Modernism," *American Quarterly*, 39 (1987), pp. 27–36.

Caws, M. A. *Manifesto: A Century of Isms* (Lincoln: University of Nebraska Press, 2001).

Chabot, C. B. *Writers for the Nation: American Literary Modernism* (Tuscaloosa: University of Alabama Press, 1997).

Costello, B. *Marianne Moore, Imaginary Possessions* (Cambridge, MA: Harvard University Press, 1981).

Cowley, M. *Exile's Return* (New York: Viking, 1934).

Crunden, R. *Body and Soul: The Makings of American Modernism* (New York: Basic Books, 2000).

Filreis, A. *Modernism from Right to Left: Wallace Stevens, the Thirties, and Literary Radicalism* (New York: Cambridge University Press, 1994).

Frank, J. *Crisis and Mastery in Modern Literature* (New Brunswick, NJ: Rutgers University Press, 1963).

Gilroy, P. *The Black Atlantic: Modernity and Double Consciousness* (Cambridge, MA: Harvard University Press, 1993).

Hegeman, S. *Patterns for America: Modernism and the Concept of Culture* (Princeton: Princeton University Press, 1999).

Hoffman, M. J. and P. D. Murphy, eds. *Critical Essays on American Modernism* (New York: G. K. Hall & Co., 1992).

Kalaidjian, W. *American Culture between the Wars: Revisionary Modernism and Postmodern Critique* (New York: Columbia University Press, 1993).

Kenner, H. *A Homemade World: The American Modernist Writers* (New York: Knopf, 1975).

Kenner, H. *The Pound Era* (Berkeley: University of California Press, 1971).

Knapp, J. F. *Literary Modernism and the Transformation of Work* (Evanston, IL: Northwestern University Press, 1988).

Knight, C. J. *The Patient Particulars: American Modernism and the Technique of Originality* (Lewisburg, PA: Bucknell University Press, 1995).

Lentricchia, F. *Modernist Quartet* (Cambridge: Cambridge University Press, 1994).

Lindberg, K. V. and J. G. Kronick, eds. *America's Modernisms: Revaluing the Canon* (Baton Rouge: Louisiana State University Press, 1996).

Nelson, C. *Repression and Recovery: Modern American Poetry and the Politics of Cultural Memory, 1910–1945* (Madison: University of Wisconsin Press, 1989).

Nicholls, P. *Modernisms: A Literary Guide* (Berkeley: University of California Press, 1995).

North, M. *The Dialect of Modernism: Race, Language, and Twentieth-Century Literature* (New York: Oxford University Press, 1994).

North, M. *Reading 1922: A Return to the Scene of the Modern* (New York: Oxford University Press, 1999).

Poirier, R. *The Renewal of Literature: Emersonian Reflections* (London: Faber & Faber, 1987).

Rabinowitz, P. *Black and White and Noir: America's Pulp Modernism* (New York: Columbia University Press, 2002).

Rhodes, C. *Structures of the Jazz Age: Mass Culture, Progressive Education, and Racial Discourse in American Modernism* (London: Verso, 1998).

Schwartz, S. *The Matrix of Modernism: Pound, Eliot, and Early Twentieth-Century Thought* (Princeton: Princeton University Press, 1985).

Scott, B. K., ed. *The Gender of Modernism: A Critical Anthology* (Bloomington: Indiana University Press, 1990).

Singal, D. J., ed. *Modernist Culture in America*: *American Quarterly*, 39 [special issue] (1987), 5–173.

Smith, T. *Making the Modern: Industry, Art and Design in America* (Chicago: University of Chicago Press, 1993).

Stearns, H., ed. *Civilization in the United States: An Inquiry by Thirty Americans* (New York: Harcourt Brace, 1922).

Steinman, L. *Made in America: Science, Technology, and American Modernist Poetry* (New Haven: Yale University Press, 1987).

Tashjian, D. *Skyscraper Primitives: Dada and the American Avant-Garde, 1910–1925* (Middletown, CN: Wesleyan University Press, 1975).

Tichi, C. *Shifting Gears: Technology, Literature, Culture in Modernist America* (Chapel Hill: University of North Carolina Press, 1987).

Wertheim, A. F. *The New York Little Renaissance: Iconoclasm, Modernism, and Nationalism in American Culture, 1908–1917* (New York: New York University Press, 1976).

Race

Bell, B. *The Afro-American Novel and its Traditions* (Amherst: University of Massachusetts Press, 1987).

Frazier, F. *The Negro Family in the United States* (Chicago: University of Chicago Press, 1939).

Johnson, J. W. *Black Manhattan* (New York: Knopf, 1930).

Johnson, J. W., ed. *The Book of American Negro Poetry*, 2nd edn. (New York: Harcourt, 1931).

King, W. *African American Childhoods: Historical Perspectives from Slavery to Civil Rights* (New York: Palgrave, 2005).

Lewis, D. L. *When Harlem Was in Vogue* (New York: Knopf, 1981).

Locke, A. *The New Negro* (1st edn. 1925; New York: Atheneum, 1992).

Myrdal, G. *An American Dilemma: The Negro Problem and Modern Democracy*, 2 vols. (New York: Harper & Brothers, 1944).

Regionalism: The South

Brooks, C. *Community, Religion and Literature* (Columbia: University of Missouri Press, 1995).

Cash, W. J. *The Mind of the South* (1st edn. 1941; New York: Vintage, 1960).

Cobb, J. C. *Away Down South: A History of Southern Identity* (New York: Oxford University Press, 2005).

Gray, R. J. *Southern Aberrations: Writers of the American South and the Problem of Regionalism* (Baton Rouge: Louisiana State University Press, 2000).

Hobson, F. *Tell About the South: The Southern Rage to Explain* (Baton Rouge: Louisiana State University Press, 1992).

King, R. *A Southern Renaissance: The Cultural Awakenings of the American South, 1930–1955* (New York: Oxford University Press, 1980).

Kreyling, M. *Inventing Southern Literature* (Jackson: University Press of Mississippi, 1998).

O'Connor, F. *Collected Works* (New York: Library of America, 1988).

Romine, S. *The Narrative Forms of Southern Community* (Baton Rouge: Louisiana State University Press, 1999).

Twelve Southerners. *I'll Take My Stand: The South and the Agrarian Tradition* (New York: Harper, 1930).

Welty, E. *The Eye of the Story: Selected Essays and Reviews* (New York: Random House, 1978).

War

Blum, J. M. *V Was for Victory: Politics and American Culture During WWII* (New York: Harcourt Brace Jovanovich, 1976).

Boyer, P. *By the Bomb's Early Light: American Thought and Culture at the Dawn of the Atomic Age* (New York: Pantheon, 1985).

Brands, H. W. *Cold Warriors: Eisenhower's Generation and American Foreign Policy* (New York: Columbia University Press, 1988).

Dudziak, M. L. *Cold War Civil Rights: Race and the Image of American Diplomacy* (Princeton: Princeton University Press, 2000).

Rhodes, B. *U.S. Foreign Policy in the Interwar Period, 1918–1941: The Golden Age of American Diplomatic and Military Complacency* (Westport, CT.: Praeger, 2001).

Weigley, R. F. *The American Way of War: A History of United States Military Strategy and Policy* (Bloomington: Indiana University Press, 1973).

Whitfield, S. J. *The Culture of the Cold War* (Baltimore: Johns Hopkins University Press, 1991).

Women

Banta, M. *Imaging American Women: Ideas and Ideals in Cultural History* (New York: Columbia University Press, 1987).

Benstock, S. *Women of the Left Bank: Paris, 1900–1940* (Austin: University of Texas Press, 1986).

Friedan, B. *The Feminine Mystique* (New York: Norton, 1963).

Gilbert, S. M., and S. Gubar. *No Man's Land: The Place of the Woman Writer in the Twentieth Century*, 3 vols. (New Haven: Yale University Press, 1988).

Jacobs, L. *The Wages of Sin: Censorship and the Fallen Woman Film, 1928–1942* (Madison: University of Wisconsin Press, 1991).

Lerner, G. *The Female Experience: An American Documentary* (Indianapolis: Bobbs-Merrill, 1977).

Rabinowitz, P. *Labor and Desire: Women's Revolutionary Fiction in Depression America* (Chapel Hill: University of North Carolina Press, 1991).

Youth Culture and Child Study

Austin, J. and M. N. Willard, eds. *Generations of Youth: Youth Cultures and History in Twentieth-Century America* (New York: New York University Press, 1998).

Fass, P. *The Damned and the Beautiful: American Youth in the 1920s* (New York: Oxford University Press, 1977).

Goodman, P. *Growing Up Absurd: Problems of Youth in the Organized System* (New York: Random House, 1960).

Hall, G. S. *Adolescence: Its Psychology and its Relations to Anthropology, Sociology, Sex, Crime, Religion and Education*, 2 vols. (1st edn. 1905; New York: D. Appleton, 1931).

Hiner, N. R. and J. M. Hawes. *Growing Up in America: Children in Historical Perspective* (Urbana and Chicago: University of Illinois Press, 1985).

Springhall, J. *Youth, Popular Culture, and Moral Panics: Penny Gaffs to Gangsta-Rap, 1830–1996* (New York: St. Martin's Press, 1998).

Wertham, F. *Seduction of the Innocent* (New York: Rinehart, 1954).

General Interest

Ahlstrom, S. *A Religious History of the American People* (New Haven: Yale University Press, 1972).

Anderson, B. *Imagined Communities: Reflections on the Origin and Spread of Nationalism* (London: Verso, 1983).

Anderson, Q. *The Imperial Self* (New York: Knopf, 1971).

Bercovitch, S. *The American Jeremiad* (Madison: University of Wisconsin Press, 1978).

Bloom, A. *Prodigal Sons: The New York Intellectuals and their World* (New York: Oxford University Press, 1986).

Brooks, V. W. *America's Coming-of-Age* (New York: Huebsch, 1915).

Brooks, V. W. *The Flowering of New England, 1815–1865* (New York: Dutton, 1936).

Brooks, V. W. "On Creating a Usable Past," *The Dial*, 64 (1918), pp. 337–41.

Burke, K. *The Philosophy of Literary Form* (Baton Rouge: Louisiana State University Press, 1941).

Croly, H. *The Promise of American Life*, ed. A. M. Schlesinger, Jr. (Cambridge, MA: Belknap Press of Harvard University Press, 1965).

Degler, C. *Out of our Past: The Forces That Shaped Modern America* (New York: Harper, 1959).

Dewey, J., *Individualism Old and New* (New York: Capricorn, 1962).

Greenblatt, S., "Culture," in F. Lentricchia and T. McLaughlin, eds., *Critical Terms for Literary Study* (Chicago: University of Chicago Press, 1990).

Greene, T. P. *America's Heroes: The Changing Model of Success in American Magazines* (New York: Oxford University Press, 1970).

Hofstadter, R. *Anti-Intellectualism in American Life* (New York: Knopf, 1963).

Hollinger, D. A. "Ethnic Diversity, Cosmopolitanism, and the Emergence of the American Liberal Intelligentsia," *American Quarterly*, 27 (1975), pp. 133–51.

Jacoby, R. *The Last Intellectuals: American Culture in the Age of Academe* (New York: Basic Books, 1987).

James, W. *Pragmatism and Other Writings*, ed. G. Gunn (New York: Penguin, 2000).

James, W. *The Principles of Psychology*, ed. F. H. Burkhardt et al. (Cambridge, MA: Harvard University Press, 1981).

Kammen, M. *People of Paradox; an Inquiry Concerning the Origins of American Civilization* (New York: Knopf, 1972).

Kammen, M. *Spheres of Liberty: Changing Perceptions of Liberty in American Culture* (Madison: University of Wisconsin Press, 1986).

Kasson, J. *Amusing the Million: Coney Island at the Turn of the Century* (New York: Hill & Wang, 1978).

Kermode, F. *The Sense of an Ending: Studies in the Theory of Fiction* (New York: Oxford University Press, 1967).

Lears, T. J. J. *No Place of Grace: Antimodernism and the Transformation of American Culture, 1880–1920* (New York: Pantheon, 1981).

Levine, L. W. *Highbrow/Lowbrow: The Emergence of Cultural Hierarchy in America* (Cambridge, MA: Harvard University Press, 1988).

Lutz, T. *American Nervousness, 1903: An Anecdotal History* (Ithaca, NY: Cornell University Press, 1991).

Menand, L. *The Metaphysical Club* (New York: Farrar, Straus & Giroux, 2001).

Ozick, C. "T. S. Eliot at 101," *New Yorker*, 20 Nov. 1989, pp. 119–54.

Rae, J. B. *The Road and the Car in American Life* (Cambridge, MA: Massachusetts Institute of Technology Press, 1971).

Riesman, D. *The Lonely Crowd: A Study in the Changing American Character* (New Haven: Yale University Press, 1961).

Rodgers, D. T. *Contested Truths: Keywords in American Politics Since Independence* (New York: Basic Books, 1987).

Salzman, J. and B. Wallenstein, eds. *Years of Protest: A Collection of American Writings of the 1930s* (New York: Pegasus, 1967).

Spiller, R. E. and E. Larrabee. *American Perspectives: The National Self-Image in the Twentieth Century* (Cambridge, MA: Harvard University Press, 1961).

Susman, W., ed. *Culture and Commitment, 1929–1945* (New York: G. Braziller, 1973).

Susman, W. *Culture as History: The Transformation of American Society in the Twentieth Century* (New York: Pantheon, 1984).

Trachtenberg, A. *The Incorporation of America: Culture and Society in the Gilded Age* (New York: Hill, 1982).

Wald, A. M. *The New York Intellectuals: The Rise and Decline of the Anti-Stalinist Left from the 1930s to the 1980s* (Chapel Hill: University of North Carolina Press, 1987).

Welters, L. and P. A. Cunningham, eds. *Twentieth-Century American Fashion* (New York: Palgrave 2005).

Reference Books

American Social History Project. *Who Built America?*, 2 vols. (New York: Pantheon, 1992).

Bercovitch, S., ed. *Reconstructing American Literary History* (Cambridge, Mass: Harvard University Press, 1986).

Bercovitch, S., ed. *The Cambridge History of American Literature* (Cambridge: Cambridge University Press, 1994).

Cayton, M. K. et al., eds. *Encyclopedia of American Social History* (New York: Scribner, 1993).

Commager, H. S. and M. Cantor, eds. *Documents of American History*, 10th edn. (Englewood Cliffs, NJ: Prentice-Hall, 1998).

Dubofsky, M. et al. *The Oxford Companion to United States History* (New York: Oxford University Press, 2001).

Elliott, E., ed. *Columbia Literary History of the United States* (New York: Columbia University Press, 1987).

Fox, R. W. and J. T. Kloppenberg, eds. *A Companion to American Thought* (Oxford: Blackwell Publishing, 1995).

Gray, R. *A History of American Literature* (Oxford: Blackwell Publishing, 2004).

Hollinger, D. A. and C. Capper, eds. *The American Intellectual Tradition*, 5th edn., vol. 2 (New York: Oxford University Press, 2005).

Kalaidjian, W., ed. *The Cambridge Companion to American Modernism* (Cambridge: Cambridge University Press, 2005).

Kurian, G. T. et al., eds. *Encyclopedia of American Studies*, 4 vols. (New York: Grolier, 2001).

Spiller, R. et al., eds. *Literary History of the United States*. 3 vols. (New York: Macmillan, 1948).

Wilson, C. R. and W. Ferris, eds. *Encyclopedia of Southern Culture* (Chapel Hill, University of North Carolina Press, 1989).

Index